D0108832

DREAM STATE

To the memory of my parents –
Daniel and Hester.

DREAM STATE

The New Scottish Poets

Second Edition

Edited by
DONNY O'ROURKE

Editorial selection and arrangement © Polygon, 2002.

Introductions © Daniel O'Rourke, 1994 and 2002.

© Copyright of poems resides with the individual poets;
the acknowledgements on pp. 305–10 constitute an extension
of this copyright page.

The title *Dream State* comes from the poem of the same name
by Stuart A. Paterson.

Polygon
An imprint of Edinburgh University Press Ltd
22 George Square, Edinburgh

Typeset in Minion and Sans by
Pioneer Associates, Perthshire, and
printed and bound in Great Britain by
Creative Print & Design, Ebbw Vale, Wales

A CIP Record for this book is available
from the British Library

ISBN 0 7486 6260 X (paperback)

The right of the contributors
to be identified as authors of this work
has been asserted in accordance with
the Copyright, Designs and Patents Act 1988.

The Publisher acknowledges subsidy from

THE SCOTTISH ARTS COUNCIL

towards the publication of this volume.

Contents

Robin Lindsay Wilson

George Gunn

Peter McCarey

Mick Imlah

William Hershaw

Contents

David Kinloch

Rody Gorman

Ken Cockburn

Maud Sulter

W. N. Herbert

Contents

ANGELA MCSEVENEY

ROB MACKENZIE

KATE CLANCHY

GILLIAN FERGUSON

STUART A. PATERSON

Contents

Roddy Lumsden

Richard Price

Anne Frater

Tracey Herd

Contents

There is no passport to this country,
It exists as a quality of the language.

'Dingle Dell' by W. N. Herbert

Introduction

Donny O'Rourke

The first edition of this book gathered work by twenty-five Scottish poets, each then under forty. It was the first sampling of those writers born in and since the mid-1950s. That such generational surveys had not previously appeared in Scotland surprised me, leading me to wonder if, in quantity, if not quality, our lot was somehow different. Carol Ann Duffy and John Burnside, each born in 1955, each brought up outside the Protestant mainstream, each living 'down South', both already stars on the metropolitan and international literary scenes, were cast as kinds of big sister and brother to the other poets in the anthology. Duffy went on to become a serious (and more interesting) candidate for the Poet Laureateship, which Andrew Motion secured; Burnside has just won the Whitbread Prize. Don Paterson, then about to publish his first collection, has enjoyed a similarly stellar career, as have Kathleen Jamie and Jackie Kay. Roddy Lumsden (for whom I broke my 'rule' that prospective contributors had to have published at least a pamphlet) made a spectacularly zeitgeisty entrance upon the scene, has been much noticed and is causing the stir his talent deserves. Born in 1966, he was the second youngest poet in *Dream State*. Praise and prizes have been heaped too upon Kate Clanchy, who had yet to write, far less publish, any verse at all when *Dream State* appeared. Although a powerful editor and publisher, Robin Robertson had still to make his debut at book length. W. N. Herbert and Robert Crawford have continued to be indefatigable, and given his influential ubiquity, as critic and anthologist, the latter had done much to shape the new British canon, which features all of the above in justifiably prominent positions. So, far from being marginalised, Scottish poets (like Scottish politicians) seem to the envious and the excluded to be 'running things' in London, as they propose for publication, edit, review and nominate for awards each other's latest books. After the relative neglect of MacCaig, MacLean and even (until shamefully recently) Morgan, this seems to me, and to most, a classic example of the adage, talent will out.

Dream State teemed with talent. Every poet and every poem were, and are, special, which, more than cultural, geographical, linguistic and gender balance (though these things were very significant), was the chief aim. I wanted to edit a book I'd want to read. But I wanted to make a case too, or more exactly cases. The case for the calibre of recent Scottish poetry has been magnificently proven and the poets have the golden opinions and silverware, or its equivalent, to affirm it. And the case for an economically, politically and imaginatively viable Scotland got the endorsement of a 'Yes, Yes' vote in the referendum that established our parliament. I know of no avowal, in prose or poetry, of the possibilities and fecundities that act of constitutional courage was waiting to release than Robert Crawford's 'Scotland' poem in *Dream State*.

Other reveries were quieter. Some reviewers felt I had slewed my selection in favour of 'state of the nation' poems, and maybe I did. The times required it. Scotland's artists did more than its politicians to dream up a new Scotland. A chasm became a cusp. I'd be pleased and proud to believe that *Dream State* wasn't just a record of, or set of hopes for, a better Scotland but a contribution to it. At any rate, because more's been done, less has to be said. In the introduction to the first edition I dilated on the merits of many contemporary poems from, and the political and cultural outlook for, this new, hallucinatory Scotland we'd one day wake up from and to. Unlike the poems, it now feels moored to the moment, but anyone wishing analysis, polemic and a consideration of each poet in *Dream State* I, will find the original disquisition miniaturised and appended here, where, given the speed at which our heads and hearts must move in order to keep pace with all the information whizzing around the frantic ether, it may already, I blush and giggle to think, be of quasi-historical interest.

Certainly the reviewers quite liked it on the whole but then introductions always get reviewed. Along with the omissions. There weren't *too* many of those. By temperament, I'm an innkeeper rather than a gate keeper, and there is nearly always room for a couple more even if the poor old publishers have to get out the folding beds. I've gone back and squeezed in people I thought were too old, or hadn't published enough, or weren't Scottish enough, or didn't get back to us quickly enough. Fair enough: they ought to have been there. I'm glad they are now. One excludee sent me threatening letters and harangued and harassed me in the small hours on the phone. Omitted again, I'm afraid. Even my tolerance doesn't extend that far. Someone I left out wrote a vengefully vituperative review rubbishing the concept, the writers and writing excerpted and, of course, the editor. Well, poet X is in this time. The politics are so dirty because the stakes are so low, Henry Kissinger said of academic rivalry. Double that for poetry. Still, I've tried to make the revised, updated and expanded selection as representative as I can within the constraints of cost and space, which at a certain point become the same thing. A big book has got bigger but could've been bigger still. Since it is my conviction that editors who take it upon themselves to make purportedly 'representative' selections should be obliged to include work that is liked, esteemed and considered valuable, even if, *particularly if, not by them*, I have dutifully, but far from reluctantly, added poets I do not myself much care for, in the full knowledge that many may find them the 'best' writers in the book. In this regard, ageing editors have an especial responsibility towards the young. When I first suggested the book I was very young myself. When it came out I was *quite* young. Seven years on? Well yes . . .

After forty, people have to choose between going forward or going back. Not all the *Dream State* veterans still look good in jeans. Architects and conductors may still be 'young' in their forties but are poets? *No.* They are however youthful. None of the people from the first edition is trying to be poetic mutton dressed as lamb. Yet there's freshness as well as maturity in the work they have allowed me to add. And their influence on the younger contributors coming into the anthology for the first time is palpable.

Most of those who helped to form the tastes and talents of Scottish poets born in the late 1950s and early 1960s have gone. Of the lustrously eminent group assembled by Sandy Moffat for his epochal painting *Poet's Pub*, only an ailing but still prodigious and prolific Edwin Morgan writes and flytes on. His brilliance, variegated virtuosity, exemplariness, difference and, in several instances, direct pedagogical intervention, made him the guiding light of the earlier book. Citing his call for a rallying of poets, I had no idea how quickly and literally it would be answered. Sure, Peter McCarey is still in Geneva, Iain Bamforth in Strasbourg, messrs Kay, Duffy, Friel, Price (and now Lumsden) in England, establishing (and constantly changing) perspectives on a Scotland they have, and have not, left. Don Paterson is back. And so are John Burnside and David Kinloch. Alan Riach has just returned to Glasgow from New Zealand. Edwin Morgan's hopes have been justified. In the *Poet's Pub* all the luminaries were white men from Presbyterian background (George Mackay Brown had converted to Catholicism). The only gay poet, Morgan, couldn't have come out in that Scotland. How altered things are now.

We needed some inspirational defiance and vision back in 1979 when Eddie took his stand. That was the year Mrs Thatcher came to power and Scotland didn't. That referendum, first flawed, then fixed, was, unlike its successor, a big 'No, No'. A stateless nation's nightmare gave rise to various sorts of *Dream State* until, pinching ourselves, we woke up to find we had a parliament, one which, despite some all too predictable sleaze and parochialism, is working well and likely to demand, deserve and get more power in due course, this in the context of, and as a challenge to, our dis-united kingdom, a Britain poised uneasily between nation and federation, a country lacking some of the confidence and cohesion Scotland has begun to acquire. 'It's not what Paris gives you, it's what it doesn't take away,' Gertrude Stein averred. At last we've started putting it back, a project in which the poets of *Dream State* are well to the fore.

Editors should always apologise, always explain. I've continued to worry about the implied definitiveness of the phrase, 'the new Scottish poets', though not enough to change it. With those new poets who feel left out, I ruefully condole; all the more so given my empathetic regard for the casualties the remorseless canonisers ignore. No anthology – particularly one that claims to be definitive – is ever remotely the whole story. To the lure of the lyric, I've perhaps too easily succumbed. Experimental work that has no desire to mean, suggest or communicate beyond its own supra-syntactic linguistic ingenuity has lost out somewhat. But *Dream State did* state; and I hope readers will seek less direct, more postmodernly occluded poetry elsewhere. Even if, back in 1994, my conscience wasn't completely clear, my criteria were. The rationale is less securely rational this time around, but caprice and whimsy have, I hope, been kept at bay.

Basically, this is *Dream State* more or less as was, with as much as practicable kept and as much as possible added. There are new poems, renovated autobiographical notes and recent photos to complement the core of previously selected work from the existing contributors, only one of whom has been 'dropped', each of whom I am exhilarated and grateful to have back: poets and poems new to this second edition, with me, as before, picking the poems I thought strongest and/or most representative. When the latter precluded too much of the former, I favoured the strong and striking. And to come clean, where I have happened upon strong poems about Scotland, I have tended to stick them in. Sadly, some such poems could not be kept on. I won't be the only one to miss the scathing urban Scots of Alison Kermack, one of *Dream State*'s stars, but she hasn't been writing and so many others have. Gary Anderson's evocative and poetic boxed collage (how many visual quotes can *you* spot?) was commissioned for *Dream State* I, and has adorned my wall ever since. If its reprise here were *Dream State* II's only distinction, it would be a considerable one. He has my thanks. And so do Lorna Copeland, who helped heroically with the first edition, and Julia Carson, to whom much is owed in the second. For a penetrating and touching (Fringe First-winning) theatrical adaptation of *Dream State*, I'd like to acknowledge Debbie Andrews. And at Polygon, Alison Bowden and Holly Roberts deserve a big vote of thanks.

Finally, because we only begin fully to appreciate what we have lost, when it can never be recovered, may I make belated and embarrassed amends by noting the impact and influence of another great poet on nearly every writer in this anthology? It was when the book had gone to press that I saw and heard just how much of Iain Crichton Smith it contained. His praise of *Dream State* meant a lot. What humility. What humanity. How loved he was. Contemplative depth, sharp yet genial wit, lyrical sonority, undeluded but never disillusioned feeling for, and adroitness in and between the languages of, Scotland: I hope this new edition has some of Iain's qualities . . .

JOHN BURNSIDE

As it happens, I'm not particularly interested in myself as a person, or even as a writer; I'm interested in a world.

I think poetry imagines, at the same time as it observes, a world. The world I imagine and observe begins with 'the natural', proceeds by exploring the lines we draw between ourselves and that world – why? where are they? why are they there and not somewhere else? – and ends in asking questions about dwelling, that is, about ecology.

For me, poetry is also a matter of repentance. To repent as in 'to wish to amend', 'to reconsider'; in my most recent poetry, then, I am engaged in an act of repentance.

I do not want people to see art, or cleverness in my work. I want a reader of a poem or story of mine to think again about the world we imagine as given. Is this where s/he wants to dwell? Is it something to be taken for granted? Why does it seem to be controlled or owned by others?

I grew up in a no-culture, a society that didn't know what it was for, though it knew what it was against. It knew, for example, that there is something unmanly about eros in any of its possible forms; it knew that culture in the broadest sense, in the sense of nourishment or investiture, was the property of others; it knew that its duty to me was to suppress any shiver of awe, or wonder, or joy that I might experience, in case I got the wrong idea about my place in the world. All of this, of course, was said to be for my own protection.

Party politics of the old right–left variety ought to be an interesting piece of history; we need to move beyond divisions of that kind. They are no longer useful. Too often, the British political poet is concerned with those old left–right dualisms. There are poets elsewhere who have moved beyond these limits – towards a poiesis, towards an ecology.

I am a poet because I am interested in living as a spirit. To the extent that we can speak of such things, I propose that we are not born with a spirit (as we are born with lungs, or a heart, say), but that we live as spirits, by an imaginative – and so magical or alchemical – process, an invention, by which we create ourselves from moment to moment, just as the world around us creates itself out of nothing.

Because this is the kind of work that engages me, any other biographical details are irrelevant.

Publications:

Poetry:
The Hoop (Carcanet, 1988)
Common Knowledge (Secker and Warburg, 1991)
Feast Days (Secker and Warburg, 1992)
The Myth of the Twin (Jonathan Cape, 1994)
Swimming in the Flood (Jonathan Cape, 1995)
Penguin Modern Poets 9 (Penguin, 1996)
A Normal Skin (Jonathan Cape, 1997)
The Asylum Dance (Jonathan Cape, 2000)

Fiction:
The Dumb House (Jonathan Cape, 1997)
The Mercy Boys (Jonathan Cape, 1999)
Burning Elvis (Jonathan Cape, 2000)
The Locust Room (Jonathan Cape, 2001)

Two Saints

My first school was a wooden bungalow
named for Brigid, patron saint of wells.
I thought she must be cold, like the closed spring
that whispered in the wood behind our house,
but later I was told of sacred fires
deep in Kildare, where monasteries were built
according to Pope Gregory's decree.
The elder Brigid glimmered in that land:
a motion under flames, the shifting greens
of dark and bright, bound in a speaking hearth.
I felt time shatter when the Normans came.

Lessons went unlearned. I played a part,
scratched the twelve times table on my cuffs
and copied spelling lists from hidden books.
But I was thinking of the undergrowth.
There would be dreams and Brigid would be there;
blue as rain her firelight on my skin.

One day I helped my father clear a pond.
We drew rakes through the water, gathered weed
and raised it dripping, shot with sudden light.
The weft was heavy, tugging for its depth.
Spread on the path, it shone like new-dyed silk.

That year we moved. There was another school:
red brick walls, locks and window bars.
It echoed like a vault when we ran out
to Christmases; the waxy corridors
swarmed with Roman numerals and names.
Saint Columba's High. If there were tales
of wicker furnaces and holy wells
I have forgotten them.
Every month we had a class exam:
History was statute books and wars,
Sixteen Hundred to the present day,
never reaching now. I started French.
All I knew of that school's saint was this:
that it was he who gave the people
books and silence at the story's end
and on an island sheltered from the stream
he drowned the oracles in chiselled stone.

URBAN MYTHS

The secret versions of ourselves,
truthful because they seem
remembered: laughing children
hidden amongst lupins,
cars by the roadside vanishing in fog:

and terrors we meant to avoid
tracking us through a long
acquaintance:
blood on the kitchen floor, blood in the roof;
networks of bone and nerve in drifted leaves

snagging the rake; a perfume of resurrection
filling our throats, sweeter than we expected,
the scent of a garden surrendered to someone else,
the ghosts in its shrubbery only this moment's loss:
a life recalled, that could not happen now,
like summering elms, or the Jesus who walks in carols.

EXILE'S RETURN

Hard to imagine it, lying intact,
folded into books: identity
to be assumed like tartan,
or spelt out on museum clocks
from heretic stones and peat-blacked pots,
history by strip light. Do we know
where we are in these tourist hills?
Is it plantain we chew to draw the taste
our childhood was? The soft, even names
come easily, we have the voice for them, we know
the stories of threadwork and burning turf
and supple hands that gather in a storm.
And when we reach the narrow, choppy loch
we remember the legends of giant fish
that no one believed and everybody told
as we drove south that morning, years ago,
pretending we could find our own way home.

OUT OF EXILE

When we are driving through the border towns
we talk of houses, empty after years
of tea and conversation;
of afternoons marooned against a clock
and silences elected out of fear,
of lives endured for what we disbelieved.

We recognise the shop fronts and the names,
the rushing trees and streets into the dark;
we recognise a pattern in the sky:
blackness flapping like a broken tent,
shadow foxes running in the stars.
But what we recognise is what we bring.

Driving, early, through the border towns,
the dark stone houses clanging at our wheels,
and we invent things as they might have been:
a light switched on, some night, against the cold,
and children at the door, with bags and coats,
telling stories, laughing, coming home.

I was an extra, walking home alone
in a matinée rain,

vaguely aware of the church, and the hunting owls
on Stenhouse Street, the house-of-horror bats

circling the lamps, a sub-fluorescent dust
of popcorn and velour, sprinkled on my clothes

like spots of light.
                Mother was Myrna Loy
in the empty kitchen,

standing at the centre of the world
with flour on her hands, in a halo of musk and steam,

and someone else was coming from the gold
of infinite distance, someone I would know

from memory: the master of the house,
plugged into the undertow of scripts

where I could happen, suddenly alive,
chosen for something, leaving my bed in the dark

and crossing the yard to meet him on the far
border of knowledge and skill,

the hero now, the one I should have been:
Walter Pidgeon. Gable. Franchot Tone.

BLUE

The way some towns would change under a rain
in childhood
and how they no longer do, or are never quite
as blue as they were: the windows turning to dusk
in the seafront cafe
and stairwells filling quickly with a thick
damp fur.
           The way we found ourselves
in waiting rooms and haberdashers' shops

gone strange in the blue of it: fish-scaled, with souls of ink;
the way we stood for hours
in the town museum,
watching that bowl of cinquecento fruit
the painter had sickened with rot – the one thing we knew
in all that gold and amber, perfect scabs
of blue-black mottling the skin
and haunted by the memory
of flies;
        and how, in snow-light, walking home from Mass
we chose it over incense and the singing
dizziness that made us think of God,
stepping away from the crib and the noise of bells
to feel the midnight darkness from the woods
cooling our faces, pagan and undefiled.

HUSBANDRY

Why children make pulp of slugs
with a sprinkling of salt

or hang a nest of fledglings on a gate
with stolen pins

is why I sometimes turn towards the dark
and leave you guessing.

only to know the butter and nickel taste
of cruelty;
                to watch, and show no sign

of having seen
                Not
wickedness, that sometimes celebrates

a tightness in the mind;
but what I comprehend

of fear and love:
cradled remoteness, nurtured by stalled desire;

willed deprivation;
the silence I'm learning by heart.

A SMOKE

The harbour's empty of water
                                gulls
wading the sweet mud

as I walk to the shell
of the lighthouse
                    the mineral kiss

of nicotine and tar
between my lips
                    each knot of smoke

fingered by a wind that tastes
of fairgrounds and far-off

dance halls
                and the burn
of exit lights in Perth or Cardenden

pleasures so small
they flicker on my skin

like cheap perfume
or someone else's rain.

A NORMAL SKIN

The wet days come like a rash:
after a month of sun, the windowpanes
are clouded with the afterlife
of cat fur and busy-lizzies,
and, gloved in her latest attack
of eczema, our silent neighbour
sits between her curtains like a burning
candle, her face turned aside,
her shoulders hunched.
She's taking apart the clocks she collected all year
at boot fairs and local fêtes
and laying them out in pieces on the table.
She knows how things are made – that's not the point –

what matters is the order she creates
and fixes in her mind:
a map of cogs and springs, laid out in rows,
invisibly numbered.
                    What we desire in pain
is order, the impression of a life
that cannot be destroyed, only dismantled.
For years you would buy those razors with orange handles,
the toothpastes and mild shampoos for a sensitive skin
I never had. For years, I took apart
the memories I thought would make me whole
being unravelled.
                    What we desire in pain
is reason: an impression of ourselves
as wounded, explained,
coerced from a destination.
                    Late at night,
our neighbour draws her curtains, disappears,
and lies in the healing darkness, half-awake,
achieving a normal skin
by an effort of will.
                    I'm not the one you thought
was sensitive, the soul you hoped to find:
arriving home, still wet with moonlit rain,
I enter the silence you left, in a dreamless house,
and reckon how little I feel,
when I stop to listen.

John Burnside

ROBIN ROBERTSON

Robin Robertson was born in Scone and brought up in Aberdeen. *A Painted Field* won the 1997 Forward Prize for Best First Collection, the Aldeburgh Poetry Festival Prize and the Saltire Society Scottish First Book of the Year Award. *A Painted Field* has subsequently been published in the States by Harcourt Brace and in Italy by Guanda. His poetry has appeared in a number of anthologies, including *The New Penguin Book of Scottish Verse* (ed. Crawford and Imlah) *The Penguin Book of Poetry from Britain and Ireland since 1945* (ed. Armitage and Crawford), *Penguin Modern Poets 13* (with Michael Hofmann and Michael Longley) and *20th Century Scottish Poems* (ed. Dunn). He publishes regularly in the *London Review of Books* and *The New Yorker* and lives in London.

His second collection, *Slow Air*, was published in early 2002 by Picador.

Publications:

Camera Obscura (Colophon Press, 1996; limited edition)
A Painted Field (Picador, 1997; Harcourt Brace, 1998; Guanda, 2002 – under the title *Camera Obscura*)
Slow Air (Picador, 2002; Harcourt Brace, 2003)

Four Views from the Camera Obscura

A herringbone of pends and wynds,
tenements in a guddle on top of each other
with a common stair like a street on its end;
the stone cliffs of the city scarped
as steep as the trap rock;
the high *lands*, smoking hives.

*

In Princes Street Gardens
a grey man holds up his daughter to pee,
her dress up about her, and him shaking.
But he is not her father,
his trousers at his knees,
their Tennent's Lager spilling in the grass.

*

To the Old Waverley: through the giant Y and H
of its sign, through the net-curtain gap
to the room inside, a lobster-pot of macramé,
sweltry, gravid: the German video on
with the sound down: the threshing hotel bed,
abandoned drinks. The red mesh of scorpions.

*

You are in another country, I know, but I did
just see you on that corner, clearly,
then passing in that cab, head down,
dashing me a note perhaps. The sap of you
still on my hands. A trace.
Wait.
Wait for me here.

FALSE SPRING

A lift in the weather: a clemency
I cling to like the legend

of myself: self-exiled,
world-wounded, god

of evenings like this,
eighty degrees and half a world away.

*

All night, the industry
of erasure, effacement,

our one mouth
working itself dry.

*

But even a god can't stop the light
that finds us, annealed,

fruitless, two strangers
broken on the field of day.

In the window-box,
the narcissi come up blind.

PIBROCH

Foam in the sand-lap of the north-sea water
fizzles out – leaves the beach mouthing –
the flecks of the last kiss
kissed away by the next wave, rushing;
each shearing over its own sea-valve
as it turns with a shock into sound.

And how I long now for the pibroch,
pibroch long and slow, lamenting all this:
all this longing for the right wave,
for the special wave that toils
behind the pilot but can never find a home –
find my edge to crash against,
my darkness for its darknesses
my hands amongst its foam.

WEDDING THE LOCKSMITH'S DAUGHTER

The slow-grained slide to embed the blade
of the key is a sheathing,
a gliding on graphite, pushing inside
to find the ribs of the lock.

Sunk home, the true key slots to its matrix;
geared, tight-fitting, they turn
together, shooting the spring-lock,
throwing the bolt. Dactyls, iambics –

the clinch of words – the hidden couplings
in the cased machine. A chime of sound
on sound: the way the sung note snibs on meaning

and holds. The lines engage and marry now,
their bells are keeping time;
the church doors close and open underground.

THE LONG HOME

I hadn't been back in twenty years
and he was still here, by the fire,
at the far end of the longest bar-counter
in Aberdeen – some say Scotland.
Not many in, and my favourite time:
the dog-watch; the city still working,
its tortoiseshell light just legible
in the smoked windows,
and through the slow delay of glass
the streetlights
batting into life.

The firewood's sap
buzzing like a trapped fly,
the granular crackle of a *Green Final*
folded and unfolded,
the sound of the coals
unwrapping themselves like sweets.
He only looked up when the barman
poured a bucketful of ice
into the sink, like a tremendous
burst of applause.

He was drinking Sweetheart Stout
and whisky, staring into the glass
of malt as if it were the past, occasionally
taking a pull on the long brown bottle.
I remember him telling me,
with that grim smile,
'I'm washing my wounds in alcohol.'
I liked a drink too,
but would always leave before him,
walking home, as if on a wire.

I'd heard what had happened
but wasn't ready for the terrible wig,
all down at one side, the turn
in his mouth and his face's
hectic blaze. He'd left here so bad
he could barely stand.
He'd got through his door, back to his room
and passed out for the night,
sleeping like a log with his head in the fire.

ABERDEEN

The grey sea turns in its sleep
disturbing seagulls from the green rock.

We watched the long collapse, the black drop
and frothing of the toppled wave; looked out
on the dark that goes to Norway.

We lay all night in an open boat, that rocked
by the harbour wall – listening to the tyres creak
at the stone quay, trying to keep time –
till the night-fishers came in their arc, their lap
of light: the fat slap of waves, the water's
sway, the water mullioned with light.

The sifting rain, italic rain; the smirr
that drifted down for days; the sleet.
Your hair full of hail, as if sewn there.
In the damp sheets we left each other sea-gifts,
watermarks: long lost now in all these years
of the rip-tide's swell and trawl.

All night the feeding storm banked up
the streets and houses. In the morning
the sky was yellow, the frost ringing.

The grey sea turns in its sleep
disturbing seagulls from the green rock.

CAROL ANN DUFFY

'I was born in Glasgow in 1955 and lived first in the Gorbals and then in Nitshill. My family moved to England in the early 1960s and I spent most of my childhood in Stafford. In 1974 I went to Liverpool University, to read Philosophy, and from 1978 have been a full-time writer. I've written a few plays for stage and for radio, but this work has always been secondary to my work as a poet. I moved to London in 1982 and lived there for several years. When my daughter was born in 1995 I moved north again and currently live in Manchester. Since her birth, I've become more and more interested in writing poems for children to read.'

Carol Ann won the Forward and Whitbread Poetry Prizes in 1993.

Publications:

Standing Female Nude (Anvil, 1985)
Selling Manhattan (Anvil, 1987)
The Other Country (Anvil, 1990)
Mean Time (Anvil, 1993)
Selected Poems (Penguin, 1994)
Grimm Tales (Faber, 1995)
More Grimm Tales (Faber, 1997)
Rumpelstilstskin (Faber, 1999)
Meeting Midnight (Faber, 1999)
The Salmon (Salmon Publishing, 1999)
Time's Tidings (Anvil, 1999)
The World's Wife (Anvil, 2000/Picador, 2000)
The Oldest Girl in the World (Faber, 2001)
Hand in Hand (Picador, 2001)

POET FOR OUR TIMES

I write the headlines for a Daily Paper.
It's just a knack one's born with all-right-Squire.
You do not have to be an educator,
just bang the words down like they're screaming *Fire!*
CECIL-KEAYS ROW SHOCK TELLS EYETIE WAITER.
ENGLAND FAN CALLS WHINGEING FROG A LIAR.

Cheers. Thing is, you've got to grab attention
with just one phrase as punters rush on by.
I've made mistakes too numerous to mention,
so now we print the buggers inches high.
TOP MP PANTIE ROMP INCREASES TENSION.
RENT BOY: ROCK STAR PAID ME WELL TO LIE.

I like to think that I'm a sort of poet
for our times. My shout. Know what I mean?
I've got a special talent and I show it
in punchy haikus featuring the Queen.
DIPLOMAT IN BED WITH SERBO-CROAT.
EASTENDERS' BONKING SHOCK IS WELL-OBSCENE.

Of course, these days, there's not the sense of panic
you got a few years back. What with the box
et cet. I wish I'd been around when the Titanic
sank. To headline that, mate, would've been the tops.
SEE PAGE 3 TODAY GENTS THEY'RE GIGANTIC.
KINNOCK-BASHER MAGGIE PULLS OUT STOPS.

And, yes, I have a dream – make that a scotch, ta –
that kids will know my headlines off by heart.
IMMIGRANTS FLOOD IN CLAIMS HEATHROW WATCHER.
GREEN PARTY WOMAN IS A NIGHTCLUB TART.
The poems of the decade . . . *Stuff'em! Gotcha!*
The instant tits and bottom line of art.

TRANSLATING THE ENGLISH, 1989

'. . . and much of the poetry, alas, is lost in translation . . . '

Welcome to my country! We have here Edwina Currie
and The Sun newspaper. Much excitement.

Also the weather has been most improving
even in February. Daffodils. (Wordsworth. Up North.) If you like
Shakespeare or even Opera we have too the Black Market.
For two hundred quids we are talking Les Miserables,
nods being as good as winks. Don't eat the eggs.
Wheel-clamp. Dogs. Vagrants. A tour of our wonderful
capital city is not to be missed. The Fergie,
The Princess Di and the football hooligan, truly you will
like it here, Squire. Also we can be talking crack, smack
and Carling Black Label if we are so inclined. Don't
drink the H2O. All very proud we now have
a green Prime Minister. What colour yours? Binbags.
You will be knowing of Charles Dickens and Terry Wogan
and Scotland. All this can be arranged for cash no questions.
Ireland not on. Fish and chips and the Official Secrets Act
second to none. Here we go. We are liking
a smashing good time like estate agents and Neighbours,
also Brookside for we are allowed four Channels.
How many you have? Last night of Proms. Andrew
Lloyd-Webber. Jeffrey Archer. Plenty culture you will be agreeing.
Also history and buildings. The Houses of Lords. Docklands.
Many thrills and high interest rates for own good. Muggers.
Much lead in petrol. Filth. Rule Britannia and child abuse.
Electronic tagging, Boss, ten pints and plenty rape. Queen Mum.
Channel Tunnel. You get here fast no problem to my country
my country my country welcome welcome welcome.

ORIGINALLY

We came from our own country in a red room
which fell through the fields, our mother singing
our father's name to the turn of the wheels.
My brothers cried, one of them bawling *Home,
Home*, as the miles rushed back to the city,
the street, the house, the vacant rooms
where we didn't live any more. I stared
at the eyes of a blind toy, holding its paw.

All childhood is an emigration. Some are slow,
leaving you standing, resigned, up an avenue
where no one you know stays. Others are sudden.
Your accent wrong. Corners, which seem familiar,
leading to unimagined, pebble-dashed estates, big boys

eating worms and shouting words you don't understand.
My parents' anxiety stirred like a loose tooth
in my head. *I want our own country*, I said.

But then you forget, or don't recall, or change,
and, seeing your brother swallow a slug, feel only
a skelf of shame. I remember my tongue
shedding its skin like a snake, my voice
in the classroom sounding just like the rest. Do I only think
I lost a river, culture, speech, sense of first space
and the right place? Now. *Where do you come from?*
strangers ask. *Originally?* And I hesitate.

ASH WEDNESDAY 1984

In St Austin's and Sacré Coeur the accents of ignorance
sing out. The Catholic's spanking wains are marked
by a bigot's thumbprint dipped in burnt black palm.
Dead language rises up and does them harm.

I remember this. The giving up of gobstoppers
for Lent, the weekly invention of venial sin
in a dusty box. Once, in pale blue dresses,
we kissed petals for the Bishop's feet.

Stafford's guilty sinners slobbered at their beads, beneath
the purple-shrouded plaster saints. We were Scottish,
moved down there for work, and every Sunday
I was leathered up the road to Church.

Get to Communion and none of your cheek.
We'll put the fear of God in your bones.
Swallow the Eucharist, humble and meek.
St Stephen was martyred with stones.

It makes me sick. My soul is not a vest
spattered with wee black marks. Miracles and shamrocks
and transubstantiation are all my ass.
For Christ's sake, do not send your kids to Mass.

THE WAY MY MOTHER SPEAKS

I say her phrases to myself
in my head
or under the shallows of my breath,
restful shapes moving.
The day and ever. The day and ever.

The train this slow evening
goes down England
browsing for the right sky,
too blue swapped for a cool grey.
For miles I have been saying
What like is it
the way I say things when I think.
Nothing is silent. Nothing is not silent.
What like is it.

Only tonight
I am happy and sad
like a child who stood at the end of summer
and dipped a net
in a green, erotic pond. *The day
and ever. The day and ever.*

I am homesick, free, in love
with the way my mother speaks.

TO THE UNKNOWN LOVER

Horrifying, the very thought of you,
whoever you are,
future knife to my scar,
stay where you are.

Be handsome, beautiful, drop-dead
gorgeous, keep away.
Read my lips.
No way. OK?

This old heart of mine's
a battered purse.

These ears are closed.
Don't phone, want dinner,

make things worse.
Your little quirks?
Your wee endearing ways?
What makes you you, all that?

Stuff it, mount it, hang it
on the wall, sell tickets,
I won't come. Get back. Get lost.
Get real. Get a life. Keep shtum.

And just, you must, remember this –
there'll be no kiss, no clinch,
no smoochy dance, no true romance.
You are *Anonymous.* You're *Who*?

Here's not looking, kid, at you.

ELVIS'S TWIN SISTER

Are you lonesome tonight? Do you miss me tonight?

Elvis is alive and she's female: Madonna

In the convent, y'all,
I tend the gardens,
watch things grow,
pray for the immortal soul
of rock 'n' roll.

They call me
Sister Presley here.
The Reverend Mother
digs the way I move my hips
just like my brother.

Gregorian chant
drifts out across the herbs,
Pascha nostrum immolatus est . . .
I wear a simple habit,
darkish hues,

a wimple with a novice-sewn
lace band, a rosary,
a chain of keys,
a pair of good and sturdy
blue suede shoes.

I think of it
as Graceland here,
a land of grace.
It puts my trademark slow lopsided smile
back on my face.

MRS DARWIN

7 April 1852.

Went to the Zoo.
I said to Him –
Something about that Chimpanzee over there reminds me of you.

LIVERPOOL ECHO

Pat Hodges kissed you once, although quite shy,
in sixty-two. Small crowds in Matthew Street
endure rain for the echo of a beat,
as if nostalgia means you did not die.

Inside phone-booths loveless ladies cry
on Merseyside. Their faces show defeat.
An ancient jukebox blares out Ain't She Sweet
in Liverpool, which cannot say goodbye.

Here everybody has an anecdote
of how they met you, were the best of mates.
The seagulls circle round a ferry-boat

out on the river, where it's getting late.
Like litter on the water, people float
outside the Cavern in the rain. And wait.

ROBIN LINDSAY WILSON

Robin Lindsay Wilson was born and raised in South Australia. When he was fourteen he returned with his parents to their native Ayrshire. He attended Kilmarnock Academy – where he began to write poetry.

A graduate of the Royal Scottish Academy of Music and Drama, he taught drama for five years in the east end of Glasgow. In the early 1980s he began his lengthy career as a lecturer in acting and theatre directing at Glasgow Arts Centre – where he worked with many young actors who have subsequently become nationally and internationally famous.

He is currently the Artistic Director of Theatre Works, based in Glasgow, and continues to teach acting to students at the Universities of Glasgow and Strathclyde as well as the Scottish Youth Theatre and the RSAMD.

His creation of the unique Actors' Labs has resulted in the publication of the first of his six books on acting – *The Actors' Lab Workshops*. These books are now being used throughout the UK to teach acting to students.

A prolific playwright, he has written for BBC radio and television and a number of professional theatre companies. In 1999 his play *Messengers* won a coveted Fringe First award at the Edinburgh Festival.

His poetry has also been awarded prizes. Two anthologies featuring selections of his poetry *The Stumbling Dance* and *Private Cities* have been printed by Stride Publications. Robin has also contributed poems to an anthology celebrating the city of Edinburgh *Edinburgh: An Intimate City*, edited by Bashabi Fraser and Elaine Greig (City of Edinburgh Council, 2001) and to one celebrating Glasgow – *Back to the Light*, edited by Donny O'Rourke and Hamish Whyte (Mariscat, 2001).

Publications:

Robin's work has appeared in:
Envoi; *Magma*; *Zenos*; *Cencrastus*; *Chapman*; *The Rialto*; *Iron*; *Northwords*; *Nerve*; *West Coast*; *Iota*; *Lines Review*; *Graffiti*; *Foolscap*; *The Scottish Review*; *Contemporary Review*; *Slow Dancer*; and *Links*.

Anthologies:
Private Cities, edited by Joel Lane (Stride Publications, 1993)
The Stumbling Dance, edited by Rupert M. Loydell (Stride Publications, 1994)
Play:
Messengers (Winner of Fringe First Award at the Edinburgh Festival)

Robin Lindsay Wilson

MARK ROTHKO'S LOCHS

Loch Doon is green and maroon
we never know what to do there
except remember the child
who returned from the war
and cast his mad hook
into the sane water –

my dad is dead
and my dad is still wading
along the sun corroded bank
of this Rothko painting

he goes into the past untitled
and the funeral lasts a thousand years

Loch Ken is worth repeating
it's number 7 pure and straight –
it has a tin of millionaire shortbread
and a thermos up its jukes
it will always be temporary and unpacked
from my mum's happy Tupperware –
its lapping yellow sweet tea
is offered until it satisfies
but she takes nothing for herself

she goes into the past untitled
and the funeral lasts a thousand years

Loch Fyne has no regrets
it knocks back the Beck's and the Gold Beer
but never gets drunk –
it's orange, gray on plum –
every summer Sandi – Rhona
Susan and the Forsyth twins

find another twist of hopeful coast –
it's a sunny lack of judgement
while the surface entertains
and the solar whoosh of friendship
fills our glasses with bubbles

they go into the past untitled
and the funeral lasts a thousand years

Loch Morar tips the balance
you are surprised at black on black
and all those lives uncoupling –
time used well and unused
falling into formless mirk
but we don't die separately –

I'm dead in you
You are dead in me
and we're under the black
of our defeated kin
and our dead preparation
at the end as tender as the dark
of our beginning
loving the sure truth
we have found in each other

I go into the past untitled
and the funeral lasts a thousand years

THE PURSUIT OF HAPPINESS

my notes are scattered
and I can't remember
why I'm bad
and why the world is dirty

perhaps it's the weather
piling up the clouds
on scared weekends
and broken promises

I'm living for the moment
but the moment

hasn't started yet
I'm living
for an Oscar nomination
and a lottery win
but I'm not an actor and
I haven't filled in the form

this pursuit of happiness
is a skirmish of snack food
snack friends snack TV

I've lost my voice
left it in a cinema
destroyed it
with home copying
under a rush
of David Byrne

and behind
the telly cables swinging,
under the tenement sky
the spine-barometer drops
and the ticking of clocks
has silenced my eyes

I should want
what I used to want
I should want
what you want
and more

but I can't remember
why I was born
and why I'm bad

perhaps it's time
to be born again
wanting nothing
but to make you happy

perhaps
that's what my work is

D. Y. Cameron's Government of Light

on this shore
I'm in bog myrtle light
picking the light
inside the sorrel stem
throwing sloe berry
dark lantern light
across the waves
warming my hands
on orange lichen

independent of windows
and city and fashion light
Loch Lomond's reservoir
of deep bright sky is
turning me upside down

I belong
to the bruised landscape
across the water
the bad luck country
where the horizontal rain
absolves me of ambition

I've only got to walk
under difficult branches
to be in a bright foreign country
which never had a future before

I could wait for a cloud
I could enter into government
I could vote for the space
between the broken bracken
and the muddy path

I could vote
for your slammed door
and your dry stane mind
or a change of heart for this
new parliament of Scotland

Continuing

nowhere special
a street without a castle
just a building society
and some municipal tulips where my family
look right and left
for a way to be modern

untouched by the fight
of this small town against gravity
they pride themselves
on their independence

no one's death has helped them
no one's love has changed them

they're disappointed in everything I do
they compare me to America

I'm bored too
I could stand by the chained pens
plastic pads and pay-in slips –
withdraw our share account
and leaving by the side door
feel as good as they do
at being unconnected to any obstacle
like time or charity

I can see my children
through the painted O of Scotland
ignoring anyone who's ordinary
they're modern while they wait
for me to spontaneously combust
or be teleported by aliens

remaining unsurprised if I used this O
as a rifle sight

left unharmed if I walked away

today
I am too ordinary
to present you with a compliment

the tenements are water stained
over new brick gable-ends
salt lichens spread

the streets
as always smell
of vinegar and burning iron

the wind is drying
the spit on my lips
the weather is petty
there's a trade
in brittle little similes

midgets are eating fish and chips
all we do is stare at cars
and I wish I had a secret list
of compliments in case
you really are my counterpart

tomorrow
when you arrive
I hope you find
this lack of a comparison
a measure of your absence
this loss of inspiration
a back-handed compliment

GEORGE GUNN

I was born in Thurso in 1956. I left school at sixteen and spent two years fishing in the North Sea. For seven years I worked on semi-submersible drilling rigs in the North and Irish Seas. Since then I've held various writing fellowships, the most recent being the Orkney Islands Council (2001). I am currently the Artistic Director of Grey Coast Theatre Company, based in Thurso, which I started in 1992.

From all of that it will come as no surprise that I believe the place for the poet is in the centre of society, not on the margins. Caithness may be in the far north of Scotland but for me it is the centre of my cultural world. I passionately believe that the local is the universal and it is in light of this I see no difference, essentially, between poetry and my other obsession, which is theatre. Poetry is the language of theatre and its public and private manifestations are part of the same human need to speak, to communicate and to be heard: a play can be a private moment, a poem can be a public event.

If I did not write poetry I would not write plays, but because I have been caught up in and concerned with the increasingly vibrant, ever evolving affairs of the theatre I have not recently published as much poetry as I should have. Although the poems here are reprinted, there is much yet which needs to be shared.

Publications:

Poetry:
Into the Anarchic (Pultney Press, 1985)
Sting (Chapman, 1991)
The Winter House (Caithness Books, 1992)
The Gold of Kildonan: Songs of the Grey Coast (Chapman, 1992)
On the Rigs (Keepdate Publishing, 1995)
Whins (Chapman, 1996)

Most recent plays:
Quiet the Dog (Highland Shorts, Traverse Theatre, Highland Tour)
Atomic City (Grey Coast Theatre, Scottish Tour)
The Year of the Burnings (Grey Coast Theatre schools' project, Golspie)

Radio:
1998 – Two series of *Islands*, BBC Radio Scotland
1999–2001 – *The Peat Bog Diaries*, BBC Radio 4

TWO ESCAPES

You will come to me one night
as I lie dying, I think
with my wet sheets & my muscles
taut like so much useless
statue marble & dreaming
of falling I will not fall
but groan & your form
because it will not be really you
will beckon to me & I shall
shrink through the wall
from fear & the guilt of sons

2
Seemingly Patrick Sellar sailed from Banff
across the Moray Firth to Helmsdale
often he would do it, from property
to property, but one day
he almost did not make it
& had to run for the shore at Portgower
his craft broken up by the swelling seas
pity then that the black creel
did not snare him, alas
the common song of Strath Ullidh

GOING DOWN TO THE CROSSROADS WITH ROBERT JOHNSON
(FOR JOHNNY MCLEOD)

I had a dream, Lyle Lovett
was playing in the Drill Hall
in Castletown, we were going to it
we'd been in the St Clair, fill

as a negro's voice & happy
summertime it was, the blues
hung around the lampposts, the crappy
bits of the village came in ones & twos

this indeed was a dream, we met Robert Johnson
across from Abrach MacKays
he ignored everything & said 'Son
play me the truth, I don't need no lies'

he pulled out a battered brown guitar
you pulled out your dented whistle
the itinerant Dounreay worker
caught a Highland bus & primed the missile

other workers forgot, the dual took place
the music of adders from your lips
McLeod, the black & white race
wurlitzed in your hips

Lyle Lovett plays to an empty hall
St Donan plays a saxophone
his music talked of a rise & fall
here we are white negroes, there is Robert Johnson

across the street going down to the crossroads
I said 'I was educated there
it was a rough school, god knows'
then I awoke to the silent air

BEHIND THE BLACKBOARD

The chalk squeaked year after year
as fields turned from frost
to potatoes to corn & the crows
cawked a liturgy of dead souls & arithmetic

as somewhere the dream of a meritocracy
grazed like an Aberdeen Angus
Granny Grind-guts chewed its cud
marched the aisles & spat out 'facts

about the Empire' & the dream world
of Canaan we on-loaded as religion
she told us everything was there
for us & Peedie Swanson winced inside

when it was slapped to us that Churchill
who was bad at sums still
became great, a misty look
crawled across her fish-head eyes

& opportunity like Johnny Onions
appeared briefly in the strange summer
biked & dangling to make us weep
far as we were from its swinging door

YESNABY

Beyond you America
behind you Stromness
far from me now
the tides changing on you
as I walk the crowded mile
of Byres Road, you curve
in my mind like a film
I would run over your top lip
through an equinoxial autumn
putting words in the mouths
of fishermen & crofters
you speak to me still
a language of salt & gull & wave
Hoy over my shoulders like an uncle

ON THE NORTH TRAIN

There is a Thurso lad whose favourite words are
fuck and cunt & his voice
stampedes up the corridor
like a herd of stirks
&, & two others outdo
each other with stories about this
& that macho doing dare

as if, as if nothing in the world
has ever happened before
he spoke, on their way home
from the rigs, from the oil field
& meanwhile Ross-shire flashes by
Sutherland, Caithness, a coast
of swearing & time on edge

PETER McCAREY

I was born on 11 September 1956 in Paisley, brought up in Glasgow, have lived in Oxford, Paris, Bradford, Leningrad, Venafro, Glasgow, and lodged in Geneva these thirteen years, helping to bring up two daughters. My work has taken me all across sub-Saharan Africa, south India and south-east Asia, though it mostly keeps me stuck in a small office. Donny has picked a few squibs from my pamphlet of dictaphone poems, which came out between two big ones, 'The Devil in the Driving Mirror' and 'Tantris'. Since then, to keep the immediacy of the short poem and the scope of the epic, I have been composing a syllabary of 2,000-odd texts, presented in a randomised but related way on screen, one at a time, with a recording of each. A beta version of the first sixth appeared in 2001 on CD-ROM; a new edition will be issued in the summer of 2002 by Punastic Press, Geneva.

Publications:

Poetry:
Town Shanties (Broch Books, 1991)
The Devil in the Driving Mirror (Vennel Press, 1995)
Double Click (Akros, 1997)
Tantris (special issue of *Lines Review*, no. 140; part 1 appeared in the 1995 *Arvon Anthology*)
In the Metaforest (Vennel Press, 2000)
Augrim, illustrated by Clara Brasca (Pulcinoelefante, 2000)
For What It Is, co-written with Alan Riach (Untold Books, 1986; reprinted from *Edinburgh Review*, no. 72)

Criticism:
Hugh MacDiarmid and the Russians (Scottish Academic Press, 1987)

Not being Bob De Niro

A colour supp. feature on Robert De Niro –
about, more like: they could pin nothing on him.
'All our negotiations were done on the phone.'
Who pays the actor
calls the shots. It's nothing personal.
Highly professional. Bang.
And then, as Jakobson says,
To attribute the feelings expressed in a work
to the author
makes as much sense as mystery play mobs
beating up the actor who played the devil.
If you're convinced, then so am I.
The mediaeval mob is on this bus, though,
reading about someone who won't be drawn
on who calls up the demon in the cage of light.
It's us that let you command those fees;
we trade our cash for folding plush
to see you, and we want to know
just who you think you are, and what
the hell you think you're playing at.
'I want to do things that will
last because they have
substance as well as quality.'
Didn't Duns Scotus say that?
And how d'you get substance onto film?
The only substance is celluloid – light,
if you count it as particles. Look at him there,
beating against that bright screen.
They can't even give him a definite shape.
People get so used with TV dinners
they think the packaging's what's underneath.
It gets gummed up, scar tissue to bone;
frozen or burnt to the throwaway ashet.
What's underneath this 9to5 job
that I'm trailing round like a ball and chain?
For don't you forget that as long as I loathe it,
it is not me and I am not it.
Go on, settle down to the company motor,
step on the gas of the global economy.
Money can buy you happiness (it says
in this ad for a fancy Toyota).
See if I pay just the VAT,
can I get the happiness and leave the hardware?

No? then I'll have to drag it about
and the weight of the world if need be because
I am not it and it doesn't own me.
You don't believe me. You're looking askance
or over my shoulder (get back to your crossword) –
He's got a job and a wife and a kid
and a house and a car and a notion to write.
I play golf myself; gets me some fresh air.
Great he's on xxK bloody yuppie
dinky moaning about no having time to write
because he's a wageslave.
Why doesn't he go on the bru then and write
about what it's like to be unemployed?
If I was on the dole I'd be writing, so
I wouldn't be unemployed.
I've got to come to some arrangement
and this way I still have one way out:
getting off the bus, though if I do that
then I'll soon be a stat in a government scheme.
O so he's admitting he could be worse off
after all he could be out sleeping rough
or nailing up curtains, keeping a family
on moonlight and supplementary.
That's right: this way I've got leisure to moan
so from your way of seeing it,
no right to do so. Away back to Possil.
The video van's on its way.

In the supp. there's this photo of Robert De Niro
what's that in his jacket – a passport?
'He's Italian, he's American, he's perfect'
I was Scottish, but British, imperfect
tense, writing not to be written out.
'Then the door flies open and he bursts in from nowhere.'
So what but. What do you mean so what?
A lot of folk bought this paper;
most of them probably read this, it's
the piece with the biggest picture and fewest words.
'He was thin; his face was gaunt.
When he came back two and a half months later
he was a different man. He looks 20 years older.
He's put on 30 pounds.'
Three pound a week: that's a strain on the heart.
Phantom parturition of selves
that life had left on the cuttingroom floor.

Turn time into space and lives
'll look like olive trees: pruned back
and cracked with the weight,
rerouted, culdesacked in shapes
they're not quite conscious of;
the level of sap in the lung of this tree
is conscience, me, the present tense.
The bus I'm on pulls in to the stop
and the traffic lights go to green.
Curdling smoke carved up in the headlights.
I say to myself: if we're stuck at this junction
I'll be stuck in this job for good.
The last one gets on, the lights go to red,
the bus pulls out and goes through them. So:
there'll be some hitch, some unorthodox move
to make, some rules to break, but I'll get clear.
I hadn't, actually, counted the queue,
I didn't know the sequence of the traffic lights either:
a moment's gamble it was. And yet
I did have an idea of my surroundings
and in some way this moment
shapes the next, the intellect and will.
Look into the branching light
where, stripped of substance, good and evil
can play at sticks and stones and break no bones.
'He knows it's a performance,
so he can be as villainous as the part calls for.'

GARDEN CITY

I met an alkie, I dispensed the small change,
he set aside the small talk and said, 'Listen,
I'm a very good person, you know',
which is to say: Possessions and professional
skills are not of the essence;
I am.
So I said 'Yes' and went away,
which is to say: The unsure strain of such awareness
is left to the likes of you. I want my tea.

It's good: I don't have far to go
from my refurbished close
to see the butcher's apron on a sign set

boldly in the weeping sump, the tobies and broken brick
where head-high rosebay willow herb
with clover, jaggy nettle and soothing dock
festoon and cloy the legend
WIMPEY SUPER SINGLES AND
1, 2 AND 3 BEDROOM FLATS
SELLING TO COMMENCE SHORTLY
or, in a city brasserie,
the porous tit on a plaster cast
poke out from ivy tumbling off a period cuspidor.
It's what the people want. It's what
the people who want it want. It's what the people
who want you to want it want you to want.

Sous les pavés – la plage

The urban sunlight comes in the window
staggering up to its knees in sand
banknotes blowing out of its seams
like scarious leaves and carious buildings
shaking dust from my shoes but it cloys,
it clogs for I'm paid to be here.

Frontiers, harbours, roads, currencies,
crowd control and corpse disposal.

Money is busy buying itself up
using what there is for collateral.

Light is said to be sculpting itself
with its only sense
of touch.

Peter McCarey

Double-click on this
and nothing happens.
23.11.95

I have on at least two occasions
got up in the night and my head as clear as day
telling me you can't live like that
and then gone back to sleep.
12.2.96

Today I scaled the ultimate
8000-metre peak of boredom
I'm not going to write a book about it
but just plant this little flag.

10.10.95

You've got fifteen seconds in which to
achieve enlightenment, pal.

7.96

Unachievable hopes and unassuageable sorrows
that lie like apples where they fall.

Maybe as some of the great religions say
we've been dropped behind the enemy lines,
Chindit, and lost our memory.

Autumn 96

I've sung in otherwise empty buildings
sometimes random, sometimes right.
I've sung until my voice hit gravel.
The open windows are the wings of the night.

19.8.96

MICK IMLAH

Mick Imlah was born in Aberdeen in 1956. He moved as a child to Milngavie near Glasgow, and then to London. He was educated at Dulwich College and read English at Magdalen College, Oxford, which he captained at rugby and cricket and in television's *University Challenge*. He subsequently taught at the University as a Junior Lecturer. Later he worked as the editor of *Poetry Review*, as a travel writer for *Departures* magazine, as poetry editor at Chatto and Windus, as a freelance editor, and as a contributor to *The Times Literary Supplement*, the *Sunday Times* and *The Independent on Sunday* among others. Since 1992 he has been on the staff of *The Times Literary Supplement*, where he is Poetry and Archaeology Editor. He is a Fellow of the Royal Society of Literature. He currently lives in west London.

Publications:

The Zoologist's Bath and other Adventures (Sycamore Press, 1982)
Birthmarks (Chatto and Windus, 1989)
Penguin New Poets 3 (Penguin, 1995)

As co-editor:
The New Penguin Book of Scottish Verse, edited with Robert Crawford (Penguin, 2000)

Forthcoming:
The Lost Leader

I Have a Dream

Seen from a car on a hill near Atlanta, Georgia
Is a model of Richmond, Virginia, built out of plywood
For burning in yesterday's remake of *Gone With The
                                Wind*;
'And that,' I lied to my friends, 'is the shell of a model
Of Toytown, Virginia, burned in the remake of *Dallas*,
A beacon of hope for the South in the *Wars of the Roses*.'

And there, in the plushest of Georgia's suburban
                        plantations
Was the campus of All-the-John-Browns State Beautiful
                        University
Where my own black girlfriend, after seven mint juleps,
Wriggled and jiggled so much in her seat that we gathered
We'd better pull up by some bushes that skirted the road
And would do for a loo. Time passed at a Southern pace;

And when she eventually crawled from a tangle of scrub
With a wig on (a blonde one), and tights round her ankles,
                        weeping
That a gang of black students had jeered her and called her
                        a 'whore',
I took it upon myself to redress the wrong
That racists and sexists too much get away with; lashed
Three twigs of magnolia into a form of birch

And found the white culprits, grouped like a circle of
                        students
In the shade of a flowering dogwood, revising the Bible.
Civil, they rushed to oblige when I dared to step forward
The one who had called her a whore: 'Yes sir, that was
                        me.'
'No, me.' 'You guys, it was *me*!' – Concluding together
'It doesn't appear, sir, as though any of us will admit

That we didn't immediately know she'd want to be paid.'
And slowly the doubts began to assail me there
Like bugs at the cracks in my own model relationship;
Couldn't I tell them apart, the whores and the victims,
The black and white? And what did the servant imply
With his sniggering pun on what passed for the state of
                        Virginia ?

Well, as I followed these difficult turns at the foot
Of an alabaster statue of Washington Booker,
'The Black Lincoln' (or was it the other way round?),
My friends' car (a black Lincoln Convertible)
Shot suddenly up the hill and away as though with
                                    tremendous impatience;
And Atlanta (or was it Atlantis?) vanished in smoke and
                                    dust.

PAST CARING

As a ship
Sees only the tip
Of the ice's pyramid
That has already scraped her bows,
We'd glimpsed that drink was something you overdid;
Now after the wreck I sift the damage you'd stowed in the house.

Eyes glazed
I fumble, amazed,
Through mounds of knickers and slips,
Extracting the bottles you'd buried there; these
I hump in their binbags, clashing against my knees
To the 'Bottlebank', by the public baths; it takes four trips.

The gin!
No wonder you're thin;
Hundreds of bottles of gin;
And feeding them singly into the ring
My arm grows weary from shifting the bottles of gin;
– A numbing collection of lots of exactly the same thing.

You were vain
As you went down the drain;
Why else would you lay up this hoard
If it wasn't one day to take stock as I'm doing
Of what an almighty amount you had taken on board?
And here am I turning your trophies to scrap at an illicit viewing!

A smear
Of lipstick, here –
Like the kiss on a valentine;

And sniffing the neck I feel suddenly near to you,
For what it gives off is your smell, if we kissed any time,
And it wasn't a cheap perfume – but the only thing properly dear
  to you.

Next week
If you're not past caring
They may let you out for an airing,
– To slump in your armchair, too burgled to speak,
The fish out of water that stubbornly stays all the more fish;
– Then how shall we drag the treasure you were back to the surface?

FLOWER OF SCOTLAND (1304–1513)

The arch-appeaser Balliol – dubbed a 'king'
By England's King (also, 'The little arse-licker') –
Whose two-faced father mined Dumfries, yet built
Oxford her nursery school – is history

The moment the Bruce appears from the priory, panting,
His sword in bloom, 'Comyn . . . the Red . . . is kilt!'
(Comyn of Badenoch, a Balliol man)
And Bruce's boys pile in 'to mak siccar'.

So by their murderous pride they raised the flag
At Bannockburn, that fell in the mud at Flodden,
Where Scotland braved a general massacre
Of soldier, sovran, noble and downtrodden.
Woe was Dunbar, mourning his sick makars.
The Highland version lasted till Culloden.

LONDON SCOTTISH (1914)

In April, last full fixture of the spring;
They'd rucked ('Feet, Scottish, Feet!') the fear of God
Into Blackheath. Their club was everything:
From the four sides who played that afternoon –
The stars, but also those on the back pitches –
All sixty volunteered for the touring squad,
Trading their Richmond turf for the Belgian ditches.

October: mad for a fight, they broke too soon
On the Ypres Salient, rushing the ridge between
'Witshit' and Messines.   Three-quarters died.

Of that ill-balanced and fatigued fifteen
The ass selectors favoured to survive,
Just one, Brodie the prop, resumed his post.
The others sometimes drank to 'The Forty-Five':
Neither a humorous nor an idle toast.

WILLIAM HERSHAW

Ma name is William Hershaw and I was born at Newport on Tay on 19th March 1957. Ma faimily muived fae Cowdenbeath tae Lanarkshire in the 1960s. Ma faither was a fireman. We steyed abuin Motherwell Fire Station for a bit and later on near Bellshill. Then we flitted back tae Fife. I went tae Edinburgh University and tuik an M.A. in English Literature and Language. In the seventies I wisnae cut out for academic life. Tae me it seemed fou o snobs, bad teachers and middle-class aspirants. Aiblins it was ma ain faut. I hope it's mibbe changed tho.

I'm Principal Teacher o English at Beath High Schuil – an establishment thrang wi fine pupils and hard-workin staff. I dinnae hae a lot o time tae write but I quite like that – I'm fair gled I dinnae hae tae depend on Scots poems for ma livin, for ma bairns wad be runnin about wi nae erse on their breeks. Poetry's the airt o ma life whaur I'm ma ain boss: I can write whit I like without haein tae souk up, network, mak ma face fit or compete for fellowships, residences, prizes and geegaws. The worst that can happen is I get ma poems sent back.

Ma ambition is tae produce a poem worth keepin within the true tradition o Scottish literature. A chuckie on the cairn. Whit tradition? Ballads and makars; David Lyndsay, Robert Fergusson, Joe Corrie – the stuff that has the wild mercury and deep humanity in it, the matter o Scotland. As you micht expect, I'm no enamoured wi contemporary 'Scottish' poetry: it's devolved poetry. I dinnae feel pairt o it. I'd raither hae Stalin and Saint Paul . . .

So whit am I daein here? Donny O'Rourke and Polygon were guid enough tae ask me and gied me this opportunity tae be an opinionated curmudgeon. Turner Prize? Whitbreid Prize? I'd tak them mair gleglike than a Labour politician up a Lordship.

Publications:

The Cowdenbeath Man (Scottish Cultural Press, 1997)
Four Fife Poets (Aberdeen University Press, 1988)
Across the Water (Argyll Publishing, 2000)
A Scots Mass For Saint Andrae (Touch The Earth Publications, 2001)

TAE MA MITHER AND FAITHER

Honest, hard-warkin, warkin-class Fife fouk,
Son and dochter o miners theirsels,
Brocht me up tae hae
Faur mair than they,
Forby, tae mind whaur I cam fae as weill.

Langtime it's taen me tae cleirly see,
So reader be mindit that if ye speir
Owre whit sma worth
These wards hae got –
They twa were the makars o me.

JOHNNY THOMSON

Johnny Thomson, lithe as Spring
An athlete and a goalkeeper
Wha could save onythin
But wan wanchancy kick tae the heid
And the lave o a young life
Gi'en scant time tae floor.

Yet ye can still fund auld men
Wha walked tae his funeral in Cardenden
Whase faces wull bloom owre and een
Moisten at memries o days lichtened;
Brocht fae Brigton, means test and dole
Bi his gracefu dives and shut-oots.

Johnny Thomson, in the thirties
Minded naethin fir politics or bigotry
And lay deein at Ibrox park;
Ahent him at the Rangers' en
The hoots and jeers grouwin like weeds
Wad hae drooned oot the crood at Nuremberg.

On Hearing the Psalms Sung in Gaelic

I hae heard them sing
Like a hert-sair bairn desertit bi its faimly.

I hae heard them sing
Sad as the wund, bleak as their corrugated kirk.

Their singin was like ma sowel torn fae ma chist
Tae speik afore me in God's leid.

They sang wi a holy dreid
That tellt o aa they'd lost.

The kythin wards unkent tae me but the hale
Hauf-kent, a tale mindit fae bairnhood.

I hae heard them sing,
Noo I maun believe their tungue was heard
In whit Eden there ever was.

Januar Winds o Revolution
From A Calendar o a Seaside Toun

A cauld, sleety wind angles doon the High Street.
It blaws aff the Forth and ower the Links,
Past the butcher's, the bookies, the pub and the Store.
It rattles the lichts on the toun Christmas tree,
It birls the newsagent's sign aroond,
It blaws like a wild Blake picter
On this mirkfu Januar efternin.
The Siberian wind kyths fae an airt lang held in ice
And has blawn whaur a biggin-wa's cawed doon.
It has blawn whaur a playwricht's heezed up president,
It has blawn ower a tyrant's bluidy heid,
Through a year o revolutions.
It blaws fae the Kremlin ower the Lammerlaws
And through the tuim heids o Burntisland fowk
On its road ti Glesgi. Syne we craw
At the deith o Socialism and nivir speir oor thirldom.
We blaw o oor culture capital – hot air.

The cauld wind o reality yowls sairly past the Labour Club
Singan that in Prague, Berlin and Bucharest
Are the fowk wi a speerit and smeddum.

SELF-PORTRAIT

Look at that moaning, greeting-faced git,
he's never happy, him.
He has a pamphlet of Lallans verse,
with his individual orthography,
and schemeless bi-lingual rhymes,
his iambics are unintentional dactyls and spondees,
his quarrels are full of morals,
his glower full of dour,
his fire filled with ire,
and the chip on his shoulder is bigger than Hugh
MacDiarmid's ego.
He's a conservative Communist with his ain hoose –
he's a party of one, him.

Just look at him –
you can tell he'll take it all as a personal affront
because he's the only living Scotsman left.
To hear him talk you'd think
he'd been in the Spanish Civil War,
yet he's younger than you.
He's a serious man but,
'cause he carries the woes of the world
in his duffel coat hood.
He's aye ready for a guid literary fecht
but inside, he's that emotional he bruises like a peach.

Haw, you, MacMakkar!
How's about making us laugh for a change?

The Visiting School Poet

I must have taught his poem a million times . . .
'The Old Women In The Snack Bar At Visiting Hour'
I must have taught his poem a million times
and now he's going to sit beside me in the Staffroom.
They'll give him a good reception . . .
too shy to ask questions,
they'll treat him like the Elephant Man.
And slowly he sits down,
and slowly he sits down beside me.
A kind looking, civilised, intensely modest man,
smoking a cigarette in the time it takes
to leave a lover, write a poem or smoke a cigarette
as my arms reach out to wring the bastard's neck.

TURNER PRIZE

A coo an a cauf
Cut in hauf.

ALAN RIACH

Born 1 August 1957 in Airdrie, Lanarkshire, then a darkly sectarian neo-industrial node of many uncles, aunts, cousins, and a singular set of parents and grandparents. Thereby closely encountered a variety of social spectra and endearing unorthodoxies. Extracted age four when mother renounced school teaching mathematics to go with Master Mariner father to Gravesend, Kent, where he piloted ships down the Thames. *Heart of Darkness* begins and ends here.

Back to Scotland whenever we could, for family and balance. First degree at Cambridge, in English. Then Glasgow for the Ph.D., on MacDiarmid. Then, after a long enough spell of strange jobs and unemployment, a post-doctoral fellowship, at the University of Waikato, New Zealand. The other side of the world: a leap into the dark.

Travels: Europe (France, Spain, Italy, Turkey, Germany, old East Berlin); across the USA, once by invitation of the USIA; Australia, a little; Samoa, once.

New Zealand: arrived 1986, went full time 1990, teaching mainly twentieth-century literature, initiating courses in Scottish, Irish, post-colonial literatures, modern poetry, creative writing, contributing to courses in American literature, New Zealand literature and convening the big first year 'Introduction to Literature' courses.

1992: trying to find an obscure Scottish novel of 1944, *Soon Bright Day* by Mary Baird Aitken, found instead a librarian named Rae. Married her. She found the book. Two sons: James and David.

1999/2000: became Associate Professor of English and Pro-Dean of Faculty of Arts and Social Sciences. Poetry published simultaneously in *The Oxford Book of New Zealand Verse* and *Dream State: The New Scottish Poets*. Hybridity? It's just a word. Think about residence.

Left New Zealand 1 January 2001. Started work at the University of Glasgow, in the Department of Scottish Literature. 1 August: Head of Department.

Publications:

This Folding Map (Auckland University Press and Oxford University Press, 1990)
Hugh MacDiarmid's Epic Poetry (Edinburgh University Press, 1991)
An Open Return (Untold Books, 1991)
General Series Editor of *Collected Works of Hugh MacDiarmid*, 16 vols (Carcanet, 1992–ongoing)
First and Last Songs (Auckland University Press/Chapman Books, 1995)
Clearances (Hazard Press, New Zealand, and Scottish Cultural Press, 2001)
The Poetry of Hugh MacDiarmid (Association for Scottish Literary Studies, Glasgow, 1999).

Radio:

Scotland's Renaissance (Concert FM, New Zealand, 1993)
Literature sections of 10-part *Fearful Symmetries: The Twentieth Century in Retrospect* (Concert FM, New Zealand, 1999–2000)
The Good of the Arts (Concert FM, New Zealand, 2001)

AT LOUDOUN HILL

At Loudoun Hill
in its sleep
on the Strathaven Road
on the dreamy edge of Ayrshire
and Lanarkshire,
        in one of the many
corners of this folding map,
where incidental blood once streaked the grass,
and I can't remember now what time
of day it was or even
if I read what time of year –

   It would be cold, like this,
sunlight like teeth, and the yellow grease
on swords and harnesses; even now –
that horse over there: its teeth
have the colour of the day,
and its sound –

        By Loudoun Hill, now,
between Arran and Strathaven,
between the submarines and the frigates
and the gardeners and the forget-me-nots
and the profiteers and the ignorant;

between Arran and the leafy burghs of small-town
Scotland, half-awake, if only that,
where (my Grandfather told me) the only
excitement seen in the streets
was the fairly regular visit of
the hearse . . .

By Loudoun Hill, its odd isolate
shoulder-shape
in the Farmers' fields
in Lanarkshire, in
the Common Market.

I was driving back,
from Arran, and
the sight of it passing
my shoulder made me think a
little about the trip, and I
couldn't imagine I had
made it alone. What does it mean
to be so modern
                    at Loudoun Hill?
with the smell of cow
dung and horsebacks,
the sheep's wool toughness in the grass,
the blotched cows in their loneliness,
the colours in the landscape mainly easy, mostly
tonally the same: redundant greys,
redundant greens. Only
the shoulder
of the hill goes into the wind, goes
                    into the mind
like another thing,
        like you pass through a door
and it's another place, there is something 'still strong
still unflinching in spirit'.

So I stopped the car
and I stood there with a gaunt eye, but not, now,
watching the armies of men on the hillside
and the men on the level fields
preparing their senses and their long blades getting
keener,
but looking at a recent incremental recognition

of who was never there, but holds it
all in balance, now, at Loudoun Hill,
                money-eyed,
watching.

A SHORT INTRODUCTION TO MY UNCLE GLEN

Glen was always building sheds. He'd buy
wood. He had a thing about building sheds. He built
six stables in his garden, then realized
he'd have to buy the horses for them (and did). He built at least
three aviaries and more kennels than I can remember.
He filled the aviaries with parrots and canaries
from Australia, Pacific Islands. He always
had dogs: Alsatians, a Great Dane he would dance with
around the kitchen, before he was married. Now,
his kitchen cupboards are full of his kids' litters of Jack Russells.
He used to like Lonnie Donegan.
He used to play the guitar and yodel like Frank Ifield.
At every piece of news today you tell him
he looks amazed and shakes his head and says: 'My, my!'
A couple of years ago some of the family took a week's
holiday in Tenerife. Glen was walking on the beach
with my father, talking. Apart from the army,
when he'd been in England and learned to be a chef
(and cook these great sweet yellow curries)
he had never been out of Scotland much. He said
to my father, 'Jimmie,' (which is his name) 'you've sailed about
the world a few times.' (Which is true.)
'Tell me,' he said,
'Where exactly are we?'
Surely,
it's the best way to travel.

THEY DREAM ONLY OF SCOTLAND
(after John Ashbery)

The dreams they dream are only of
Scotland to be looking for it through
hundreds of islands and millions

of acres of gorse, to be tasting
this honey is delicious, but it
burns the throat
                    Or hiding from twilight in offices
(they can be adults now, all grown up)
and the murderer's swagger is easily
seen in the shadow on the oblong, lilac loch.
He holds keys in his right hand.
                              – That was before
we could drive for miles, for hundreds of miles
at night on roads through bracken, and when my headache grew
worse, would stop
at a petrol station. Now I care
much more about signs. What sign
does the honey give? What
about the keys?
                    I am going into the bedroom slowly
                    I would not have been hurt
                    had I not fallen against the
                    living-room table. I am back
                    against the bed, doing nothing
                    but waiting in the horror of it
                    for our liberation, and lost
                    without you.

THE BLUES

The lights are on all over Hamilton.
The sky is dark, blue
as a stained glass window in an unfrequented church
say, by Chagall, with grand and glorious chinks
of pinks and purples,
glittering jewels on those glass fronted buildings
where the lifts are all descending
and the doors are
being closed.
                    You're out there somewhere,
going to a concert in wide company or maybe
sitting somewhere weaving a carpet
like a giant tapestry, coloured grey,
pale brown, weaving the wool
back in at the edges of the frame, your

fingers deft as they turn the wool in tight and
gentle curves.
> Or somewhere else.
> What do I do
> except imagine you?
> The river I keep crossing
> keeps going north. The trains
> in the night cross it too.
> Their silver carriages are blue.

NECESSITY OF LISTENING
(for John Purser)

Love makes belief in miracles,
and future brings its own time, not the past's
predictions. You're right enough,
John: we should be content, contented.

Today, your new boat rests
in chuckling water, moored near Glasgow.
Soon you will take her to Skye.
Your hand will rest and move upon the tiller.

Tonight, my wife: her hand upon my arm
now knows no source for its resting;
her sleeping smile is unknowing as I am;
her comfort content is my own, her husband.

KILMARTIN GLEN

I never saw the intricate connections
with quite this sunny clarity before,
such intimate revealing of relations
in brilliance, and at such an hour:
the West and Islands open to the sea
and Ireland, always seemed to be
alive with colour: bright blue waters,
emeralds and snow; but shapes and movement,
glacial striations, ox-bow lakes, tidal rivers,
hill-tops making patterns to each other –

all connect in vision as the art of men
and women finds its laws in natural
reciprocation: raindrops in a quiet pool
form expanding spirals on the bending plane:
an ancient brooch, the lanulae –
silver, gold: water, sunlight, eyes
to see the clearness of design. And this
takes place in mind, imagination:
across 10,000 years, while now
outside the car my father drives, the rain
drives down on grass and bracken, heather
rocks and hills and lochs and lochans,
midges and elusive little fish. The forestry
have camouflaged the earth's wet dark
antiquity; the road between Kilmartin
and the ferry just approaching Oban is
impatient, twisty, a hard fast exit through
this valley of old ghosts. And yet the vision stays
perception, the clarity of sunlight's
careful disposition, in
this undifferentiated time.

CLEARANCES
for James

The clouds go over
singly, or in fleets, trailing
raggedly back, against a sky
where looming vaults of rain
come over too. Then the sky lets loose:
the shades of grey become uncountable,
the rain comes down on everything, diagonal, banks:
the windows, roof, the wooden deck,
the trees around, the green slopes run
with mud, the fields below are soaked and fill;
the road becomes a grey and moving river.

The baby hasn't heard this sound before: the heavy rain
on the iron roof, and cries himself
to sleep, at last, as the downpour
eases off. It must be time to leave.
The weather is an actual farewell.

I used to think the old Gaels of Ireland,
or the west of Scotland, knew
so little of our modern world.
It seemed they were a pastoral people
and burdened with a culture of conservatism.
But clearances are always strong in the mind,
the images recurrent, the rubble of the ruined homes,
the ghosts of children, animals, and men
and women helpless in the face of the event.

Farewells and birth, there are some things
no clues or forms of knowledge alter
in themselves. I won't say they can't help.
They knew about departure, those old people,
and the kinds of life we deal with here
require that inherited wisdom. Now
the heavy showers have passed, but different shades of grey
reflect, refract unnumbered tones of light.
It's time to pack what we have and can carry.
It's time to take what we can, and go. The boy
will not remember this, the landscape
of his parents, unless we do.

ELIZABETH BURNS

I grew up in Edinburgh, have done a degree in English and worked in a variety of jobs, most recently as a creative-writing tutor with the Open College of the Arts.

Of the poems included here, 'Sisters' and 'Poems of Departure' both explore an idea I've often returned to, that of invisibility – in this case, how someone far away is made more real by the presence of objects, dreams and memories. I'm also interested in writing about invisible, unrecorded lives in history, particularly those of women. 'Valda's Poem', for example, gives an imagined voice to the poet's wife. 'For W. S. Graham' also enters, in imagination, the world of a poet, in this case a Scottish poet living in Cornwall. I'm interested in the differences between Scotland and Cornwall, both Celtic, and how Cornwall, with its lighter, less Calvinist feel, may have influenced Graham's poetry.

Publications:

Ophelia and other poems (Polygon, 1991)
The Gift of Light (diehard, 1999)
The Time of Gold (Galdragon Press, 1999)

POEMS OF DEPARTURE

I
in the dream we are in New York   walking the
humid streets
under an orange sunset   blurred with smog
but the houses seem too old and foreign   to belong
here
we cannot find   5th avenue   east 12th street
and everywhere's too quiet and too beautiful for
New York City

an old man with a horse and cart   shuffles past
along deserted gutters   selling white roses

it becomes in the dream   a city of the old world
of quaint houses   the scent of roses in the streets

Europe and America   split by an ocean   the two of us
wrenched between   the old world   and the new

II
I feel as a child about to be abandoned
who screams at her mother 'I don't love you anyway'
I have a stack of sharpened words inside me
that I pull out to wound you with
make little nicks in your skin
instead of kisses   but at the same time
I want to be curled in the crook of your arm
I want things like lullabies and cocoa
an abundance of tendernesses

III
of these last days together I will remember
the motherly holding of one another
the placing in my lap   of the grey and white shell
that you found on the beach at Ardalanish

and your calm voice reading poetry into the night
keeping sadness at bay   though how sibling close it
creeps
until its breath is all over me   inside my imagination
making the tears come at my throat   a blue-grey
sobbing

IV
fat globe   I want to punch you
batter away   at your enormity
I hate you for the   gaps you make
for your infinite   wildernesses
of continents   and oceans
you smug   plump   planet

V
I dream of infidelity   of a woman who discovers
her husband's unfaithfulness abroad
knots silk scarves together   into a noose
pulls it tight   around her neck

VI
we are living in a limbo   in a half life
in the almost colourless place   where the limp tongue
of the last of day   licks the sky with faint colours
slight flickers of green or apricot
these are the shades   we live with
in the place between daylight   and darkness
in the place between your being here   and leaving

VII
the white candle of our last evening   still burns
the white flowered violet that you gave me   blossoms
light falls   on your gift of the rose garden painting

the room is ghosted   with your presence
and remembrances   pungent as rosemary
seep through   the muslin of the heart

SISTERS

Even when she moved
five hundred miles away
telepathy was alive between them
and love as strong as ever

She sends in the post
pressed tulip petals
slivers of shell from the day at the beach
wrapped in tissue paper

She, a book of stories
golden earrings

and she, the painting of a windy day
the daffodil bowl

Even before the letter
saying, between the lines, 'come',
she is on her way

Valda's Poem/Sleevenotes

Sleevenotes to Hugh MacDiarmid's record Whaur Extremes
Meet:
*'Recorded at Brownsbank, the home of Valda and Chris
Grieve, near Biggar in the Lanarkshire hills on two sultry
days in June 1978. Chris, in his chair by the window, talking
with his friend, the poet Norman MacCaig, a wee dram in
every glass. Valda in swimsuit, working in the garden, or
keeping the soft-coated Wheaten and Border Terrier quiet
for the recording.'*

June sun presses on my back as I bend
sweat gathers at my neck and under my arms
I am naked as I can be in my bathing costume

I step out onto the flowerbeds
making light footprints with my bare feet
Spray trails from the watering-can
falls in dark circles round the plants

I want to lie out on the parched grass
and let the sun's hands touch me everywhere
let them finger the frail flesh of my breasts
rub gold into the crease and wrinkle of my stomach

At the open window edged with ivy
they sit, two old men in their shirt-sleeves
On the table between them a bottle of whisky
the two fat volumes of collected poems
and a tape-recorder lapping up their words

The dog flops in the shade of the back door
I go to her when she stirs, stroke her hot fur

give her water, keep her from barking
I hear their talk and laughter, his and Norman's
I hear the rise and fall of Chris's voice
the rhythms of his favourite poems, over and over

In the afternoon I sit against the apple tree
feeling the dent of bark on my bare shoulders
I close my eyes and the murmur of their voices
blurs with the birdsong that maybe
when we listen to the finished record
will have swum inside the poems

FOR W. S. GRAHAM

Sydney, I took a pint of Tinner's Ale
as you took yours: down at the pub at sunset light
when the Zennor sea grows fiercely blue

round this windblown spit of knotted land
where you fled from the knuckled whack of the Clyde,
ran into the lap of the lazy Atlantic.

Was it here that language had you in its clasp,
tossed you like a slip of driftwood on an ocean,
caught you in its net like silvered mackerel?

Did it nip at your tongue on winter days
as you strode the icy edges of the cliffs
and cranked your frozen bones with whisky?

Did it enter your skin when spring came in
with the flecks of blossom, the cuckoo-spit,
the honeyed smell of bluebells in the woods?

Did it spin in your head in sun-plumped summer
when Zennor meadows grow drowsy with bees
and hedgeflowers spill tipsily into the lanes?

Did it hurtle about you in blackberry autumn
when bold winds blow in from the end of the land,
making you cower from the gale and growl of it

down by Madron where the rain in the trees
lulls you to sleep in the wide-eyed dawn
when sea is milky-green and dreams are fleet

and fat with words and you wake with a salt taste
on your tongue? Was this how it had you, Sydney,
all those years? And was the ale always this good,

this golden?

ROBERT ALAN JAMIESON

'Poetry', says Delmore Schwartz,[1] 'is its own reward,' retelling the tale of Orpheus' visit to the older – and at that time better known – poet, Agathon. He has just had his work dismissed by Agathon, and this is his response. 'Poetry is its own reward.' 'Poiesis' is simply 'making' in Greek. And in Orpheus' justification to himself, it is the process of making, rather than the product and the response of any reader, which is emphasised.

To live in a poetic manner, making/creating, that is really all there is to it. We are not lonely without readers, for we are already in a relationship, making response to the world, the countless stimuli it throws at us. By recording with subtlety of mood and feeling, the fleeting sense of possible comprehension, of some kind of order, or 'rightness' beyond the chaos and cruelty we witness, we create a temporary calm. Writing poetry is the search for some means of expressing and so capturing the elusive/allusive sense of understanding that comes upon a person every so often. Different writers have expressed it differently: the 'atom of delight', the 'spot of time', the 'epiphany' and so on. Whatever it is called, and somehow I think it must remain nameless, it nevertheless lies behind the idea of writing/making at all. As we explore the world in the hope of discovering that perfect point in the chronotope, we explore language/ write in the hope of approaching the still centre, the perfect phrase, the felicitous expression, where word, image and idea reach an equilateral agreement. Sometimes it happens.

Poetry is a flexible, living matrix of possibility. It can stretch to carry an involving and memorable narrative, it can snap-shot a split-second and render it as clear as any camera lens. It can fix in words the relationship between abstract entities, it can make concrete the consistency of surface and appearance. I wander around in this place made of language. I try to keep my ears and eyes open, to smell the smells and feel the air. My feet

---

[1] Robert Phillips (ed.), *The Ego is always at the Wheel: Bagatelles, Delmore Schwartz* (Carcanet, 1987).

remain on the ground, but my hands and head are always, somehow, making. And my tongue is ready to speak.

Publications:

Soor Hearts (novel) (Paul Harris, 1984)
Thin Wealth (novel) (Polygon, 1986)
Shoormal (poetry) (Polygon, 1986)
A Day at the Office (long poem/novel) (Polygon, 1991)
Beyond the Far Haaf (libretto) (Vanderbeek and Imrie, 1992)
Mount Hiddenabyss (poetic dialogue with Graeme Todd), (Fruitmarket Gallery, 2000)

Poetry in the following anthologies: *The Best of Scottish Poetry*, ed. Bell (Chambers, 1989); *The Faber Book of Vernacular Verse*, ed. Paulin (Faber, 1991); *The New Makars*, ed. Hubbard (Mercat, 1992); *Ahead of its Time*, ed. McLean (Jonathan Cape, 1997); *Love for Love*, ed. Burnside and Finlay (pocketbooks, 2000); *Wish I Was Here*, ed. Macneil and Finlay (pocketbooks, 2000).

SANG ODA POST WAR EXILES

Harry listen Harry please
We canna bide nae langer.
Da aert is tired man, sae is du,
We'll sell da sheep, we'll sell da coo.
Gie up da lease.

Come man awa
For we maun ging
Across da Soond o Papa.

Harry listen Harry please
Du'll git a better job.
Somethin maer reglar, wi reglar pey,
Dis croftin wark, hit'll never pey.
Life wid be aesier.

Come man awa
For we maun ging
Tae a cooncilhoose in Scallwa.

Meg Meg, du canna ken,
Du døsna understaand.

Foo muckle dis is pairt o me,
Dis affbidden bit o pøramus laand.
Hit gies me strent.
Hit gies me stimna.

Resistin the National Psychosis
(April 9th 1992)

I'm a diamond –
I will never fuckin crack –
Rough uncut an smaa
I roll aroond yer jeweller's scale
but I am unassayable –
Rockin in the gyral cradle
I'm unassailable –
a speck o haillness, fixed an stable –
my name is the single caa
I'll answer tae –
I bear nae makar's braand –

I love the puzzle madness poses
tae yer need fir diagnosis

Lios Mhor

As strangers
we came to
the island of broch,
of Culdee haven, of
Norseman's
lonely castle,
of the high
churchman's
palace. But,
green isle in
Gaelic deep,
your
limestone
teeth were
pushed from

sea to air by
the same
force that
split the
earth from
Shetland

This the line my
heart defaults to you
along, links Scotland,
Norway north to
Ireland west, to
Sodoroy beyond –
and here we bring our
children home –
where Somerled hid,
half-breed of Gael
and Norsemen, here
too I hid among the
undergrowth of
youth with deer, and
my imagination
mountain-real

Green isle, the
time-tides swell
around you;
Glensanda's hills are
scarred by weeping
quarry-sores while
you yourself smooth
out, eye of the great
ravine, that Nevis to
Cruachan, Morven to
Jura, welcomed any
sea-bound stranger
landing in a coracle,
hopefully, down at
your gentle shores

The hand of the saint
which is missing a
finger points to the
heavens above, and
then to the earth at

his feet – these
strangers bring
mysteries, they build
up enclosures against
ghostly Fianna who'd
strike off the
newcomer's cross-
bearing arm.

The weaver loops
from age to age, a
picture-memory
looms the threads of
one into the other.
Flight is possible here
without a plane, until
the Phantom swoops
the glen, buzzing
and the white-tailed
eagle lifts from the
kirk roof, shrieking,
'Here thunder
moves!' The silence
returns

All that the
noises were,
is gone. The
stranger
children go
back on the
ferry, away
from the
crofthouse
sinking
slowly in an
unfarmed
bogland.
Wet green
isle, see how
the stillness
goes with us
now,
rippling
outwards till

among the
echoes, it
finds a
narrow
mountain
pass, or tidal
seaward
channel to
the world

Robert Alan Jamieson

SAXBY FIVE
BEING MEDITATIONS ON FIVE WORDS/PHRASES
FROM JESSIE M. SAXBY'S 'SHETLAND LORE'
IN NO PARTICULAR ORDER

'DA HUMLABAAND'　(the strap that holds the oar)
　pull du de rem　　pull on your oar
　an bliss da leddir　and bless the leather
　it hadds de t'dy koors　that holds you to your course

'SWEEIN FIR IT'　(karmic retribution)
　laek meths swees oo　as meths burns wool
　affa shiep's hied　from a sheep's head
　da Mukkil Mester redds wis　the Devil sorts us

'DA INNBJU'   (the 'bowing in' of a guest)
  kum de wis   come this way
  innaboots   into the house
  du'll tak a drap a tae   you'll have a cup of tea

'DA MODER-DY'   (the mother wave)
  rys apo da nynt waev   rise upon the ninth wave
  it aalwis braks da shoar   that always breaks the shore
  an draas da raagir haem   and draws the wanderer home

'DA HAAGRIES'   (the ancient boundary markers)
  twartree bitsa staen   two or three stones
  an a helloa   and a hell of a
  lokka gowlin   lot of crying

Speaking to the Ocean, Glasgow

What are you to me, red city of the western sun,
    but a warm womb? Your European chic,
    your transatlantic cheek so deep ingrained.

Warmth – even from that wee otter-man
    the other night – pished an pissed himsel –
    the stink of puke around him, who
    on the late-night Queen Street platform
brought me the spark of light I needed
    in return for a speed-rolled fag
    (his hands were shivering).

Is it that your stone retains the evening's warmth –
    enough to see the hapless, somehow, through?
No, people die here too, hungry and empty,
    unborn potential scattered through your rainy streets
    unravelling, like a broken string
    that might have led them to the surface, now
    a pointlessness that sweeps around the labyrinth
of alleyways and all the crumpled papers.

Something garrulous about you makes me wander anyway,
    draws me to the river and its empty banks,
    as if your energies still drift towards that setting sun –
braving the channels with a big braw heart,
    then full sail set for liberty,
    an wi a wee bit luck, a fortune too.

'Born again at forty',[1] I drew my last 'first breath' in you,
    your air hanging like the reek over Babylon,
    blessed by the presence of running water.

---

[1] Edwin Morgan, 'The Second Life'.

GRAHAM FULTON

I was born in 1959. I went to school and left school. I went to art college and left art college. Since then I've worked in a number of places culminating in the one I'm in just now. I live in Paisley.

The way it is. Ordinary people doing ordinary things. But what we take for granted, if looked at long enough from a different angle, can become funny, bizarre, claustrophobic or frightening. Normal behaviour is all around us. The humdrum is the source of poetry. That's what I try to capture on sheets of white paper.

Some of the poems seem as if they've been dipped in cynicism. Probably so. It's a dangerous place out there. Hopefully there's enough humour and concern, alongside the stuff coughed up by old uncle subconscious, to balance the picture. There's a thin line between comedy and tragedy, madness and sanity, ugliness and beauty. It's all interchangeable. I've got no gasp-inducing message to ram down unsuspecting throats. I just report on what's going on as seen through my eyes. What else is there but what we remember and what we see now. Tiny incidents pounced on years later can have a resonance and significance that wasn't apparent at the time. Tiny clues to something or other. Sometimes the landscape can change from Scotland to Paris or New York or wherever, but it's all the same. People are at the centre of all the poems. People trying to find a kind of dignity. People left behind on the lower floors.

I've learnt from a small pool of poets, all separated by decades and distance but all unified in their celebration of the astonishing world of the ordinary as well as their attitude and approach to writing. Find your own rhythms and vocabulary and say what you see as truthfully as you can. Anything can be written about. It's all waiting. Nothing is unimportant or taboo. It's just a question of really seeing what's always been there in front of your face.

Publications:

Tower of Babble (with Bobby Christie, Ronald McNeil and Jim Ferguson)
(Itinerant, 1987)

CHARLES MANSON AUDITIONS FOR THE MONKEES

'We're just trying
            to be friendly'
he sings to the suits
                who make
the choice.
A truly groovy
            American boy.
Dolenz!
        Polanski!
                Underage sex!
An X
    for outcast
between his eyes,
                a guitar
slung across
        his back.
Charlie wants
        to be an Axe-hero,
Charlie has mastered
                tricky chord changes,
Charlie has memorised lines
                        that
the Beatles haven't written
                    yet.
He knows about
            Rickenbackers,
knows about
            Revelations,
knows he didn't
            get much
education,
        knows
he hasn't
        a hope

in hell.
He should invest
            in a pom-pom hat,
swap his uniform
            for another
loveable grin,
            puddingbowl trim.
Nesmith!
      LaBianca!
            Tork!
A man
      with murder
in his heart
            is not what they want
in a primetime slot,
            not what's required
for the ratings
            war,
not what they need
            for the decade
of flowers.
He hasn't
      grown
a beard
      so far.
He thinks
      'There's
plenty of time
            to tell my girls
to lift their knives
            and make their mark,
sneakout and freakout
            in Beverly Hills,
shoot the high-school creeps
            in the head,
slice the starlets
            with babies inside them,
be the American monster
            that Americans
like their monsters
            to be.
San Quentin!
      Piggies!
            Sharon Tate!

Let the powermen
    see my face
on the cover of
    LIFE Magazine,
let them all
    be believers,
let them be
    in love
with my version of
    The American dream
as they taste their
    root
beers,
  as they bite
their cookies
    but
till then I'll sing
    my saddest song,
let the judges know
     "We get the funniest looks
from
  everyone we meet –
Hey! Hey! . . ."'

The Unmasking Scene

Tinted purple and
  in synchronisation
with an upright piano

  Mary Philbin unmasked

Lon Chaney

  to reveal a wire
trussed nose and
  a receding hairline

which were essential
  credentials for an

artist in the Twenties

until my mantis baby
with varnished toenails
        gave me her halo to stop me
growing out of my trousers

        and asked me where it
all went wrong
        to which I offered

'Spineless and spiteful or

        something or other'

and she gave me her popcorn
        to stop my tummy rumbling
and I enquired what

        I required to be an
artist in the Eighties

        for I realised she had
an answer to everything
        and she replied with a sigh

'A vicious streak is

        fine and dandy

a fucked-up life can
        come in handy'
and she searched for her toothbrush

        to help flush the dreaming

while I sent postcards
        to my brylcreem friends
until the leeches
        were delivered and

Lon disappeared

        beneath the Seine

Goodnight John Boy

Action, adventure
and a long sea voyage that starts
at six in the morning
and all the Harlem whores
in hotel corridors
you can afford. Someone young
and violent
turning the handle of your bedroom door
in the spooky dead of night
with only a chink of light
from the keyhole,
but don't be alarmed ladies and gentlemen

these chains are made of chrome steel
so unwrap the soap,
put your thumb in your mouth,
snuggle beneath Colonial sheets and think
of her cold shower junk-buck gymnastics.
The cockroach in the medicine cabinet,
the middle-aged negro with sweat
in his armpits in the yum yum sausage bar
looking for the syrup for the pancakes
'gimme some syrup, ah wawn some syrup'

of Abraham Lincoln
preaching peace but waging war
as he went marching through Georgia
pretending he was black
and wearing a top hat
and looking a bit like Jane Fonda's dad,
who is dead,
or Gregory Peck who isn't
but nothing at all like Buster Crabbe
who didn't know if he was Bucking
or Flashing or clean living Doris Day
with a cute button nose on the Deadwood stage
whip cracking away
if that's what

turns you on,
and King Kong climbing to the top
of the Empire State building
to have his wicked Simian way

a roll in the low budget hay with Fay Wray
in a torn silk dress
and strawberry blonde wig
or so we were led to believe
by the Senate of the day,
but I know for a fact he was a
regular, blueberry-pie guy
who beat up his wife between picking fights
with lame-brained lizards back on Skull Island
THE LAND OF OPPORTUNITY
where a puppet's gotta do
what a puppet's gotta do
and the niggers know their place
and that is trampled underfoot.
He only wanted to be loved

just like everybody else,
but he should have bought
a Statue of Liberty ashtray,
he should have bought a JFK rubber mask
to smother his conscience
just like everybody else
he should have heard the headboard
of the bed next door
slamming
against
the partition.
Ambulance music, steam hiss.
The smell of roasting chestnuts.
The smell of roasting gooks. The smell
of Mary Tyler Moore

having her all-American breakdown.
And I should have known
that the bi-planes get us all in the end,
but I still stood up on the New York City subway
to give my seat to a woman
who looked at me as if I was a

rolled

trousers to knees and
danced a weird waltz.

Chucked bangers at club-feet,
snow at girls' faces,
crisp bags full of frogspawn slop.

Sat among rocks, wore Harlequin socks,
rabbit ear collars and baratheas, spat
on the heads of waggy yap dogs
allowed to run free by owners.
Rolled

jumper sleeves to elbows
and pretended to be Thalidomide.
Smoked
singles
bought from ice cream vans,
scuffed mushy leaves with best shoes, kicked
puddle-twigs at the dumb sun as the wind
swiped through big branches, scurried
among big shadows.
Tumbled,

yelling, from dizzy swish roundabouts,
pelted the swans in the dam with cans,
tore the pages from brainyboy's books
then tipped his schoolbag upside down,
lit fires just for the hell of it, splashed
scruffy steam gold against the oaks

that had seen it all before.

Ate banana and marmite rolls
as gloom curdled in the cloakroom.
Looked at photos of whopper breasts,
studied photos of open legs,
fell over each other to sniff
the future.
Fumbled
in panties at puberty parties,
swallowed Pale Ale, Newcastle Brown,

Breaker Malt Liquor and Eldorado.
Gathered at night to sit on walls
or topple sun-dials onto grass.
Made scratchy marks on sheds and lamp-posts,
squirted stinking, chemist perfumes
onto clothes of teeth-brace boys,
spluttered over thick Panatellas,
chewed on borrowed plastic pipes.
Dropped lit matches into postboxes,
said the words 'fanny', 'gobble' and 'spunk',
spooned in shagalley toothpaste dark,
fell over each other to reach

the sex.
Grew
hair long, got it chopped off,
did everything wrong, everything
right.
Threw slushballs at respectable windows,
stones at clocks, rocks at stars
and cruised cobbled wynds with springs
in heels,
skated, laughing, into the void, fell over
each other to ask

the time.
Rolled

trousers to knees and
danced a daft can-can.
Rolled back to ankles, hobbled
for home, the whipped

cream of Scotland's dream.

QUIZ NIGHT

In the pub
the hospital worker tells me

'Some of the things
you wouldn't believe.
A woman who watched her breast
get eaten by cancer,

slow.
A cold black hole.
She didn't want to make a fuss.
She was just scared.
Her family knew she smelt
but thought it was something else.

I've seen the breast,
it's kept in a box.'

The quizmaster with the frightened eyes
blows into his mike and asks the throng

are there any monsters in tonight?
are there any angels in tonight?

'A cyst they removed
the size of a table.
The woman just thought
she was putting on weight.
A length of bowel
packed tight with excreta.
Swollen, years of keeping it in.
The nurses forced
it down the sink.
A man who strolled into a propellor,
sliced to bits, a little bit pissed.
His face like a Halloween mask
on the slab, funny
if it wasn't so sad.

He took the wrong
turn in the dark.'

The quizmaster with the big bow tie
blows into his mind and asks the throng

is there anyone here who's afraid to die?
is there anyone here who's afraid to live?

'Lots of questions,
none of the answers.

Perfect, unmarked. Floating in space.
I've seen the face,
it's kept in a drawer.'

GERRY CAMBRIDGE

I lived in a caravan in Ayrshire from the age of thirteen until I was thirty-eight. Then for two years I lived in Hugh MacDiarmid's cottage as the poet-in-residence. I now live just outside Glasgow.

I am of Irish-Catholic background. As far as I know, I was the only Catholic at Irvine Royal Academy in Ayrshire in the mid-1970s. So I had a more than typically anxious, as well as guilt-ridden and hypochondriacal, Catholic adolescence. As I also lived four miles outside of town and was terrified of women, I became obsessively interested in ornithology, by way of sublimation. Later, I grew interested in nature photography. And still later, in my early twenties, by way of freelance journalism, my own peculiarity of temperament, and a crush on a librarian at the Dick Institute in Kilmarnock, I discovered poetry. As Professor Hamish MacAmbrose, in a libellous essay on my work, has observed:

> The literary productions of this questionable psyche were visited on the world initially in the poet's first book, *The Shell House*. One would expect . . . that the volume would contain frequent mentions of caravans, guilt-wracked lust, and disbelieving doctors. Not a bit of it. Here is a bard evidently entranced by light and as apparently incapable of writing about sexuality as his most recent incarnation, as will be seen, is incapable of not writing about it.

The Shell House had a photographer's fascination for light and the visible world. My second full collection, *'Nothing But Heather!'* brought together my own nature photographs and poems. It was written during my sojourn at MacDiarmid's cottage. My latest collection, *Madame Fi Fi's Farewell*, is in part an overt celebration of the arrival of miracle – Eros – into the life of an individual. While Eros may not be the subject of a particular poem, it is always surely the fount from which the energy of poetry, and every other worthwhile thing, comes.

Publications:

The Shell House (Scottish Cultural Press, 1995)

The Dark Gift and Other Poems (St Inan's Press, 1996)
'Nothing But Heather!': Scottish Nature in Poems, Photographs, and Prose
(Luath Press, 1999)
The Praise of Swans (Shoestring Press, 2000)
Madame Fi Fi's Farewell (Luath Press, 2002)

As editor:
The Dark Horse, the Scottish–American poetry magazine

PRAISE OF A CROFTER

You'd shove, unknocking, into the croft on the hill where I sat in easy
    despairing
Over the page's bounded snow, and mutter about the rain-soaked hay,
The tatties you brought in your bucket, and how the beasts were
    faring –
Storm-unignorable, sweeping my bland blue heaven of choices away

With the one word, *Now*. Old drunkard, stubbly abstraction-hater,
    washer 'Wunce a week',
When you'd strip to a vest that hung there in rags as if you were
    freshly tiger-mauled,
Mocker, your laughter bright as the skies, of the folly of what I
    sought, or seek;
Jim Harcus, Jim Harcus, if forever's a lifetime, the name you are
    forever called,

When I went to the north expecting to praise elementals and skies,
There you awaited, wheezing like a steam-train, blunt as a hail
    shower –
And more remarkable soon your gale-blazed brow and the watery
    blue of your eyes
Than argosies dreamt on the seas in a golden hour;

Exemplar of the actual, of the sense I'd have in my every line,
You, clang-solid, brine-bitter, standing over the West's Atlantic,
    clouds arranged about your head,
Or hunching, tractor-borne, through showers, to mend a fence to
    keep in your beasts with twine,
No sipper at bottles, drinker at the fresh original spring of the unread,

Dreader of the kirkyard's harbour, you hoarded in boxes and letters a
    life, served up dire home-brew;
Island Apemantus, godless religious man, digger of friends'
    deep graves,

Funeral attender out in unboundaried air on your tractor, beside the
    expansive blue
Drowning the sight of the eye, the final resolving brine that dooms
    and saves,

Thank you, for the many a dark-encircled night we sat up late;
No case of liking you or not: simply there, in your
    wire-twist-buttoned coat;
Reliable as tatties in your bucket, and strong as an iron gate;
Perching the bird of the real in my mind – and anchor, for the
    spirit's boat.

THE STARS OF AUTUMN

We stood below the stars of autumn, and
Whispering with me you proved you knew
That they, also, die. I touched your hand.
We stood below the stars of autumn. And,
Shivering, I tried to say what I had planned,
But did not (though it all came true).
We stood below the stars of autumn, and
Whispering with me, you proved you knew.

LINES TO ANOTHER EMILY

I sense as I sit close that you're aware of me,
who notice your neck's slenderness, too frail.
You're a watercolour, bone-china vase, and pale
as a bare page still to be written on. See,
my large strong hands are like birds, restless. We
spark such opposites, you and I; my blood-heat
blazes here in my red-bearded face; neat,
you sit like the form for a sonnet, whitely.

Watch me. I am the gale you lock your door to
that nightlong tests your buttressed walls.
I am the life you fear and lust for, charged and new,
that roars in the woods at your silent calls;
force to break through your charmed ring, and enter,
to touch to glad sorrow in your dark centre.

THE DARK GIFT

Pure white and buff flight feather, tawny owl's.
I found it by the lane as I walked home,
kept it for your interested son, its comb[1]
and furriness, despite his adolescent scowls
and rancour, fascinating. I used to search
far woods round here, confused teenager, for
lush primaries of those birds I rarely saw,
on mornings when my mother thought the church

contained me. Tonight you drive me back
up the Glasgow road towards the city's
knives and angers, all the human pities
and our own. Dazzling road signs mark the black.
And you hit the wheel, as I clutch this tawny's feather,
as we speed on through the autumn night together.

---

[1]'Comb' refers to the comb-like design of the leading edge of the first primary feather
in an owl's wing, which serves to soften the air flow over the wing, and aids silent
flight.

ROBERT CRAWFORD

Poems are leylines of language through the world. Emanating from the underground of words, they surface unexpectedly, till you can sense them sometimes following, sometimes cutting across the usual routes. However surprising, a good poem will seem completely just. It'll give you the sense that it's jumped to the right conclusions. If you follow the contours of language as closely as you can, poems will often start to emerge, helping you tune into something that seemed beyond you, or was hidden in everyday chatter. When you're in a state of poetic receptivity (a 'dream state', if you like), words, phrases and images come in from different angles, and start to coalesce. Even when you've got the shape of the poem, there's usually a good deal of honing, cutting, refining to be done. Sometimes poems get longer as you work on them; more often they get shorter as you prune back to the real essentials. As I've grown older, I've become aware of a wish to write poems that are short, pithy, quite crammed, and of a desire for poems, sometimes long ones, that expand as richly as I can make them. Dr Who's tardis is an emblem of my ideal poem. I like reading poems aloud, and feel they should be acoustically interesting, as well as working on the page.

Born in Bellshill in 1959, I grew up in Cambuslang, Lanarkshire, though for a good deal of the time local-government reforms turned it into Cambuslang, Glasgow, a transformation I enjoyed. My parents had left school in their early teens, and worked as bank tellers. A late, happy, only child, I went to Glasgow University to study English, then wrote a doctorate on T. S. Eliot at Oxford. I had a job for three years there, in a women's college, then at Glasgow University for two years, during which time I got married. In 1989 we moved to St Andrews, where I work as Professor of Modern Scottish Literature at the University, and where I live with my wife and two children. For eleven years I was founder editor of the international magazine *Verse*. Involved in various editorial projects, as well as writing literary criticism, I've always liked making poetry under the deep cover of a regular job, as poets as different as Burns, Eliot and

Edwin Morgan did. But it's important to keep room for the inner space where (in reaction with the outside world) poems happen.

Publications:

Main poetry publications: *Sterts & Stobies*, Scots poetry pamphlet, with W. N. Herbert (Obog Books, 1985); *Severe Burns*, Scots poetry pamphlet, with W. N. Herbert and David Kinloch (Obog Books, 1986); *Chatto Modern Poets II*, contributor (Chatto and Windus, 1987); *A Scottish Assembly* (Chatto and Windus, 1990); *Sharawaggi: Poems in Scots*, with W. N. Herbert (Polygon, 1990); *Other Tongues: Young Scottish Poets in English, Scots and Gaelic*, editor (Verse, 1990); *Talkies* (Chatto and Windus, 1992); *Masculinity* (Jonathan Cape, 1996); *Penguin Modern Poets 9*, with John Burnside and Kathleen Jamie (Penguin, 1996); *The Penguin Book of Poetry from Britain and Ireland since 1945*, ed. with Simon Armitage (Penguin, 1998); *Spirit Machines* (Jonathan Cape, 1999); *The New Penguin Book of Scottish Verse*, ed. with Mick Imlah (Penguin, 2000); *Scottish Religious Poetry: An Anthology*, ed. with Meg Bateman and James McGonigal (St Andrew Press, 2000); *Six Poets Live at the DCA*, CD with John Burnside, John Glenday, Tracey Herd, Kathleen Jamie, Don Paterson (Dundee Contemporary Arts, 2001).

Literary criticism: *The Savage and the City in the Work of T. S. Eliot* (Oxford University Press, 1987); *About Edwin Morgan*, ed. with Hamish Whyte (Edinburgh University Press, 1990); *The Arts of Alasdair Gray*, ed. with Thom Nairn (Edinburgh University Press, 1991); *Devolving English Literature* (Oxford University Press, 1992; second, expanded edition Edinburgh University Press, 2000); *Reading Douglas Dunn*, ed. with David Kinloch (Edinburgh University Press, 1992); *Identifying Poets: Self and Territory in Twentieth-Century Poetry* (Edinburgh University Press, 1993); *Liz Lochhead's Voices*, ed. with Anne Varty (Edinburgh University Press, 1993); *Literature in Twentieth-Century Scotland: A Select Bibliography* (British Council, 1995); *Robert Burns and Cultural Authority*, ed. (Edinburgh University Press, 1996; Iowa University Press, 1996; Polygon, 1997); *The Scottish Invention of English Literature*, ed. (Cambridge University Press, 1998); *The Modern Poet: Poetry, Academia, and Knowledge since the 1750s* (Oxford University Press, 2001).

OPERA

Throw all your stagey chandeliers in wheelbarrows and
    move them north
To celebrate my mother's sewing-machine
And her beneath an eighty-watt bulb, pedalling
Iambs on an antique metal footplate
Powering the needle through its regular lines,
Doing her work. To me as a young boy

That was her typewriter. I'd watch
Her hands and feet in unison, or read
Between her calves the wrought-iron letters:
SINGER. Mass-produced polished wood and metal,
It was a powerful instrument. I stared
Hard at its brilliant needle's eye that purred
And shone at night; and then each morning after
I went to work at school, wearing her songs.

SCOTLAND

Semiconductor country, land crammed with intimate
    expanses,
Your cities are superlattices, heterojunctive
Graphed from the air, your cropmarked farmlands
Are epitaxies of tweed.

All night motorways carry your signal, swept
To East Kilbride or Dunfermline. A brightness off low
    headlands
Beams-in the dawn to Fife's interstices,
Optoelectronics of hay.

Micro-nation. So small you cannot be forgotten,
Bible inscribed on a ricegrain, hi-tech's key
Locked into the earth, your televised Glasgows
Are broadcast in Rio. Among circuitboard crowsteps

To be miniaturised is not small-minded.
To love you needs more details than the Book of Kells –
Your harbours, your photography, your democratic intellect
Still boundless, chip of a nation.

A SCOTTISH ASSEMBLY

Circuitry's electronic tartan, the sea,
Libraries, fields – I want the lot

To fly off and scatter, but most of all
Always to come home to roost

In this unkempt country where a handicapped printer,
Engraver of dog collars, began with his friends

The ultimate encyclopedia.
Don't expect any rhyme or reason

For Scotland remaining an explosion reversed
Or ordinariness a fruited vine

Or why I came back here to choose my union
On the side of the ayes, remaining a part

Of this diverse assembly – Benbecula, Glasgow, Bow of
    Fife –
Voting with my feet, and this hand.

ALBA EINSTEIN

When proof of Einstein's Glaswegian birth
First hit the media everything else was dropped:
Logie Baird, Dundee painters, David Hume – all
Got the big E. Physics documentaries
Became peak-viewing; Scots publishers hurled awa
MacDiarmid like an overbaked potato, and swooped
On the memorabilia: *Einstein Used My Fruitshop*,
Einstein in Old Postcards, Einstein's Bearsden Relatives.
Hot on their heels came the A. E. Fun Park,
Quantum Court, Glen Einstein Highland Malt.
Glasgow was booming. Scotland rose to its feet
At Albert Suppers where The Toast to the General Theory
Was given by footballers, panto-dames, or restaurateurs.
In the US an ageing lab-technician recorded
How the Great Man when excited showed a telltale glottal
    stop.
He'd loved fiddlers' rallies. His favourite sport was curling.
Thanks to this, Scottish business expanded
Endlessly. His head grew toby-jug-shaped,
Ideal for keyrings. He'd always worn brogues.
Ate bannocks in exile. As a wee boy he'd read *The Beano.*
His name brought new energy: our culture was solidly based
On pride in our hero, The Universal Scot.

FUR THI MUSE O SYNTHESIS

Interkat intercommuner, intercommunin
At aw leid's interfaces, skeich
Tae interpone a hooch that intermells
An interverts auld jorrams tae reconduct
Aureat thru lingua franca, intercommoun
Thru joie-de-vivre-wurds, guttir thru dictionar, it's
       yirsel's
Thi ane I T, thi richt wurdbank, fettle
Thru thi hert's printoot, wi'oot figmalirie tae spairge
Or jevel thi speerit. Interclosin delicht,
Wulcat dotmatrixed fur aye fae Jamieson
Lik a delicut pomerie oar thi epitaxy layerin
Crystals wi a pink o molecular beam, yi kythe hirdum
       dirdum
Tae gowks, mebbe, but yi've a gledge o beauty
That'll magnetize lummles, an yir lusbirdans o
      phonemes hae sprent
Tae staun oan thi mune, tae ratch licht fae skau, an tae
       sacre
Fowk vivual an vieve again whan thi makars wha cam
Tae thi keyburd o thi leid lik piper's invites
Richt-furthe find it an interteneyare that maks
Regenerate thi stolum o Scoatlan.

Intricate negotiator between factions at variance, having intercourse at all language's interfaces, apt to startlingly interpose a cry of joy that intermingles and appropriates to a new, unfamiliar use old slow, melancholy boatsongs to reconduct high diction through common speech, the language of conversation through exclamations of delight, gutter through dictionary, it's you who are the only Information Technology, the true word-bank, speech-energy through the heart's printout, without whim to spatter or joggle the spirit. Intercepting delight, wildcat dotmatrixed forever from Jamieson's *Dictionary of the Scottish Language* like a delicate orchard or the epitaxy layering crystals with a perfect glitter of molecular beam, you appear confused nonsense to fools, maybe, but you have an oblique look of beauty that will magnetise metal filings, and your pygmies of phonemes have leapt to stand on the moon, to dislocate light from total ruin, and to consecrate people alive and lively again when the poets who came to the keyboard of the language as if they were the last folk to be invited to a party immediately discover it to be an entertainer of guests which makes regenerate the large, broken off fragment of Scotland.

Ghetto-Blastir

Ghetto-makars, tae the knackirs'
Wi aw yir schemes, yir smug dour dreams
O yir ain feet. Yi're beat
By yon new Scoatlan loupin tae yir street

Wi a Jarre-lik puissance, ghetto-blastin
Auld sangs crooned doon
Yir reedy beaks, wastin an tastin
O deid pus. See us? We're foon

Wi whit's new, wi aw that's speerin oot
An cummin hame tae roost, tae set the feathirs
Flyin in yir kailyard. Scoot
Tae yir hales, tak tae yir heels, blethirs,

Wee naethins aye feathrin yir ain nests
O douce semis! Yir psychadelic tartan's
Shite tae oor white nichts an aw the guests
Oor laughtir's aftir. Sook yir fozie cartons

O guttir music, mak the Muse seik uttir-
lie wi yir gabbin, stabbin, sabbin
Ochones. Gang tae the Gents an muttir.
Ladies tae! Bicoz we're grabbin

Whit's left o the leid tae mak anither sang
O semiconducters, Clydes aw dancin fastir
Than yir feart shanks. Ye'll scraich tae hear amang
Pooer-clubs an cliques, twee pubs o freaks,
When cockiedoodlin doon yir beaks

The raucus sweet soon o oor Ghetto-Blastir.

ochones – lamenting noise made by a Lowlander
when imitating Gaelic speech; *scraich* – cry like
an alarmed hen.

MASCULINITY

At our school sexes were colour-coded
Blue for a boy and blue for a girl;
A different shade, though, more skyish
On the soft, hard woollen blazer.

Evenings we'd lie up in our rooms
Learning masc. and fem. declensions,
Mensa, mensae. Our diningroom table
Had squat, chunky, rebarbative legs

Unlike those of my lithe first girlfriend
Who crossed hers when she came to tea.
That term I became her Latin lover,
My whole world zinging with testostericity,

All I touched shocked by another language –
Trees, ships, houses, horses, roads
Masculine or feminine, caressed
And confused, the way next term Greek

Gendered things just a little differently,
Maybe because it was older.
It took me years to understand
Erotic grammar and the answer given

By the boy at the back who raised his hand
Erect as a spear, 'Please, sir, please,
Masculinity's not much to do
With sex. It's all about gender.'

THE RESULT
1707–1997; for Alice

Moments after death, I found my voice
Surprising, hearing my own

Ansafone saying, 'I'm not here just now,
Please speak after the tone.'

You saw it in my eyes – release
Back to the world. More, more

You, Scotland, sea, each lost and re-elected.
I toast debatable lands, the come-go shore

Of living here. 'Thanks!' My full, bannock-smeared glass
Rises to you, our son, and our new, blonde

Daughter. We dance, in grey St Michael slippers,
Cancerless, broken out, and passed beyond.

MEG BATEMAN

I was born in Edinburgh and educated at the Mary Erskine School. My upbringing was privileged and slightly bohemian, and probably set up a longing in me for a society that was rural and homogeneous rather than urban and class-based. Consequently I took Celtic Studies at Aberdeen University, during which time I spent a very happy year in South Uist as an auxiliary nurse. It was during the unfocused and solitary years of researching for a Ph.D. that I started writing poetry myself. At first it was therapeutic but soon a fascination with the craft took over. After six years' part-time teaching in Edinburgh, I returned to the Celtic Department in Aberdeen, where I lectured for seven years. Then I moved to Skye with my young son to work at the Gaelic College, Sabhal Mòr Ostaig.

My aesthetic in poetry has been shaped by what I admire in Gaelic. Sorley MacLean excited me in the way he could accept paradox even while leaving it unresolved. I also admired the supra-moral frankness of some early Gaelic songs. I want to write poetry that is pared down, with a minimum of adjectives or adverbs, so letting the nouns and verbs take on a lapidary quality. Some people say my poetry is very personal but I disagree. While I would shudder if someone read the raw feelings of my diary, I never release a poem until I feel I have achieved a level of abstraction that takes it beyond the embarrassingly confessional.

My writing is squeezed awkwardly between the demands of an academic job and single motherhood. I only write when I have to, maybe half a dozen poems a year. I find writing exacting as I try to find a form that seems inevitable to fit an understanding that I believe to be true. I seek to balance the emotional and intellectual, so a poem is neither self-indulgent nor rhetorical. I have also had a lot of fun from poetry and met a lot of people through it. It seems to constitute an enduring human need to bear witness to our lives.

Publications:

Poetry (collections and anthologies):
Fresh Oceans (Stramullion, 1987)

Duncan Glen, *Twenty of the Best* (Galliard, 1987)
Meg Bateman, *Òrain Ghaoil/Amhráin Ghrá* (Coiscéim, 1989)
Robert Crawford (ed.) *Other Tongues* (Verse, 1990)
Christopher Whyte, *An Aghaidh na Sìorraidheachd/In the Face of Eternity*
(Polygon, 1991)
Donny O'Rourke (ed.), *Dream State* (Polygon, 1993)
Meg Bateman, *Aotromachd agus Dàin Eile/Lightness and Other Poems*
(Polygon, 1997)
Simon Armitage and Robert Crawford, *The Penguin Book of Poetry from
Britain and Ireland Since 1945* (Penguin, 1998)
Meg Bateman, Nicholas Moore and Fred Beake, *Etruscan Reader IX* (Etruscan
Books, 1999)
Alec Finlay and Kevin MacNeill, *Wish I was here* (pocketbooks, 2000)
Robert Crawford and Mick Imlah (eds), *The Penguin Book of Scottish Verse*
(Penguin, 2000)
Bashabi Fraser and Elaine Greig (eds), *Edinburgh: An Intimate City*, one poem
(Edinburgh City Council, 2001)

Academic (editing and translation):
The Gaelic section (pp. 12–113) in Catherine Kerrigan (ed.), *An Anthology of
Scottish Women Poets* (Edinburgh University Press, 1991)
Colm Ó Baoill and Meg Bateman, *Gàir nan Clàrsach/An Anthology of 17th
Century Gaelic Poetry* (Birlinn, 1994)
'Women's Writing in Scottish Gaelic since 1750' in Douglas Gifford and
Dorothy McMillan (eds), *Scottish Women's Writing* (Edinburgh University
Press, 1997)
contributor to Peter Davidson, etc, *Cavalier Verse* (Clarendon Press, 1998)
Robert Crawford, Jim McGonigle and Bateman (eds), *An Anthology of Scottish
Religious Verse* (St Andrew Press, 2000)

Thigeadh e thugam
nuair a bha e air mhisg
a chionn 's gu robh mi measail air.

Dhèanainn tì dha
is dh'èisdinn ris
a chionn 's gu robh mi measail air.

Sguir e a dh'òl
is rinn mi gàirdeachas leis
a chionn 's gu robh mi measail air.

Nist cha tig e tuilleadh
is nì e tàir orm
a chionn 's gu robh mi measail air.

Because I was so fond of him

He used to come to me
when he was drunk
   because I was so fond of him.

I'd make him tea
and listen to him
   because I was so fond of him.

He stopped drinking
and I was pleased for him
   because I was so fond of him.

Now he comes no more,
indeed he despises me,
   because I was so fond of him.

AOTROMACHD

B' e d aotromachd a rinn mo thàladh,
aotromachd do chainnte 's do ghàire,
aotromachd do lethchinn nam làmhan,
d aotromachd lurach ùr mhàlda;
agus 's e aotromachd do phòige
tha a' cur trasg air mo bheòil-sa,
is 's e aotromachd do ghlaic mum chuairt-sa
a leigeas seachad leis an t-sruth mi.

GILLE A' SIREADH OBAIR

Duilleag bhàn-bhuidhe
a' tionndadh air a faillean 's a' tèarnadh,
a' fàs nas lugha, nas rèidhe,
mar d aodann an-diugh
aig *roundabouts* is *slipways*
air na rathaidean gu deas,
a' sleamhnachadh bhuam
sìos ioma-shlighe m' aineoil.

Agus fhathast laigh thu nam ghàirdeanan
fad na h-oidhche raoir,
's dh'fhàg do chruinnead ghrinn òg
a lorg air mo bhoisean,
gam phianadh leis a' chùram
a bha air Eubha mu Adhamh,
mise, boireannach gun ainm,
's tusa, gille bho thuath.

LIGHTNESS

It was your lightness that drew me,
the lightness of your talk and your laughter,
the lightness of your cheek in my hands,
your sweet gentle modest lightness;
and it is the lightness of your kiss
that is starving my mouth,
and the lightness of your embrace
that will let me go adrift.

BOY LOOKING FOR WORK

A pale-yellow leaf
turning on its twig and dropping,
growing smaller, flatter
like your face today
at roundabouts and slipways
on the motorways south,
sliding away from me
down a labyrinth of difference.

And yet last night you lay in my arms
all night long,
and your neat young roundness
left its imprint on my palms,
hurting me with the tenderness
Eve knew for Adam,
me, an anonymous woman,
and you, some boy from the North.

CEÒL SAN EAGLAIS

'S toil leam an coithional a fhreagras gu greannach,
dòchas a' dìosgail tro bheathannan doirbhe;
's toil leam còisirean ghuthanna geala,
solas a' lìonadh àiteachan dorcha;
ach is annsa leam an coithional nach seinn ach meadhanach –
an salmadair nach buail air na puingean àrda,
an tè a cheileireas os cionn na h-uile,
an t-organaiche a thòisicheas air rann a bharrachd;
oir 's ann an sin a thèid an gaol a dhùshlanachadh,
eadar àilleasachd is dìomhanas is breòiteachd daonna,
's ann an sin ge b' oil leam a nochdas am beannachadh –
am fios nach eil lorg air ceòl nas binne.

UGH BRISTE
(do Cholm, aig trì bliadhna a dh' aois)

Sheas thu air ugh na Càisge
a bh' agam bho aois m' òige
's tu dannsadh mun teine cas-rùisgte.

Smaoinich mi mar a chomharraicheadh na Sìnich
le duilleig de dh' òr
an sgoltadh ann an soitheach briste,
is iad a' dèanamh toileachas às a bhreòiteachd,
às a chàradh eadar bith is neo-bhith . . .
ach 's ann a bha an t-ugh na mhìle pìos.

Is ged nach robh càil de bhreòiteachd
mun ràn a thàinig asad
's tu bàthadh a' chiùil
ris an robh thu a' dannsadh,
no mu na deòir theth
bha a' taomadh far do ghruaidhean,
chuirinn-sa òr air do phianadh aig an àm ud
's tu ag aithneachadh nach buan a' bhòidhchead.

MUSIC IN CHURCH

I like a growling congregation,
hope creaking through difficult lives;
I like choirs of bright voices,
light filling dark places;
but best I like indifferent singing –
the soloist who gets the high notes flat,
the warbler who makes herself heard over all,
the organist who embarks on an extra verse;
for here is the greater challenge to love,
amid fastidiousness, vanity, human failing,
here too, appears the greater blessing,
on knowing it sweeter than any singing.

BROKEN EGG

(for Colm at three years old)

You stepped on an Easter egg
I had kept since a girl
as you danced round the fire bare-footed.

I thought how the Chinese
would mark out with gold
the crack in a broken vessel,
taking a delight in its fragility,
in its state between existing and not . . .
but the egg was in a thousand pieces.

And though there was nothing fragile
in your roaring
that drowned the music
you'd been dancing to,
nor in the hot tears
streaming off your cheeks,
what I would mark with gold
was your pain then
as you understood that beauty does not last.

EALGHOL: DÀ SHEALLADH

Choimhead mi an t-seann chairt-phuist,
na taighean mar fhàs às an talamh,
na h-aonaichean nam baidealan os an cionn,
nan comharra air mòrachd Dhè,
mus d' rinneadh goireas de bheanntan,
no sgaradh eadar obair is fois,
eadar an naomh is an saoghalta . . .
is shìn mi chun a' bhodaich i.

'Eil sin cur cianalas oirbh, a Lachaidh?'
dh' fhaighnich mi, 's e na thosd ga sgrùdadh.
'Hoi, òinseach, chan eil idir!
'S e cuimhne gun aithne a bh' agam oirre-se,'
is stiùir e ri bò bha faisg oirnn san deilbh,
'Siud a' Leadaidh Bhuidhe, an dàrna laogh aig an Leadaidh Bhig –
dh' aithnichinn, fhios agad, bò sam bith
a bhuineadh dhan àite rim bheò-sa.'

ELGOL: TWO VIEWS

I looked at the old post-card,
the houses like a growth from the soil,
the peaks towering above them,
a sign of the majesty of God,
before an amenity was made of mountains,
or a divide between work and play,
between the sacred and the secular . . .
and I passed the picture to the old man.

'Does it make you sad, Lachie?' I asked
as he scrutinised it in silence.
'Sad? Bah! Not at all!
I just couldn't place her for a moment,'
and he pointed to a cow in the foreground,
'That's Yellow Lady, Little Lady's second calf –
I'd know any cow, you see,
that belonged here in my life-time.'

IAIN BAMFORTH

I was in Scotland for a year in 1993, to complete my GP training and settle down – as I thought – for a contented life on the pastures. Once a week I used to drive the fifty miles from our house on Luce Bay, south of Stranraer, to the hospital in Ayr for an afternoon teaching session most trainees called 'playschool'. It was a moment when driving freed the mind, although anyone who knows the road will be familiar with its frustrations as well as with the spectacle of the 'omphalos' of Ailsa Craig. Defoe, Burns and Keats all had something to say about the stretch between Dumfries and Ayr, and that cone of quartz and feldspar in the Firth of Clyde, known to an earlier generation as Paddy's Milestone.

Now, sitting in a valley in the centre of Europe, I allow myself an ironic smile at my expression 'the social contract and its bad-faith Tory echo/masquerading as a *citizen's*/charter'. The 1990s, for me, were dominated by a rather sinister development: the politicisation of health care, and not just by the Tories. I suspect I wouldn't be living here at all (Strasbourg) were it not for my conviction, despite all the enjoyment I got from ordinary GP work, that a vital sense of freedom was being stamped out of my profession. The doctor's sense of accountability has been changed from one of ethical commitment to mere contractual obligation. Everything that has happened since confirms my hunch: medicine is, in fact, becoming an instrument of social control, and health a species of tyranny. Most discomfiting of all is that nobody seems to give a hoot.

Things aren't much better in France, not even in Europe's 'capital', largely because the fall of the Berlin Wall made utopian thinking suspect. But without a utopia, politics makes no claims on the will; citizens become consumers. Any landmarks I have now, hundreds of miles from the sea, were left by Edwin Muir, the most complete critic Scotland has ever produced (and good critics are rarer by far in Scottish letters than good poets); he came to Europe, too, to find out more about the historical forces that had wreaked such havoc in his own life. Then he came back to write *Scottish Journey*. Driving through Galloway one fine sunny day in 1934 his brakes went on fire. He stopped and had a smoke till they cooled. In that sinister decade of political tensions and economic doldrums, the 1930s, he found parts of Scotland purgatorial. Yet in the closing pages of his book he imagines a country which would be 'a harmoniously working and interdependent unity from the Borders to the Shetland Islands'. History and the great capitalist machine for creating wealth and inequality, which Muir was so suspicious of, have made the prospects for Scotland uncommonly cheerful. Now there's a chance of something better. We can be citizens of Europe (and Scotland has probably had more influence on Europe's civic sense of itself than it knows), but let's not be consumers ourselves. A little Scotland would be just as degrading as a little England.

Publications:

The Modern Copernicus (Salamander, 1984)
Sons and Pioneers (Carcanet, 1992)
Open Workings (Carcanet, 1996)
Poets on Poets (selection of Dunbar's poems) (Waterstone's/Carcanet, 1997)
Without Day: Projects for the New Scottish Parliament (anthology) (Canongate, 2000)
The Order of Things (anthology) (Canongate, 2001)

MEN ON FIRE

Being a land of dissent and magnificent defeats
it evolved a subtle theology of failure, stealing its own thunder
wherever two or three were gathered together
and the occult plumbing groaned querulously beneath the boards.

These days, it grows owlish with hindsight –
recounting itself as a salvo of rain far north on mappamundi,
who's who of a supernumerary Creation myth
that swallowed the serpent's tail, ate the offspring whole.

When Rousseau exhumed the weather over Waverley
its civil imaginary became a fast diminishing return.
Few Encyclopaedists recall the genealogy backpacked out of Troy
or the vernacular of a silver-tongued Golden Age.

Later it saw itself arsy-versy, a nation after the letter;
but common cause outreaching the Dutch
it sold its birthright for a cut of the glory . . .
a mere idea, it seemed invincible.

Yet it thrived on its own lost cause, and the mark of Cain
was a lefthandedness it practised righteously –
its sentinel cities on the plain a gritty paradigm
for an industry of calloused hands.

Guilt was one thing it exported to the new world;
ballast to the quantum energy ascending through midnight suns
as a monument of candour, men on fire:
here, in the old, sorrow recurs as a brief downpour,

dream-fug, supplements to a Journal of the Plague Year
when the gospel of virtues, that manic uprightness,
laid blame at nobody's door but its own . . .
beyond reach of heaven was a legislature pining for hell.

Out of it, sons and daughters have no clear sighting
of how an apple-tree opens the debate
but know it does, since they find themselves
on a mission without a motor, reciting the plot backwards

while pavements become rain-sleeked and lustral
and an oddly buoyant cargo gospel
swims through anti-matter to the hard edge of the landscape.
Like a native technology, it starts from what's left

and salvages its own future, a startled Doric narrative
stalking the wet track, tongue and tinder
to its radical children, shy to touch the incontrovertible ores
of a faith that has lately outgrown its disappointment.

CALVINIST GEOGRAPHY

– *A northern supremacist monad!*
It eavesdrops, shrewd dissertation:
goes out to shoot converts
when light drips through the roof
and the day leans to, a gob
of consternation at the easy drama

of the dark. Novel as any nation
it grows on you like a fuggy absence,
archaic body, story's end.
What's left limps back to first

causes, the old betrayals –
though no one's wiser now

the fire's smoored and a soft smirr
drifts in across the moors. *Or*
it blows wrong, a chill family epic
kept wrapped for redemption:
when the renegade sermons start up
again, from clumps of rock

and scraggy deserts between estates,
they tell you more than you want
to know about persistence
and extinction, the risen towns
gravid with herring, crazed fiddlers
making a palaver in the square –

or here on one of Wade's roads
where the servile myths skite home
to sour news, the barracking
of a threadbare ruinous country.
It holds an accent out, in self-defence.
Sweet as failure, you can taste

feral voices on the tongue:
success, they say, will always
ring a hollow change, like sorrow.
Attrition, diaspora: they're children
from an illfitting marriage;
shipped off to weather continents

without a say-so in the sublimations
of unreadiness. Trite tradition,
it leaves its interpreters
stuck on voes, shouting across islands
for the pure light of justice.
Underfoot, it's the usual unison,

granite voices thinking they're already
home, though the sun could tell
why happiness is hostile. Hard
breathing, flight's nervous feathers,
always get goosed. *Wind scolds*
like a mother and soon the moon

has pale ideas of its own, none new
to the narrator. Names are maps
among the oxbows and civic drumlins;
open secrets. They inhale
surprise, subtilised by circumstance,
a blunt determination to make good

that could easily spend another century
riddling for old catastrophes,
cleared spaces, idylls, odd ideals.
There's no new peak, hardly even
a pent Sunday or an underground edition.
Irony's a glib surface like the sea:

a spit of land, a cold promontory
where goodness has to be spat on too
when the day's done. No thought
of comfort or compensation:
the joke about deserters wasn't one.
Work it out, then: either rescue it

from its talk of beginnings or know
you might be right, being wrong.
It drives off through rain
and conflagrations, in all directions,
passes proof to the snug compass.
Now it's dark it's almost dawn.

ALIBIS

It was a barely perceptible affront.
Mr Wordly Wiseman took sentimental fright
in the arms of a carnival victim who spoke no English
and a bulemic variety of the patois . . .
métro, boulot, dodo of an hexagonal affair.

Beneath my window, the Street of the Dry Tree
led down to the Pont Neuf: new to the ancien régime
and still new to a discredited 18th Brumaire –
those bourgeois sins, complacency and self-regard,
strode out of their century, asking why we needed this . . .

The other side, past the eviscerated belly of Paris,
was a tour through the skin trade: fast food, fast sex

and a gallic Punch giving Judy the once-over;
little secrets Maigret might have kept from his wife
and the big-time vendors of the naked truth.

By the door, I'd stacked the empties, my cadavers.
I was reading Brecht on the hell of the disenchanters
and watching my deaf-dumb neighbour watching me . . .
Twice weekly to buy milk, and long afternoon surveillances
till the pigeons hauled the daylight home.

Every evening, I drowsed to an upstairs *Liebestod*.
Someone was dreaming of being a frontiersman in America
or stalking Flaubert to the lower reaches of the Nile:
watermarks on the wall of the local morgue.
Tracking sun-spots, I compounded my dream-interest.

I was glossing the storyline as fast as I dared
in a place my grandpa called Babylon, the Antichrist *chez lui*.
Deaf to domesdays, it was still crossing itself
or chafing the epochs like a cod-accordion . . .
scraping by on Piaf-naif dreams of glory.

To the silent majority this was never the End-of-Days.
In Figaro's marriage, their namesakes had forced the hand;
centuries later they were still living off the dowry . . .
That retro-radical flight from history
was the snore of the old world outliving itself.

Before the continental drift of two wars
I could imagine Nerval trailing home his livid lobster
to a draughty grammar and the past's Latin drone.
After Haussmann, every lamppost was an orator
interrogating the breezy dispersal of the Communards.

Candid, the swans hissed from the oil-slicked Seine
and made me a duvet beneath the rafters.
After the rest went south one always stayed behind,
its head beneath its wing, flim-flamming the current;
undemocratic, a hesitant Belgian joke.

Halfheartedly I studied the semiotics of couscous
or watched the French devour their colonies.
I bore my life to the Deux Magots and left the ashes there;
a diagram of detours, another unfinished novel.
I took a visceral interest in my precarious species.

Curdled leftovers occluded the windowsill.
Whatever they meant was there to keep me in my place
till the damp became a sticky resurrection.
In one myth of the private life I was killing time
even as I joined them in exhaustion, passion's last logic.

Better to play the medicine man, overhauling the rich
with pop-Oedipal recipes out of Dr Pangloss.
I listened to the histories of hundreds of bodies,
anaesthetic, *involontaire*, subsumed in the mesmeric aura
of everlasting life, an odd entropic metaphor.

Back came the comic echo, news of my four bare walls . . .
I was a novice, fingering the sacramental relics,
eaten whole by the culture fetishists.
Satisfaction was the gape-mouthed, cruel, pacific god
who gave me everything, even the need itself.

And art or absinthe a way of swamping Giant Despair!
Faute de mieux, I made a virtue of my contradictions –
humour was the one weapon to unseat the era.
But when I started hearing panic behind the mockery
the joke had come too close to home.

Tomtoms drummed me back at night from the Big Arch –
Speer's neo-geo paradigm, marmoreal in white Carrara –
to a counter-city in the galleries at Châtelet.
I took the pons asinorum to maturity,
chose a destiny, lit up, went back to my subterfuge.

Beside me, in the next block, lived the ultimate collector.
I never saw him, only heard the poisoned whisperings:
one day they called the *pompiers* in to clean him out,
houseproud among a decade's scatological relics,
each one labelled, wrapped and catalogued.

RAIN DIARY

You hardly have to say the word and it's here, hauling
Banff Bailiffs across the streets of Europe
to one of Joyce's reclaimed 'funams of waste arenary soil',
Nora breathing 'O Jim!' the very day he stopped
in the Bleibtreustrasse and watched it pour down flights,

his nation's *esprit de l'escalier*. Reading it
is like explaining a heresy, its one-offs and torrents
soodling, dropwise, sklent notations of delight.
It takes women of the sun cultures indoors, fingers
in every recess. Damp clothes drop like names
in the rue du Cherche-Midi, soft exclamations
and no talk of respite, only poor men and pike staves.
Half an hour later, like Mercutio, it recalls them
to the ordinary. Beyond the comic the credible;
but that was before it had gone a while down-under
and swept a town off its feet. It disappears inside itself
like an enharmonic pun; its iron cataracts yielding
a blue moon to the platitudes of assent
blowing upwards sheer off mountains. Vigil levels out
in its aftermath. It mists futures, pocks stone
with slow acids, leaving no one outside
dragging neighbours to his wake while the moon
slumps in the midden. Some keep it in clay pots, hoping
a flaff will dry it on the change or temper
the peaty spirit, its sublimation of the very worst.
Like Vico's history, it's a spatial form of coming back;
rigorously errant, faithful to its origins.
Hospitality grows from watersigns, its toponymic limbo.
Undemonstrative, it dumps chill messages,
finds lovers everywhere, scuffing down from saga-steads
like serendipity, striking out the excursus
it once made to an attentive rapt face on the watergaw
fixed half a childhood over the Broomielaw. Our pluvial towns
step out of history, and watch themselves get wet.

UP AND DOWN THE AYR ROAD
for Gerald Mangan

Had you been up and down the Ayr Road once
or twice in a full moon,
you might have seen him too, a man with only
three things on his mind:

convoys of U-Haul juggernauts in front
that won't let him pass,
Covenanters on the shooting crests at Ballantrae
where Burns, at Shanks' pony's pace,

wrote back 'Life is all a VARIORUM', and Keats,
knee-deep in St John's-wort,
peered over the drop
and thought Ailsa Craig more 'omphalos' than Hellespont –

volcano stump of a glacial
slick that had shovelled topsoil south
from this granitic
anti-Greece. (There's probably a tourist-path

leading out across the schist and gneiss,
rich sea-tangs
of the ploughshare, exuberant clumps of lamb's lettuce
and the committed songs

of those who've looked over
Lear's shirt-tails, and seen the greenest grass
thriving on the plummet of the void.)
You might have seen him giving gas

to his hundred-horse-power, no doubt reflecting
he'd likely – more than not –
be clinging to a pencil when the seas go dry
and Scots clacks from one empty palate

to the next. So, as he skirts the potato fields
and creameries, bound this afternoon for the hill
flailing across the windscreen
and the giant hospital hull

where he'll be left to worry out
the social contract and its bad-faith Tory echo
masquerading as a *citizen's*
charter, open the window and you might hear Diderot

decanting 'Knowledge is Happiness' and believe it,
counting field after field of shy
dandelion-heads blown suddenly adrift
into another space

of seed-scatter vectors, effortless
upward soarings of chromosomes. Defoe the spy,
too, delimited these cloud-deft
gables, the spruce

herring-town anchors
interred inland, but didn't think it such a bind,
life that had reached one bend
in the road to Ayr.

DONNY O'ROURKE

I was born on 5 July 1959, in Port Glasgow. Back then, its reason was its river and its river was its reason. My father, who had served his time in the Yards, died a couple of years ago, no longer knowing, what his home town was for. Mum was from County Antrim. It's romantic and sentimental, but I persist in thinking of myself as a Scot, in the original sense of the word, meaning Irish. Dad loved to sing and tell stories; my mother liked to reminisce – traits I hope my poetry has inherited.

As a poet unless (or until) you're very good, you are what you read. So Paul Blackburn's in there and Frank O'Hara and Tom Paulin and lots of the other mostly Irish and American writers I've lovingly ransacked since leaving Glasgow University in 1981. I don't think university taught me how to write poetry; but it probably taught me how to read it. I started writing in my early teens. Puberty, poetry and the guitar all seemed to arrive at around the same time and remain headily commingled in my memory. I wanted to be Leonard Cohen rather than Hugh MacDiarmid . . .

The discovery of a viably imagined Renfrewshire in the work of Alan Sharp, Bill Bryden, Peter McDougall, Gordon Williams and others made me want to try something other than song lyrics. Douglas Dunn had grown up in the next village; John Byrne had gone to my Paisley school. Poetry was not only permissible, it was possible.

But tricky. I was in my mid-twenties before I happened upon anything resembling a 'voice' of my own. Mind you, I took comfort from the fact that so many Scottish poets didn't hit their stride until they were older than any of the writers in this anthology: Muir, MacCaig, Morgan, late developers, every one.

I worked in arts TV for years but haven't made a film since 1996, when I decided to concentrate on writing, performing and teaching, and the travelling they entail. I direct a Scottish Studies programme at the Glasgow School of Art, where the students aren't just permitted to be artists but are encouraged, indeed obliged, to be artists. At present I'm on sabbatical at Pembroke College, Cambridge. Poetry has taken me all over the place, most recently to the Friedrich Schiller University of Jena.

Performance interests and rewards me more and more as I get older. Stories and songs are a big part of my stage act and life act. Even my writing is a sort of performance but then identity isn't simply formed it's performed. As a (more or less) full-time writer, I'm living as I have wished to since I was five years old. All you have to do is write. Right? If only, but, despite the doubts and dreads, I just keep hoping the next poem will be really GOOD . . .

Publications:

Poetry:
Second Cities (Vennel Press, 1991)
The Waist Band and Other Poems (Polygon, 1996)
Modern Music (Vennel Press, 1998)
Jenarbeit/ Jena Drafts (Friedrich Schiller University, 2001)
On a Roll (Mariscat, 2001)

Songs:
Still Waiting To Be Wise, CD with tunes and performances by Dave Whyte (Birnam Records, 1998)

For the theatre:
On Your Nerve: A Wake for Frank O'Hara, with David Kinloch and W. N. Herbert (CCA Glasgow, 1997)
The Kerrera Saga, with George Wylie (Gilmorehill Theatre, 1998)

Television Drama:
Burns on the Box (BBC Scotland, 1995)

As editor:
Dream State: The New Scottish Poets (Polygon, 1994)
Ae fond Kiss: The Love Letters of Robert Burns and Clarinda (Mercat, 2000)

As co-editor:
Across the Water: Irishness in Modern Scottish Writing (Argyll Publishing, 1999) and *Back to the Light Mariscat* (Glasgow City Council, 2000)

Poems in a number of anthologies and textbooks, including *Twentieth Century Scottish Poems* (Faber, 1999), *Mungo's Tongues* (Mainstream, 1994), *Working Words* (Hodder and Stoughton, 1995) and *Understanding Poetry* (Harvester Wheatsheaf, 1996)

Algren

I picture you profiled in Film Noir tones
shirt-sleeves rolled back, cigar smoke

coiling like an unpent spring
as you type at a card table

in some Clark St. cathouse
in '48 or '49

before Korea and McCarthy
made it hard for Reds to work.

The book you're writing,
'The Man with the Golden Arm'

will make a movie star of Sinatra
and not one royalty cent for you

last of the bare-knuckle poets,
more famous in the end

for being the first man
to make Simone de Beauvoir come

than for anything you wrote.
Travelling to Chicago

and later, here in the burg
you called a busted flush,

I read *The Neon Wilderness*
and *City on the Make*

serenades to the low lives
and losers of these streets.

As well, after your hobo
wanderings, the time you did

for stealing a typewriter,
that you remained constant to Chicago

her soda jerks and crap games
pastures new then

reduced to scuffed
green baize.

Glasgow, you look beatific in blue
and I've a Saturday before me
for galleries and poems,
a house full of Haydn,
and beneath my kitchen window,
tennis stars in saris
lobbing backhands at the bins.
French coffee, and who knows maybe
Allen Ginsberg in my bath!
then round to the dairy
where scones are cooling on the rack
and Jimmy won't let me leave
till I've tried one there and then,
here, where the new Glasgow started –
an old grey city going blonde
whose Asian shops are full of fruits
we owe to Cap'n Bligh
and I'm so juiced I could walk clear
to Loch Lomond,
past busses stripping the willow
all along Great Western Road
but I just browse bargains in banjos
and pop-art knitted ties,
before checking out the crime section
at Caledonia Books,
finding Friesias in the flowershops
and in the second hand record store,
Bruckner's Third,
The Cleveland
under Szell:
so sad; like falling for passing students
with that black haired, blue eyed look,
or buying basil and chorizos . . .
In the afternoon I'll look at paintings
in Dougie Thomson's Mayfest show,
maybe stroll down to the studio
to view some archive film,
past the motorways and multi-storeys
of Grieve's Ultimate Cowcaddens,
the peeling pawn at George's Cross
where, today, everything is redeemable
because tonight there'll be guitar poets
from Russia at the Third Eye Centre.

And later I'll cook zarzuela
for a new and nimble friend.
God Glasgow it's glorious
just to gulp you down in heartfuls,
feeling something quite like love.

MILK

Your custom often
when the house was still

to brew milky coffee
and reminisce.

Child care experts would have frowned
on my late hours,

the bitter adult drinks
and frothy confidences.

Yet your stories stopped my mewling
and continued as I grew

me tending the fire,
you talking of Ireland,

more real to your first born
than the younger ones who slept.

Those nightcaps, Mother,
were our hushed bond.

And though, for twenty years now,
I've drunk my coffee black,

I'm not weaned yet
of that rich, warm milk.

Primary

Every word I've ever read or written
I owe to you Miss Hughes –
dream colleen and crabbit queen
of primary one

With your round white face
and russet perm you could have modelled
Ireland for *The Book of Kells*

and green –
       your eyes
              and swankiest
                      sweaters

green

the lightest
       brightest
             tightest
                  green

Those first terms were mostly religion
sums and reading but you
grew hyacinths in the dark
curdling in that cupboard also
school milk into cheese.
Our first solid achievement.
Your muslin miracle.

It was 1964; we bought 'Black Babies'
wept and wet ourselves
but were excused –
Pees and Queues for the 'lavatory'
never the toilet
A stickler for proper English
and Catholic self-improvement
praying we'd pass for higher class
you spruced up where we came from
helped us out:

'Port Glasgow' was articulated sternly
and in full
                'The Port, Daniel O'Rourke

is vulgar
                    teeth and tongue now, Porrtt
Glass go.'

You pulled out all the glottal stops
corrected nearly everything we learned
at home.

Miss Hughes, you had magnificent breasts
and I loved you.

You turned all our cream to crowdie.

WINE AND WOOING
(A song lyric)

I wasn't the first one
I wasn't the worst one
You called me your baleful boy
After all the losers
And cynical users
There was no cause to be coy
So what you wanted you named and took
And the name you chose was mine
Yours was the first grown woman's look
That I knew to be love's sign

You taught me wine and wooing
I learned by candlelight
To do what needed doing
To do it slow, and right?

It was your proud prime
And my first time
You wept but wouldn't say
What joys or fears
Had caused the tears
As the dark spring night turned grey –
Again that look, but what you took
Was your loving leave of me
The callow shallow lad mistook
How a woman's heart comes free

You taught me wine and wooing
I learned by candlelight
To do what needed doing
To do it slow, and right?

On other nights
When brighter lights
Glow in younger eyes
Older now and bolder now
Still waiting to be wise
All I know and show of love
was learned that night we shared
Long ago in Glasgow
When you looked at me and dared.

DAVID KINLOCH

I was born in Glasgow in 1959 and was educated there, graduating from Glasgow University in 1982. From then until 1990, when I returned to Glasgow, I travelled around quite a bit, studying and teaching French in a variety of places, including Oxford, Paris, Swansea and Manchester. It was only after leaving Glasgow that I realised how important Scotland was to me and that I wanted to return. Scotland has remained an abiding concern and my most recent collection of poems, *Un Tour d'Ecosse*, offers a vision of the country from the handlebars of the ecologically friendly machine the French call 'la petite reine'.

I enjoy mixing and matching very different kinds of poetry in my work and like to work through fairly large-scale structures as well as individual poems. What happens when 'traditional' musical (the music is very important) lyrics cohabit with more experimental prose-poems and fables? This idea is central to 'Dustie-Fute', which is the first part of a poem in three sections. In this poem, the old Scots word for a troubadour or jongleur, juggler or merchant, jumps out of Jamieson's dictionary and, rather like Orpheus, sails off on the Renfrew Ferry into an Underworld of secret or suppressed languages. 'Dustie-Fute', however, is not a poem about old words, nor is it simply a poem about the difficulty for many writers of my generation who would like to write in Scots more fluently than they are able. These unexpected, boisterous words become in the course of the poem a kind of metaphor for the queer and wonderful tongue that died prematurely in the mouths of many young men killed by Aids. The more recent poems of *Un Tour d'Ecosse* revisit some of these concerns, but satire and humour become an ever more important weapon against disillusionment in poems that seek to suggest some of the amusing overlaps between areas of sexual, linguistic and national marginality.

Publications:

Poems in *Other Tongues* (Verse, 1990); *Dustie-Fute* (Vennel Press, 1992); *The Thought and Art of Joseph Joubert* (Clarendon Press, 1992); *Reading Douglas Dunn,*

co-edited with Robert Crawford (Edinburgh University Press, 1992),
Paris-Forfar (Polygon, 1994), *Une Nouvelle Alliance: influences francophones
sur la littérature écossaise moderne*, co-edited with Richard Price (Ellug,
Grenoble, 2000), *Un Tour d'Ecosse* (Carcanet, 2001).

THE REV. ROBERT WALKER SKATING ON DUDDINGSTON LOCH

The water tensed at his instruction
and trout gazed up at his incisive feet.
We felt that God must be in clarity like this
and listened to the dull glens echo
the striations of his silver blades.

Far out on Duddingston loch
our true apostle sped
with twice the speed of Christ
who walked on waves.

We saw him harrow ice
with grace of the elect
and scar the transubstantiation
of wintered elements.

With a sense of real presence
he crossed our loch
what need of vestments
with such elegant legs?

DUSTIE-FUTE

When I opened my window and reached for the yoghurt cooling on the
outside ledge, it had gone. All that remained was a single Scottish word
bewildered by the Paris winter frost and the lights of its riverbank motor-
ways. What can *dustie-fute* have to say to a night like this? How can it
dangle on its hyphen down into the rue Geoffrey L'Asnier, where Danton
stayed on the eve of revolution? How can it tame this strangeness for
me or change me into the cupolas and flagstones I so desire yet still
notice every time I walk among them? Does the 'auld alliance' of words
and things stand a chance among the traffic and pimps in the Publicis
Saint-Germain? For it's not as if *dustie-fute* were my familiar. I could

easily confuse *dustie-fute* with *elfmill*, which is the sound made by a worm in the timber of a house, supposed by the vulgar to be preternatural. These words are as foreign as the city they have parachuted into, dead words slipping on the sill of a living metropolis. They are extremes that touch like dangerous wires and the only hope for them, for us, is the space they inhabit, a room Cioran speaks of, veering between dilettantism and dynamite. Old Scots word, big French city and in between abysmal me: ane merchand or creamer, quha hes no certain dwelling place, quhair the dust may be dicht fra hes feete or schone. Dustie-fute, a stranger, equivalent to *fairand-man*, at a loss in the empty soul of his ancestors' beautiful language and in the soulless city of his compeers living the 21st century now and scoffing at his medieval wares. Yet here, precisely here, is their rendez-vous and triumphantly, stuffed down his sock, an oblique sense, the dustie-fute of 'revelry', the acrobat, the juggler who accompanies the toe-belled jongleur with his merchant's comic fairground face. He reaches deep into his base latinity, into his *pede-pulverosi* and French descendants pull out their own *pieds poudreux*. Dustie-fute remembers previous lives amid the plate glass of Les Halles. They magnify his motley, his midi-oranges, his hawker lyrics and for a second Beaubourg words graze Scottish glass then glance apart. In this revelry differences copulate, become more visible and bearable and, stranger than the words or city I inhabit, I reach for my yoghurt and find it there.

THE LOVE THAT DARE NOT

Even the illness that extinguishes it comes in borrowed clothes, not one name but many, forming the syntax of your end. Unravelling its hidden meanings, side-stepping tears that dare not fall yet because they would admit the last page of this dictionary has been turned, I trace you back, nudging you, as I used to, from word to word:

the days you called me *rinker*, a tall, thin, long-legged horse, a bloody harridan, I called you *rintherout*, a gadabout, a needy, homeless vagrant, like the tongue we spoke beneath the sheets. Our life as mobile and happy as the half a dozen Scottish verbs I'd push across a page on Sunday afternoons, trying to select a single meaning.

Here it is: under *Ripple* or *Rippill*, a squat paragraph which tells us we must separate the seed of flax from the stalk, undo our badly-done work, separate and tear in pieces. And when we are birds, must eat grains of standing corn, when clouds, open up, disperse, clear off. Its noun has you in its grip: an instrument with teeth for rippling flax.

Or you might find us under *set* which seats, places hens on eggs in order to hatch them, assigns work, settles, gets in order; puts milk into a pan for the cream to rise, sets fishing-lines or nets, works according to a pattern, plants potatoes, makes, impels, includes, besets, brings to a halt and puzzles, nauseates, disgusts, marks game, lets, leases, sends, dispatches, becomes, suits, beseems, sits, ceases to grow, becomes mature, stiffens, congeals, starts, begins, sets off

The love that dare not. Except that now, so near the end, when I would like to hold you and have been forbidden, I search for it in your eyes, daring their definition.

ENVOI: WARMER BRUDER
(a slang expression for homosexual, literally, 'hot brother'. It gave rise to many vicious puns in concentration camps like Sachsenhausen and Flossenburg.)

i

Concentrate hot brothers:
Shovel snow with me
In Sachsenhausen
From one side to the other
And back again.

Then in the silence
Make an angel of the snow
Which falls unceasingly
On camp and foe.

The lights of Grangemouth
Dance their triangles
Into tears,
Its smoke the ghost of blood,
The melting snow.

ii

Concentrate hot brothers:
Make an angel of the snow
And shovel Sachsenhausen
Silence from one side to the other
And back again.

O warmer bruder
Tonight you fall
Shaping car windows
With triangles of Grangemouth light.

Smoke, the ghost of blood,
Fills up the melting sky.

iii

Blood dropped on Sachsenhausen
Snow was silenced,
Shovelled out of history.
But here in Scotland
It does not melt

And cloaks the Grangemouth
Sky with red triangles.
This is no sunset
But concentrated smoke
That stings the eye.

iv

Triangles of smoke
Blood the Grangemouth skies.
Along the Forth the hospice
Workers shovel snow

From drives that keep the patients
Bound, while silence, like an angel,
Visits and stays on.

THE TEAR IN PAT KANE'S VOICE

The tear in Pat Kane's voice
Offers you the shadow of a bi-plane
Unutterably high just next to silence:

Off the grain, it thinks more quickly
Than the images of his songs
And each true thought concludes
In the break where each true note begins.

The tear in Pat Kane's voice
Offers you a man's name,
Whiter and harder than Alba:

Adorno at his plain table,
Rubbing out the barbaric lyrics
Of post-Auschwitz poets

And cleansed children,
Desperately seeking a river crossing
In a blown-up ferry,
While we sit like empty cars
In a reconverted bauble,
Crossing from one song to
Another over the nailed-down waves.

BED

for Eric

The moment the light goes out,
He sleeps: a gift from the dark.
There is the small chime
Of the moon on the wall,
The deep freeze digesting
In the kitchen. He floats
From head to toe on the buzz
Of his snore, dreaming the calm
Glide of a Jaspar ski-lift,
The summer elk that trotted
Out of forest beneath our
Dangling feet. His arm
Crooks the violin of my head.
I elbow him away intent on
Sleep but suddenly unpegged
By a gust of dreams we roll
Together in the hot hole
Of his mum's old bed,
Dribbling on the pillows.
Waking, he has me in an
Arm-lock, our legs a single
Rope of flesh, my ear-lobe
Tickled by his breath. I reach
Behind me and shove my hand

Between his thighs. He stretches,
Opening briefly like a centre-
Fold, a light smile of welcome
On his lips. But more than this
Is the scrape of the two-o'clock
Beetle, the nip of a dust-mite,
My scratch: my love disturbed
By me, awake but patient
In the dark.

FROM THREE WEE FREES
To John MacLeod

I HINNIE-PIGS
   (or Wan wee free)

thur wiz this wee free rite
an hi wiz doazin aff in a pew
wi the meenister goan on'n'on

sittin oan hiz hauns hi wiz
jist like at school when hi pleyed
hinnie-pigs. hinnie-pigs

wiz when wan o the boys
tried tae lift ye up by thi
oxters an gave ye three shakes.

if yer hauns went aw flabby like
ye wur a rite wersh wee git
an a bent shot intae thi bargain!

a woofter man! if yer hauns
steyed pit ye wur a hinnie-pot or
pig an *youz* got a shot at thi liftin.

wull. thur wiz this wee free rite
sittin tite oan hiz hauns
skretchin his erse as hi snoozed

dreemin o hinnie-pigs when
all o a sudden it's Jeezusiz' turn.
Aye Jeezus! Christ! hi seez Jeezus

dayin sum liftin. Jeezus thi hinnie-
merchant feelin fur sweet oxters an
sour yins. wull blow me if hi didni

chooz thi biggest harry hoof
o thi lot! am tellin ye hiz hauns
wur everywher. bloody whirligig hi wiz

an thi wee free wiz fair gobsmacked
when hi jalouzed that thi guy doin
thi jack'n'thi boax wiz thi wee free

hisel an Jeezus seyin tae him: it's yoor
turn noo son. it's thi nippy sweetie's turn.

Braveheart

O Mel! Mel of the hair extenders! Braveheart!
O Mad Mac Mel! It is I,
Walt, Walt Whitman, who salutes you.
When I heard at the close of the day
That your heroic film of the Wallace
Would premiere in Stirling, I floated

From Mount Florida, high above Glasgow, floated
From the residence of my comrade Kinloch, a brave heart
Like you, I crossed the hummock-land of Shotts as Wallace
Did on leaving Elderslie, I
Sped through that dun-coloured upland (beside the great M8)
                                                    that day
To celebrate your epic but most of all to be with you

O Mel! But also to petition you,
Dark singer of Democracy, you who floated
Like a Moses through Scottish bogs, waiting for the day
To release your noble, simple people, their brave brave heart
Clasped in an English vice. O Mel, I
Confuse you, mix you in my mind with Wallace.

And who could blame me? For you and Wallace
Commingle in my scented breast, you
Two and I, comrades all, shooting the film of liberty I
Crave above all else, I crave and lost as my successors floated

Back up stream to a land of villanelles and sonnets. Bravehearts!
Brave Walt! a bearded Ariel imprisoned in a bad sestina
                              who would this day

Be free again by your example, free today
To live today, to sing the love of comrades as Wallace
Did. He could not rhyme, his only beat the braveheart
Quad-pumping the eclectic plaid about his knees
                              (What knees!). You
Saw him Mel, as clearly as I see you who floated
From Australia via Hollywood to this premiere. I

Name the perfumed guests as they arrive, I
Shake the manly hand of Jodie Foster, day
Dream as Christian Slater – he of the slow doe-eyes – floats
In. We sit transfixed as the credits of your Wallace
Roll but I have eyes alone for you,
Peach of a biceps – your musk white thighs – muncher of
                              power-breakfasts, Braveheart!

Mel Wallace, Will Gibson, this day
Your barbaric yawp injects its braveheart
Into me. You and I floating and free.

Customs

Customs vary: Rapunzel always
Sleeps on planes like this, slumped
Forward, waterfall of hair
Stepped over by a steward

As my gaze climbs it to the Prince
Beside her. Tenderly he pretends
To read a book, quite stomached
By her beauty, portholed

Sunsets nesting on her crown.
The long-haul of my lover's
Snores fizzle up close by me.
We are dimmed. My spotlight

Aims optician's letters
At me through the glare:
Bug-like, icarian, they fall
Away and will not make a story.

This is patience. Half-
Sleep fugs peripheral vision
And I am five again, intently
Glueing a balsa bi-plane

Until we touch the tarmac and it
Tenses like ryvita. We're stopped
At customs, two men travelling
Together. They ferret out the hidden

Freight of our pornography:
A Birthday card, a Christmas
Valentine. 'Sweetpart' to
'Sweetpart' and sillier names

Crease the fake gravitas
Of their faces. We haven't
Landed. My balsa plane dips,
Lurches over unexpected

Cliffs and as they gingerly
Remove each layer of sweaty
Socks, request receipts,
I ache for the reassuring

Touch of discreet fawn bark,
The ghost of tree rings,
The flight of your hand on mine.
Patience love. Wait

In the fearful patience
That is ours now
And forever. Soon the officer
Will close our case so the flight

Back may resume.

RODY GORMAN

I was born in Dublin on New Year's Day 1960 – approximately ten minutes after my twin brother, than whom I am legally older according to the Irish Succession Act 1965. I was raised by Gaelic-speaking parents from Derryoober and Bloomfield in the counties of Galway and Mayo, attending schools under the De La Salle Brothers in Ardtona, Ballintemple, Rahogue, Kilmacoda and Rathmanus. After school, I worked in the Registry of Deeds in Dublin as an Irish Language Officer and Staff Association Representative.

In 1986 I moved to Scotland, where I have lived in Oban, the Inner Hebrides, Edinburgh and Portlethen, working as barman, fisherman, gardener, lexicographer, translator, librarian, lecturer, researcher and editor. I attended the University of Aberdeen (1995–8), where I studied Onomastics, Linguistics and the poetry of Dafydd ap Gwilym. I started writing poems in Scottish Gaelic in 1994 and have since published in English, Irish and, most recently (Yn Queigad), Manx Gaelic. In 1995, I was awarded a Scottish Arts Council Writers' Bursary. In 1996 I visited Ireland as a Scottish Gaelic poet on a cultural exchange organised by the Gaelic Books Council and the Department of Foreign Affairs in Ireland. From 1998 to 2001, I was employed as SAC Writing Fellow at Sabhal Mòr Ostaig in Skye.

The house in which I live with my family in Sleat was, according to legend, once occupied by a village poet who drowned himself in nearby Cruard Gardens.

Publications:

Fax and Other Poems (Polygon, 1996)
Cùis-Ghaoil (diehard, 1999)
Bealach Garbh (Coiscéim, 1999)
On the Underground/Air a' Charbad fo Thalamh (Polygon, 2000)

Forthcoming:
Faoi Shlí Cualann (Coiscéim)
Siubhal an Fhuinn (diehard)

Fax

Tha 'm fax anns an oisean
Na thrèan-ri-trèan anns a' chluain

No na mhuc a' gnòsail
Ann an guth ìseal

Is tha 'm printer taobh ris na leum na eas
Agus duilleagan bàn' a' sruthadh às

Is tha seallaidhean gan sgrìobadh
A chaidh a dhraghadh

A grinneal a' Chuain Siair
Air sgàilean m' annalair

'S iad uile cur an cruth fhèin gu seòlta
Air saoghal an latha.

Doras-Cuartachaidh

Choisich i mach orm
A-mach air an doras-chuartachaidh
Ach 's eudar gun deach rud air choreigin ceàrr
Air an uidheam,
Oir, a dh' aithghearr
'S ann a thill i gam ionnsaigh.

Fax

The fax in the corner
is a corncrake in the meadow

or a pig grunting
in a low voice

and the printer beside it is a waterfall
with white pages gushing out of it

and scenes are being depicted
that were trawled

from the bed of the Atlantic
on the screen of my computer

and they all put their own form neatly
on today's world.

Revolving Door

She walked out on me,
Out through the revolving door
But something or other must have gone wrong
With the mechanism
Because, shortly afterwards,
She came back to me.

A' FAIREACHDAINN T' FHÀILIDH

Bidh mi a' faireachdainn t' fhàilidh
A nochdas gu ciùin
Gun fhiosd' air feadh an àile
'S mi a' sreap ri cabar na beinne:

Dithis chearc-fhraoich air dùsgadh,
Na fèidh às dèidh sin
A' rùsgadh air falbh mar chuimhne
Gu h-obann gu dlùth na coille.

CATCHIN YER WAUCHT

I catch the waucht o yer scent
the merest thochtie o't
o a suddenty, throw the air
as I sclimm the ben:

Twa grice, frichtit
syne the deer
meevin aff like a flaucht
o memory,
tae the derkest pairt o the wid.
(Translation: Sheena Blackhall)

GETTING YOUR WHIFF

I get your whiff,
which appears subtly
and suddenly throughout the air
as I climb the mountain:

Two grouse roused,
then the deer
moving off like a flash of memory
to the densest part of the wood.

Do Gheas

Cha dèan do gheas mo leas. Ach tha mi coma's mi un comas Air sineadh sìos air leabaidh—fhlocais, 'S mo chneas a' sineadh ri do chneas.

SPELL

Your spell won't do me any good
but I don't care so long as I'm able
to snuggle with you under the downie,
my skin stretched out over yours.

Hosai

A' sealltainn air ais air an tràigh,
Fiù 's làrach mo chois' air falbh.

Looking back at the beach,
even my footprints
have disappeared.

KEN COCKBURN

I was born in Kirkcaldy, where I went to primary school; for secondary school I travelled through each day to Edinburgh on the train, along the Fife coast and over the bridge, which opened up new social and imaginative worlds to me. I read French and German at Aberdeen University and Theatre Studies in Cardiff, staying on in Wales for six years to work with touring theatre and dance companies. I returned to Edinburgh in 1990, where I worked with the gallerist and publisher Graeme Murray, latterly at the Fruitmarket Gallery. Since 1996 I've been the Fieldworker at the Scottish Poetry Library, undertaking talks and workshops across Scotland. Currently I also work with Alec Finlay on the pocketbooks series of anthologies and artist books, and teach occasionally at Glasgow School of Art. I live in Edinburgh with my wife Tamsin and daughters Alice and Isobel.

At school, and more so at university, I was turned on to literature both in and beyond the classroom, but had to emerge from formal education before I could find a space for writing myself. The impulse was a couple of unhappy love affairs, and I've never written many love poems, identifying with Orpheus for whom the death of love was the birth of poetry.

I'm not very good at making things up, which is maybe why I prefer writing poems to writing stories, and why the poems are based on actual events, or dreams and myths, or use 'found' material. I subscribe to the notion that poems exist already in the world in a 'raw' state, and the role of the poet is to reveal them. I'm also taken with the idea of recurrence, that things which have happened once will come round again, which ties in with this kind of recycling. It may be a story which has already been beautifully realised as a piece of literature, perhaps something overheard or misheard, or even (as in the case of the Lorca 'flower') a bad translation from another language.

Publications:

Orpheus (Red Sharks Press, 1988)
Given: Seven Poems, Seven Days (Instant Republic, 1995)
Souvenirs and Homelands (Scottish Cultural Press, 1998)

As editor:
The Order of Things: Scottish Sound, Pattern and Concrete Poems, edited with
Alec Finlay (pocketbooks, 2001)
The Jewel Box: Contemporary Scottish Poems, audio-CD, edited with Alec
Finlay (Scottish Poetry Library, 2000)
*Brilliant Cacophony: Connecting the Contemporary of Art and Architecture on
Edinburgh's Royal Mile,* edited with Lise Bratton (Scottish Sculpture Trust,
1998)

A FLOWER FOR FEDERICO GARCÍA LORCA

House-Museum Federico García Lorca, Fuentevaqueros, Granada

Visitors carrying suitcases, rucksacks,
and other objects of big size,
are not admitted.

Photographs may be taken in the patio,
but not inside the rooms.

Smoking is forbidden in the rooms of the house.
However they may do so in the patio provided they use ashtrays.

Food is not allowed inside the house,
though visitors may drink fresh water in the patio.

years of silence

a geranium flowerpot

remember his laughter

'In this town I had my first dream of remoteness.
In this town I will be earth and flowers.'

Spins and Turns

After the bells we'd had enough
of the country danceband's steady beat
and straightaway I found some jazz
that was nearer the mark: light, quick,
trying to catch itself out with spins and
turns dreamt up then and there.
I danced round the bed you lay on with
the end of the wine, that was nudging you
the other side of sleep
and you switched out the light, suggesting
I should switch off the radio too
but the music was suiting my mood, and besides,
then it stopped. The announcer announced
there was only time for one more number
and they'd do the *Doctor Kildare* theme.
I knew you wouldn't mind too much.
So I sat at the foot of the bed you were falling
asleep in, almost, but not, in darkness,
light from lampposts and maybe the moon
seeping in through the curtains, and I listened
as they revived *Doctor Kildare*
slowly becoming aware that
in front of me the lemon geranium
was oozing oxygen into
the atmosphere of the room, you know,
one of those meaningful insights that come
when you're half-asleep and half-pissed.
Applause. I switched the radio off
and joined you, gratefully, in bed.
Once I realised
I hadn't caught the band's name
I realised
I wasn't about to lose sleep over it.

Blank

Berlin.
A city new to her.
Talks on the prospective exhibition
although progressing
require tact.

At the museum one afternoon
in a section recently repainted
and, still pictureless, awaiting a rehang,
she puts to the chief Curator
(a young man, bearded, slender but imposing)
awkward questions concerning the availability
of particular works which are central to the show.
He opts not to respond directly
but neither does he evade her approach. Instead

he proposes that they dance
twirls her across the varnished parquet floor
whose sheen reflects white walls, unsmudged
– the rehang, he confides, as their clicking steps echo
in corridors, offices and lumber-rooms,
the rehang he'll be keeping secret,
at least until the *Vernissage*.

SHANDWICK STONE

As jets without the black box of memory
startle sheep in deserted glens
the stone hunters stalk their various prey.

Chaotic and recurrent as the tides
incised patterns swirl underneath them.
The Pictish beast, that composite

bird-fish-mammal, harbours a smile
having already weathered eras and elements
untraceable by radar.

The rain-clouds gather above an unyielding sea.
Wildflowers and seeding grasses rustle
in anticipation of the next downpour.

MAUD SULTER

My life has been a fascinating parlay of complementary opposites: yin and yang, white and black, cold lands and hot lands. I was a social experiment produced by my parents to challenge the prejudice of both my family lines. Luckily for me, given the immensity of the task, from the day I was born I have been beloved of the ancestors.

Named after my maternal grandmother Maud and my paternal great-great-grandmother Nana Benyiwah, I feel a great responsibility for preserving the memory of my foremothers and am deeply honoured to bear their names.

In some ways my role as poet echoes that of the traditional West African linguist, for although I was born and grew up in Glasgow, Oatlands, Hutchesontown, and educated in the Gorbals, my ancestral home is the village of Ano in Ghana. The red soil there draws to it the bones and the spirits of those departed. It is there that my father, Doctor Claud Ennin, who was also the village chief, is interred. Although if truth be told, he, like me, spent much of his life in exile.

The poem 'Africa Beckons' was written in the mid-1980s a long time before I had returned to my village in the company of my Aunty Marion and the Queen Mother of Ebirum. That was a very special day for me and I was very pleased to be in the company of Lubaina Himid, my companion throughout the 1990s. I would later accompany her to her birthplace in Zanzibar, Tanzania.

For me, writing poetry is an act of empowerment both for the writer and the reader. I like to think my poetry helped not only Lubaina and I to return to our African roots but also gave strength to many others around the world encouraging them to reconnect to their history.

To quote from 'As a Blackwoman', the title poem of my first collection for women of African descent the world over, 'The personal is political holds no empty rhetoric'.

Publications:

History of art books:
Passion: Discourses on Blackwomen's Creativity (UFP, 1990)

Poetry collections:
As a Blackwoman (Akira Press, 1985)
As a Blackwoman (reprint) (UFP, 1989)
Zabat: Poetics of a Family Tree (UFP, 1989)
Zabat Narratives (UFP/Rochdale Art Gallery, 1989)

Anthologies:
Dancing the Tightrope (The Women's Press, 1987)
Charting the Journey (Sheba Press, 1987)
Watchers and Seekers (The Women's Press, 1987)
Through the Break (Sheba Press, 1987)
Let It Be Told (Virago, 1988)
Original Prints III (Polygon, 1988)
Gossip (Onlywomen Press, 1989)
Sleeping with Monsters (Polygon, 1990)
The Crazy Jig (Polygon, 1992)
Daughters of Africa (Jonathan Cape, 1992)
Dream State: The New Scottish Poets (Polygon, 1994)

AS A BLACKWOMAN

As a blackwoman
the bearing of my child
is a political act.

I have
been mounted in rape
bred from like cattle
mined for my fecundity

I have
been denied abortion
denied contraception
denied my freedom to choose

I have
been subjected to abortion
injected with contraception
sterilised without my consent

I have
borne witness to the murders
of my children
by the Klan, the Front, the State

I have
borne sons hung for rape
for looking at a white girl

I have
borne daughters shot
for being liberationists

As a blackwoman
I have taken the power to choose
to bear a black child
– a political act?

As a blackwoman
every act is a personal act
every act is a political act

As a blackwoman
the personal is political
holds no empty rhetoric.

DRICH DAY

Ice cold steel gray sky ahead
entering the Kingdom of Fife

Walk through ruins
of castles ancient, a priory
tombstones cold as death itself
of people past, children lost
to disease poverty the
harsh reality of life

Sea a blanket of September sorrows
unremitting drich and drizzle
permeates our light outerwear

Walking the links at St Andrews
we kissed holding each to the other
treasuring the moment
for the sake of itself
nothing between us and Denmark
except that tomorrow you leave me.

IF LEAVING YOU

If leaving you
was as easy
as the falling
in love
with
a
total
stranger

– not total

our blackness
a bond
before speech
or encounter

I could walk
from you now
into the hustle
and bustle
of Waverley
station
and checking
my ticket
– depart.

A Poem of Love

Africa beckons us with her bittersweet call.

In our mind's eye we see the soil pass through the sands of time to our present
uneasy phase in the belly of this retrograde beast that is the land of our birth.
Our surrogate home. The consumer of our culture. Of our communal soul.
Do not allow our oppressor, of whatever hue, tell us that we in our blackness
are not African children. Are not the warriors of time.

Perpetually in motion
towards our goal. Liberation. Lover your body meets mine and I resist its
consuming wave of desire as it ricochets like the plastic bullet of yesterday's
dawn into the barren wastelands of my undisturbed unloved soul. Graciously
you resist. I express my desire. Then you approach. Your body; victimised,
illigitimised, used as a weapon in the war of sexual terror implicit in the
Western mythology of sex. Unambiguous its tender radiance, its compassionate
glow. Come close my lover. Let us Love in the face of our enemies.

Let us create a union of spirit for the mutual soul. Time is come to rebel.
We grow in the face of those who talk black but sleep white. Chant Africa
but despise her. The heady odours sour and sweet. Spices intoxicate us
as we step amongst the high piled seasonings and scents. A stench. The bodies
of our new born rot in the freezing sunlight of another day of hunger. We find
pleasure in each other's caress. We find ourselves in pain that we can feel so
much love. We tear at each other when we feel we cannot go on.

Our love will
hold us close as budded leaves. Ours is the future we dared not hope to imagine
least of all create. Yours is the fire that ignites. The flame sparked from the
flint buried beneath this harsh veneer which is my shield in this hostile world.
Come let us burn Babylon to the ground. Raze the beast. Free our souls.
We are African Peoples. The time is come. To reclaim the line of forebearers.
Recognise in profile grandmother's brow. Kiss the mouth that sang the song
of our spirit while Europe was still a bare and barren land. Now. Much later.
We find ourselves. Here. In a white ethereal cultural void. Stand firm. So.
When those detractors who want to divide us, for in our strength is Revolution,
speak of some political survival over Culture, let us call with a voice in unison
Echoing from Europe to the Americas and back to the continent of Africa herself.
'We' we shall chant 'Are African people' 'We are going home'
The seed of our future is planted within us. Where we go it follows. Feeding
on warm African soil, a warm and inviting reservoir in our bellies. Carried into
diaspora. The entire world can be our rightful home.

AFRICA AFRICA AFRICA

'We are African people and we are going home'.

W. N. HERBERT

I was born in Dundee two hundred(ish) years ago, the idiot bastard son of Robert Burns and Mary Wollstonecraft, and brought up in a kilometre-high tenement. Each morning I stirred the brains of McGonagall into my gruel, each night I donated hair to Billy MacKenzie's wig. Eventually I escaped over the Wall into Northumberland, joining the stylish monastery of IKEAfarne. Here I illustrated seagulls. I began to trace an enormous dog-leg from Newcastle to Lancaster, where at night I howled like an enormous dog. Meanwhile, I fathered a child (Isobel) and became a disused lighthouse-keeper on the Firth of Tyne.

No. I was born in Dundee in 1961. I went to Oxford and did my D.Phil. on that auld iconoclast MacDiarmid. I did residencies in Dumfries and Galloway and Morayshire, then in 1994 I was selected as a New Generation poet. I became Northern Arts Literary Fellow, then Fellow in Creative Writing at Lancaster, then the first Wordsworth Fellow at Dove Cottage. Until recently I lectured at Lancaster in one of the oldest Creative Writing departments in the country, established by the Scottish poet and critic David Craig. I now teach at Newcastle University. I live on Tyneside, in North Shields.

I'm a polystylist, obsessed by how different modes of writing interact – not just Scots or English, but also formal or free verse, poetry on the page or in performance, long poems, forty-line lyrics. Everything's a dialect. Because they cross these borders, my books reject the orthodoxy of the slim volume, exploring the different concision of a large canvas. My next book examines how English has become infected by Scots; it's smitten with the love of difficult things – myths, cities, mythic cities, furniture, lemurs – how these help us mourn our dead and celebrate our living.

No. I was born in Constantinople in 961 . . .

Publications:

Pamphlets:
Sterts and Stobies, with Robert Crawford (Obog, 1985)

Severe Burns, with Robert Crawford and David Kinloch, (Obog, 1987)
Other Tongues, with Meg Bateman, David Kinloch and Angela McSeveney
(Verse, 1990)
Dundee Doldrums (Galliard, 1991)
Anither Music (Vennel Press, 1991)
The Landfish (Duncan of Jordanstone, 1991)

Collections:
Sharawaggi, with Robert Crawford (Polygon, 1990)
The Testament of the Reverend Thomas Dick (Arc, 1994)
Forked Tongue (Bloodaxe, 1994)
Cabaret McGonagall (Bloodaxe, 1996)
The Laurelude (Bloodaxe, 1998)
The Big Bumper Book of Troy (Bloodaxe, 2002)

Critical/editorial:
To Circumjack MacDiarmid (Oxford University Press, 1992)
Contraflow on the Super Highway: An Informationist Primer, edited with
Richard Price (Gairfish/Southfields, 1994)
Strong Words, edited with Matthew Hollis (Bloodaxe, 2000)

Video/tape/CD:
Dour Fun (dir. Valerie Lyon), STV, 1999
Poetry Quartets: 7, with John Burnside, Liz Lochhead, Don Paterson (The
British Council/Bloodaxe, 1999)
BON: Book of the North (edited) (*New Writing North*, 2001)

A BACKLOOK

(To my father)

Presleyan, yi didnae waant
ti be a tigir
rinnan aflemm thru gloaman
o tennyments
hittan thir tap-note o grey,
Sportan Post tichtfurlit in
yir haund.
Uncranglan lyk
a quiff, i thi glistiry room
whaur men ur biddubil.

gloaman – early evening; *uncranglan* – uncurling,
relaxing; *glistiry* – hot, sweaty, flickering with light;
biddubil – cowed, obedient.

MARIPOSA PIBROCH

If the Grunewald *Crucifixion*'s like
the skeleton of a butterfly, that

gnarling into the blackish, ragged
filaments through which my memory

is falling into the back garden
like pancake-large snowflakes;

then the mosquito I pressed against
this kitchen window yesterday,

the emptiness between its sap and
the pulse of my apologising finger,

is bringing me back, like swinging
from a balcony by the nail caught

in my jean's rump; landing in Elie,
in the grounds of a manse, cruciform,

clouting the earth like a sack
of floury potatoes, back emptied

of air. I'm facing a piper outside
Selfridges, playing airs sentimental

enough to summon drunks to shake
my penniless hands and beg; airs

that are built into the childhood
but aren't genuine. The giant

mosquito drone that alone demarks this
foreign music I feel kin to, salutes

or seems to the offerings I cannot
make: only the hearing is authentic.

Dingle Dell

There is no passport to this country,
it exists as a quality of the language.

It has no landscape you can visit;
when I try to listen to its vistas

I don't think of that round tower, though
only two exist in Scotland, though

both are near me. There are figures on
an aunt's old clock, cottars; Scots

as marketed to Scots in the last century:
these are too late. I seek something

between troughs, a green word dancing
like weed in a wave's translucence,

a pane not smashed for an instance
through which the Dingle Dell of Brechin

sinks into the park like a giant's grave
from which his bones have long since

walked on air. Into this hole in
the gums of the language I see a name

roll like a corpse into the plague pits:
Bella. It is both my grandmothers'.

Beauty, resilient as girstle, reveals
itself: I see all of Scotland

rolling down and up on death's yoyo.
There is no passport to this country.

BALLAD OF THE KING'S NEW DIALECT

When Jamie ran to London toon
tae tak up his new throne,
he drapped his pack o playin bards
wi jist thi wan 'Ochone'.

Fur he wiz noo thi Roses' king
and spak thi Roses' speak,
and kent nae mair thi Thistle's leid
than he did thon o thi Leek.

Though noo and then a traitrous burr
lyk bad wind could be whiffed
or sticky-wullie haein a cling
ontil a hizzie's shift.

Syne aa thi king's abandont crew,
his auld pleyed-oot Pleiades
did girn oan hoo pair Scots wiz deid
lyk fuitba-lossin laddies.

And wan or twa o them began
tae treh oan English laurels
which seemed a chic improvement oan
a cap o kail an sorrels.

There wiz wan doon-drag wi this speak;
that when they trehd tae spake ut,
though cleidit up in fustian dods
thir tongues still felt stark nakeit.

But naewan thocht tae waarn thi king
though ane and aa could hear ut;
thi English nobles foond ut fun,
thi Scots bards were too feart.

Ye're thinkin: whas thi laddie then?
thi usual wan wha caas
oan seein thi king paradin past
'Eh speh thi royal baas!'

Insteid that pairt o Jamie's coort
frae Embro's landit clique
devestit utsel quite literally
and sae uts scions still streak.

Sune oor toons' puir began tae ape
this style they could afford
by tearin oot o thir urbane mous
ilka rural wurd.

And this is whit thi London lug
finds better than erotica –
thi anely 'haurd' word left is 'fuck':
narcoticised demotica.

Fur ivry Rabbi that proclaims
anither Booker Crisis
some Jockstrap's gettin stuffed wi cheques –
remember: pets win prizes.

Sae here's the chafe – gin wan o us
frae Jamie's former *Heimat*
should think tae wear mair wurdy claes
in this appallin climate,

thi creh gaes up fae fowk roond here
'That jessie's wearin a jaiket!'
Gab's garb's aa inauthentic when
ut's casual tae gang nakeit.

ochone – alas; *leid* – language; *sticky-wullie* –
goose-grass; *hizzie* – hussy; *shift* – underdress;
girn – complain; *doon-drag* – drawback; *cleid-
it* – swaddled; *dods* – garments; *jessie* – effem-
inate male.

CABARET MCGONAGALL

Come aa ye dottilt, brain-deid lunks,
ye hibernatin cyber-punks,
gadget-gadjies, comics-geeks,
guys wi perfick rat's physiques,
fowk wi fuck-aa social skills,
fowk that winnae tak thir pills:
gin ye cannae even pley fuitball
treh thi Cabaret McGonagall.

Thi decor pits a cap oan oorie,
ut's puke-n-flock à la Tandoori;
there's a sculpture made frae canine stools,
there's a robot armadillo drools
when shown a photie o thi Pope,
and a salad spinner cerved fae dope:
gin ye cannae design a piss oan thi wall
treh thi Cabaret McGonagall.

We got: Clangers, Blimpers, gowks in mohair jimpers,
Bangers, Whimpers, cats wi stupit simpers –
Ciamar a thu, how are you, and hoozit gaun pal,
welcome to thi Cabaret Guillaume McGonagall.
We got: Dadaists, badass gits, shits wi RADA voices,
Futurists wi sutured wrists and bygets o James Joyce's –
Bienvenue, wha thi fuck are you, let's drink thi nicht away,
come oan yir own, or oan thi phone, or to thi Cabaret.

Come aa ye bards that cannae scan,
fowk too scared tae get a tan,
come aa ye anxious-chicken tykes
wi stabilisers oan yir bikes,
fowk whas mithers waash thir pants,
fowk wha drink deodorants:
fowk that think they caused thi Fall
like thi Cab McGonagall.

Fur aa that's cheesy, static, stale,
this place gaes sae faur aff thi scale
o ony Wigwam Bam-meter
mimesis wad brak thi pentameter;
in oarder tae improve thi species' genes,
ye'll find self-oaperatin guillotines:
bring yir knittin, bring yir shawl
tae thi Cabaret McGonagall.

We got: Berkoffs, jerk-offs, noodles wi nae knickers,
Ubuists, tubes wi zits, poodles dressed as vicars –
Gutenaben Aiberdeen, wilkommen Cumbernauld,
thi dregs o Scoatlan gaither at Chez McGonagall.
We got: mimes in tights, a MacDiarmidite that'iz ainsel
    contradicts,
kelpies, selkies, grown men that think they're Picts –
Buonaserra Oban and Ola! tae aa Strathspey,
come in disguise jist tae despise thi haill damn Cabaret.

Panic-attack Mac is oor DJ,
thi drugs he tuke werr aa Class A,
sae noo he cannae laive thi bog;
thon ambient soond's him layin a log.
Feelin hungry? sook a plook;
thi son o Sawney Bean's oor cook:
gin consumin humans diz not appal
treh thi Bistro de McGonagall.

Waatch Paranoia Pete pit speed
intil auld Flaubert's parrot's feed,
and noo ut's squaakin oot in leids
naebody kens till uts beak bleeds
and when ut faas richt aff uts perch,
Pete gees himsel a boady search:
thi evidence is there fur all
at thi Cabaret McGonagall.

We got: weirdos, beardos, splutniks, fools,
Culdees, bauldies, Trekkies, ghouls –
Airheids fae thi West Coast, steely knives and all,
welcome to thi Hotel Guillaume McGonagall.
We got: Imagists, bigamists, fowk dug up wi beakers,
lit.mag.eds, shit-thir-beds, and fans o thi New Seekers –
Doric loons wi Bothy tunes that ploo yir wits tae clay;
ut's open mike fur ony shite doon at thi Cabaret.

Alpha males ur no allowed
amang this outré-foutery crowd
tho gin they wear thir alphaboots
there's nane o us can keep thum oot,
and damn-aa wimmen care tae visit,
and nane o thum iver seem tae miss it:
gin you suspeck yir dick's too small
treh thi Cabaret McGonagall.

There's dum-dum boys wi wuiden heids
and Myrna Loy is snoggin Steed,
there's wan drunk wearin breeks he's peed –
naw – thon's thi Venerable Bede;
in fack thon auld scribe smells lyk ten o um,
he's no cheenged'iz habit i thi last millennium:
gin thi wits ye werr boarn wi hae stertit tae stall
treh thi Cabaret McGonagall.

We got: Loplops and robocops and Perry Comatose,
Cyclops and ZZ Top and fowk that pick thir nose –
Fare-ye-weel and cheery-bye and bonne nuit tae you all,
thi booncirs think we ought tae leave thi Club McGonagall.
But we got: Moptops and bebop bats and Krapp's Last
    Tapeworm friends,
Swap-Shop vets and neurocrats, but damn-aa sapiens –
Arrevederchi Rothesay, atque vale tae thi Tay,
Eh wish that Eh hud ne'er set eye upon this Cabaret.

dottilt: daft, confused; *oorie*: dirty, tasteless; *gowks*: fools; *ciamar a thu*: how are you (Gaelic); *kelpies*: river spirits in the shape of horses; *selkies*: seals which can take on human form; *leids*: languages; *Culdees*: members of the Columban church; *loons*: young men; *Bothy tunes*: ballads from the rural north-east; *ploo*: plough; *foutery*: excessively fussy.

Jacobite's Ladder

Once I dreamt that my head was a stone
shoved beneath a throne in London,
and that a troop of kings and queens
in progressively cleaner regalia
came and sat on my head
for a period of years,
breaking their royal wind into my ear.

As I lay stifled there, I saw
a ladder stretching from the top of the Law Hill
into the soup-flecked clouds,
and climbing up and down this blue ladder
were a series of patriots, some historical,
some fictional: all more real
than the town spluttering beneath them,
at least to the monarchs, who shifted
their faith-defending buttocks
uncomfortably throughout.

There were the renowned Pictish heroes:
Drost of the hundred battles; Brude,
son of Pontius Pilate; and Nechtan,
slayer of mere Northumbrians, all
wearing unknown costumes and recounting

unknowable legends. There were
the triumvirate of television, stage and screen:
Wallace, Bruce and Scottish Play, all
preceded by their faithful definite articles.
There were the terrible Caledonian twins: North
and the Shepherd, Burns and McGonagall,
Louis and Stevenson; and there
were the tribe of Trocchi, all
of whom drank of the waters of Leith and acquired
the power of literary amnesia. That's right:
they didn't know they were born.

Then I was wrestling with Big Tam
dressed as a galley slave
and as we fought he whispered
the history of the golf ball in my other ear:
'Wooden, feathery, Haskell.'
And when he got to gutta-percha
I nutted him with my stony pow,
and as he fell he muttered,
'You'll never get to Marbella
with a shwing like that.'

Then I was the hammer Mjollnir
driving spikes into the blue palms of the sky,
nailing a saltire of jet-trails into place
over Cambuslang. There was writing on
my temples, words cut into the stone,
but I found no one who could read them, nor
could I find a mirror, and yet I knew
these were my land's commandments.
When I awoke, I named the place
where I had rested 'Stonehaven'
and journeyed on my way rejoicing
beneath a great pyramid of cloud.

ODE TO SCOTTY

We kent ut wiz yir accent that
they couldna tak much mair o –
thae engines – foarmed somewhaur atween
Belfast and Ontario.

O Mister Scott, weel may ye talk
aboot WARP Factor Seven:
you tuke thi clash o Brigadoon –
transpoartit ut tae Heaven.

But still we luve ye tho ye werr
a Canuck in disguise:
tho Spock an Banes baith fanciet Kirk
you luved thi Enterprise.

Noo that we aa could undirstaund
fur ilka Scoatsman dotes
oan engines – see hoo Clydesiders
still bigg thir wee toy boats.

An syne therr wiz yir pash fur booze
fae Argyle tae Arcturus;
ye ootdrank Klingons grecht an smaa –
anither trait no spurious.

We kent dilithium crystals werr
(tho in thir future foarm)
thi semm gems that ye find gin you
crack stanes aroond Cairngorm.

An whit a bony fechtir, eh?
Sae martial a revure,
while Kirk left you in oarbit fur
three-quaartirs o an oor

while he an Spock an Banes plunked aff
tae some furbidden planit –
ye kent they werr oan lusty splores
but still ye birled lyk granite.

But maist o aa we luve ye coz
ye saved oor naishun's fiss:
ye nivir whinged aboot Englan but –
ye beat thum intae Space!

clash – conversation, local speech; ilka – each; bigg
– build; syne – then; gin – if; revure – a look of calm
scorn or contempt; plunked off – played truant;
splores – jaunts, antics; birled – spun.

JACKIE KAY

Jackie Kay was born and brought up in Scotland. She has published three collections of poetry for adults – *The Adoption Papers* (winner of a Forward Prize, a Saltire Award and a Scottish Arts Council Book Award), *Other Lovers* (which won the Somerset Maugham Award) and *Off Colour* (which was shortlisted for the 1999 T. S. Eliot Award).

She has also written three collections of poetry for children – *Two's Company* (which won The Signal Award), *Three Has Gone* and *The Frog Who Dreamed She Was An Opera Singer*, winner of the 1999 Signal Award.

Her first novel, *Trumpet*, recently won the Guardian Fiction Prize, a Scottish Arts Council Book Award and The Author's Club First Novel Award. It was also on the shortlist for the IMPAC award in 2000.

She has written for the stage and television and a libretto of hers, *Twice the Heart*, was performed at the Aldeburgh Festival and the Queen Elizabeth Hall with composer Mark Anthony Turnage.

She lives in Manchester with her son. A new collection of short stories, *Trout Friday*, and a new novel for children, *Strawgirl*, will be published in 2002.

Publications:

Poetry:
The Adoption Papers (Bloodaxe, 1992)
Two's Company (Puffin, 1992)
Other Lovers (Bloodaxe, 1993)
Three Has Gone (Blackie Children's Books, 1994)
Off Colour (Bloodaxe, 1998)
The Frog Who Dreamed She Was An Opera Singer (Bloomsbury, 1998)

Fiction:
Trumpet (Picador, 1998)
Trout Friday (Picador, 2002)
Strawgirl (Macmillan, 2002)

Ma mammy bot me oot a shop
Ma mammy says I was a luvly baby

Ma mammy picked me (I wiz the best)
your mammy had to take you (she'd no choice)

Ma mammy says she's no really ma mammy
(just kid on)

**It's a bit like a part you've rehearsed so well
you can't play it on the opening night**
She says my real mammy is away far away
Mammy why aren't you and me the same colour
But I love my mammy whether she's real or no
**My heart started rat tat tat like a tin drum
all the words took off to another planet**
Why

But I love ma mammy whether she's real or no

**I could hear the upset in her voice
I says *I'm not your real mother,*
though Christ knows why I said that,
If I'm not who is, but all my planned speech
went out the window**

She took me when I'd nowhere to go
my mammy is the best mammy in the world OK.

After mammy telt me she wisnae my real mammy
I was scared to death she was gonnie melt
or something or mibbe disappear in the dead
of night and somebody would say she wis a fairy
godmother. So the next morning I felt her skin
to check it was flesh, but mibbe it was just
a good imitation. How could I tell if my mammy
was a dummy with a voice spoken by someone else?
So I searches the whole house for clues
but I never found nothing. Anyhow a day after
I got my guinea pig and forgot all about it.

**I always believed in the telling anyhow.
You can't keep something like that secret**

I wanted her to think of her other mother
out there, thinking that child I had will be
seven today eight today all the way up to
god knows when. I told my daughter –
I bet your mother's never missed your birthday,
how could she?

Mammy's face is cherries.
She is stirring the big pot of mutton soup
singing *I gave my love a cherry
it had no stone.*
I am up to her apron.
I jump onto her feet and grab her legs
like a huge pair of trousers,
she walks round the kitchen lifting me up.

Suddenly I fall off her feet.
And mammy falls to the floor.
She won't stop the song
I gave my love a chicken it had no bone.
I run next door for help.
When me and Uncle Alec come back
Mammy's skin is toffee stuck to the floor.
And her bones are all scattered like toys.

Now when people say 'ah but
it's not like having your own child though is it',
I say of course it is, what else is it?
she's my child, I have told her stories
wept at her losses, laughed at her pleasures,
she is mine.

I was always the first to hear her in the night
all this umbilical knot business is nonsense
– the men can afford deeper sleeps that's all.
I listened to hear her talk,
and when she did I heard my voice under hers
and now some of her mannerisms crack me up

Me and my best pal
don't have Donny Osmond or David Cassidy
on our walls and we don't wear Starsky and Hutch
jumpers either. Round at her house we put on
the old record player and mime to Pearl Bailey
Tired of the life I lead, tired of the blues I breed

and Bessie Smith I can't do without my kitchen man.
Then we practise ballroom dancing giggling,
everyone thinks we're dead old-fashioned.

WATCHING PEOPLE SING

Carrie Carrie Anna. My mum's away.
Gie it laldy. Gie it laldy.
Our room shifts and tips axis
crashes towards her jaw
dropped, slack and quivering.
Closes the eyes. Dreams the song.

I am old enough to do the buffet.
Pass a bit of this, a bit of that.
When Alec sings *Ae fond kiss*
his soft lips part like petals.
He is another life away.
Someone's with him. *Ae fareweel.*

I grow up with party social.
Dress for it in two-inch platforms.
The chorus sways on the couch;
banners with big words. *For a' that.*
The mouths of the people of the past.
Everyone has their way of singing.

Peter's chin, doing its dinger,
judders, hings on to the last note –
a massive electric shock. *Put your sweet
lips a little closer to the
flooooooooooooooorrrr.* Margaret's conceded
after the tenth *come on Margaret*

g'on yourself hen. She sings and smokes
Any old time you want to come back home.
Her man replies *It's a quarter to three* in a semi-
American accent learnt in the Glasgow Odeon.
I can't sing. All I can do is watch
and clap, and clap, and clap.

My dad's up now for the rest
of the night. Songs like roll calls.

Far away in the hills of Croft-amie
Smoke dances across, swish, swish
in its soft skirts, moves me to tears,
the salt of the songs – *where the white man*

fears to tre-ad. He throws his head
back for the high note coming
in like a keen north wind *there's a*
dah de-de dah de-de DAH DAH DAH
Come on John. Another song.
The shirt's unbuttoned. Centre stage.

The farthest I've climbed in a windie SILL
The wee cigar held, a conductor's baton.
I'm the bar room mountaineeeeeeer.
Betty Toner upstages him; smooth dance
across the blue ice-rink, she glides
and turns *sing me a song of Bonnie Scotland.*

Her voice is a pattern on the floor.
Any old song will do. Everybody claps
in time. *Take it away Betty.*
The music swirls out the chimney.
The whole house trembles and remembers,
songs with the wrong words, the right sentiment

a heavy scent behind our ears.
People are what they've been in this room.
A good dancer. A patter merchant. *What a night, eh?*
How many. Nights with the same songs
growing on the skin like hairs. I am
sixteen. I blow-dry my mother's hair.

Too old for this really, I move
between glasses, topping up
the Teacher's whisky. Yet still, Anna's voice
singing *John Anderson my Jo John*
makes the song mine. I know him.
I can see him coming down the hill.
Nae we maun totter down John
And hand in hand we'll go
And sleep thegither at the foot.
Oh God, I think, Oh God, who will
sleep at my foot, who will sing to me like that
eyes brimming with love and change and spark.

IN MY COUNTRY

walking by the waters
down where an honest river
shakes hands with the sea,
a woman passed round me
in a slow watchful circle,
as if I were a superstition;

or the worst dregs of her imagination,
so when she finally spoke
her words spliced like bars
of an old wheel. A segment of air.
Where do you come from?
'Here,' I said, 'Here. These parts.'

THE BIRTH AND DEATH OF BETTE DAVIS

On her way down
the birth canal
she shouted,
Fasten your seatbelts it's going to be a bumpy night.
She came out
smoking a cigarette saying,
I never ever want to do that again.
In the room was a pale nurse and a silver bowl.
Oh – and a momma.
In the bowl was the placenta, lush purple stuff.
Make this into puff pastry placenta pie
and feed it to my father,
she said, and then sucked for a moment on her mother.
One second was enough for her.
Goddam, fetch me a gin,
she roared at the feeble midwife.
She flicked her cradle cap, tossed her single curl.

It was the one part
she never wanted:
one day she went out looking for her looks
and lost them.
Her skin was lined, bad dialogue on cellulite.
Her eyes were covered in film.

Her bow and arrow eyebrows were stuck in a tree.
In the room was a man
who never loved her, the bastard.
He told little lies under his coat.
She swore at him and fought the morphine
her last line was her first.

She had the stars.

The Broons' Bairn's Black
(a skipping rhyme)

Scotland is having a heart attack
Scotland is having a heart attack
Scotland is having a heart attack
The Broons' Bairn's Black.

Pride

When I looked up, the black man was there,
staring into my face,
as if he had always been there,
as if he and I went a long way back.
He looked into the dark pool of my eyes
as the train slid out of Euston.
For a long time this went on
the stranger and I looking at each other,
a look that was like something being given
from one to the other.

My whole childhood, I'm quite sure,
passed before him, the worst things
I've ever done, the biggest lies I've ever told.
And he was a little boy on a red dust road.
He stared into the dark depth of me,
and then he spoke:
'Ibo,' he said. 'Ibo, definitely.'
Our train rushed through the dark.
'You are an Ibo!' he said, thumping the table.
My coffee jumped and spilled.

Several sleeping people woke.
The night train boasted and whistled
through the English countryside,
past unwritten stops in the blackness.

'That nose is an Ibo nose.
Those teeth are Ibo teeth,' the stranger said,
his voice getting louder and louder.
I had no doubt, from the way he said it,
that Ibo noses are the best noses in the world,
that Ibo teeth are perfect pearls.
People were walking down the trembling aisle
to come and look
as the night rain babbled against the window.
There was a moment when
my whole face changed into a map,
and the stranger on the train
located even the name
of my village in Nigeria
in the lower part of my jaw.

I told him what I'd heard was my father's name.
Okafor. He told me what it meant,
something stunning,
something so apt and astonishing.
Tell me, I asked the black man on the train
who was himself transforming,
at roughly the same speed as the train,
and could have been
at any stop, my brother, my father as a young man,
or any member of my large clan,
Tell me about the Ibos.

His face had a look
I've seen on a MacLachlan, a MacDonnell, a MacLeod,
the most startling thing, pride,
a quality of being certain.
Now that I know you are an Ibo, we will eat.
He produced a spicy meat patty,
ripping it into two.
Tell me about the Ibos.
'The Ibos are small in stature
Not tall like the Yoruba or Hausa.
The Ibos are clever, reliable,
dependable, faithful, true.

The Ibos should be running Nigeria.
There would be none of this corruption.'

And what, I asked, are the Ibos faults?
I smiled my newly acquired Ibo smile,
flashed my gleaming Ibo teeth.
The train grabbed at a bend,
'Faults? No faults. Not a single one.'

'If you went back,' he said brightening,
'The whole village would come out for you.
Massive celebrations. Definitely.
Definitely,' he opened his arms wide.
'The eldest grandchild – fantastic welcome.
If the grandparents are alive.'

KATHLEEN JAMIE

'There are figures in much of my work: queens, princesses, anchorites, wandering monks. I think these are forms of energy; or aspects of the self, like the figures on tarot cards. I think my work is a means of exploration for me. Some explorations result in dead-ends'

Kathleen Jamie was born in Renfrewshire, Scotland, in 1962. She has published four collections of poetry and has also written a travel book about northern Pakistan, *The Golden Peak*.

She has received several prestigious awards for her poetry, including the Somerset Maugham Award, a Forward Prize, a Paul Hamlyn Award, and, recently, a Creative Scotland Award. She has twice won the Geoffrey Faber Memorial Award – the only person to have done so.

As well as poetry, Kathleen writes for radio, specialising in drama and specially commissioned long poems. She is a popular reader and tutor; and in 1999 was appointed Lecturer in Creative Writing at St Andrews University. She lives in north Fife with her young family.

Publications:

A Flame in Your Heart, with Andrew Greig (Bloodaxe, 1986)
The Way We Live (Bloodaxe, 1987)
Black Spiders (Salamander, 1992)
The Golden Peak (Virago, 1992)
The Autonomous Region, with photographs by Sean Mayne Smith (Bloodaxe, 1993)
The Queen of Sheba (Bloodaxe, 1994)
Jizzen (Picador, 1999)

The Republic of Fife

Higher than the craw-stepped
gables of our institutes – chess-clubs,
fanciers, reels & Strathspeys –
the old kingdom of lum, with crowns agley.

All birds will be citizens: banners
of starlings; Jacobin crows – also:
Sonny Jim Aitken, Special P.C.
whose red face closed in polis cars

utters *terrible, ridiculous*
at his brother and sister citizens
but we're no feart, not of anyone
with a tartan nameplate screwed to his door.

Citizen also: the tall fellow I watched
lash his yurt to the leafy earth,
who lifted his chin
to my greeting, roared AYE!

as in YES! FOREVER! MYSELF!
The very woods where my friend Isabel
once saw a fairy, blue as a gas flame
dancing on trees. All this

close to the motorway
where a citizen has dangled,
maybe with a friend clutching
his/her ankles to spray

PAY NO POLL TAX on a flyover
near to Abernethy, in whose tea rooms
old Scots kings and bishops in mitres
supped wi a lang spoon. Citizens:

our spires and doocoots
institutes and tinkies' benders,
old Scots kings and dancing fairies
give strength to my house

on whose roof we can balance,
carefully stand and see
clear to the far off mountains,
cities, rigs and gardens,

Europe, Africa, the Forth and Tay bridges,
even dare let go, lift our hands
and wave to the waving citizens
of all those other countries.

Things Which Never Shall Be

I shall be your wife.
Behind the doors of our house
which are wooden, and plentiful:
dogs and other animals, eager to play.
Rooms of grasses and flowers give out
to further rooms, our house
will be settled among woodland and hills.
So go. And take the dogs with you.
Leave me to work and fecundity in everything:
trees, hedgerows, weather-signs, poetry,
quirks you'll love and mock
only in jest. Our bedroom
will gather bouquets of sunshine,
we'll be home there in winter, I'll play
the spirit and you'll catch your breath.
We'll inhabit a huge place,
where I could move between rooms
with books in my arms,
and our home will be home to all comers.
We'll become skilled in art and endurance,
experts in love, and each other.

Ships/Rooms

Though I love this travelling life and yearn
like ships docked, I long
for rooms to open with my bare hands,
and there discover the wonderful, say
a ship's prow rearing, and a ladder
of rope thrown down.
Though young, I'm weary:
I'm all rooms at present, all doors
fastened against me;

but once admitted I crave
and swell for a fine, listing ocean-going prow
no man in creation can build me.

PERMANENT CABARET

Our highwire artiste,
knowing nothing of fear, will take
sparkling risks fifty feet high.
Her costume, ladies, is iced with
hard diamonds.
While she mounts all those steps
our old friend the clown will stand
upside down in a shower of confetti
and chirp 'Love me!'

Their lamp is the last on camp to go out.
Coco reads Jung, sometimes aloud to
Estelle, if she's sewing on sequins.
More often she practises alone in the ring
for the day she enters permanent cabaret,
perhaps in Zurich. Coco cracks his knuckles,
thinking vaguely of children, or considers
repainting the outside of their van.

Half way across Estelle glitters like frost.
She has frozen. 'Remain professional.' She
draws breath through her teeth, wavers
her hand: 'Let Coco sense something for once!'
His red boots are edging towards her. He
coaxes, offers aid – his absurd umbrella.
The audience wonder: is it part of the show
this embarrassing wobbling,
this vain desperation to clutch?

XIAHE

Abune the toon o Xiahe
a thrast monastery,
warn lik a yowe's tuith.

The sun gawps at innermaist
ingles o wa's.
Secret as speeders

folk hae criss-crosst a sauch
seedit i the yird flair
wi rags o win blawn prayer.

Xiahe. Wave droonin wave
on a pebbly shore,
the *ahe* o machair, o slammach,

o impatience; ahent the saft saltire
i trashed, an sheep;
wha's drift on the brae

is a lang cloud's shadda.
the herd cries a wheen wirds
o Tibetan sang,

an A'm waukenet, on a suddenty mindit:
A'm far fae hame,
I hae crossed China.

Xiahe (pronounced Shi-ah-e) – a Tibetan town in
the now Chinese province of Gansu; *sauch* – willow;
yird – earth; *slammach* – cobweb.

THE QUEEN OF SHEBA

Scotland, you have invoked her name
just once too often
in your Presbyterian living rooms.
She's heard, yea
even unto heathenish Arabia
your vixen's bark of poverty, come down
the family like a lang neb, a thrawn streak,
a wally dug you never liked
but can't get shot of.

She's had enough. She's come.
Whit, tae this dump? Yes!
She rides first camel
of a swaying caravan

from her desert sands
to the peat and bracken
of the Pentland hills
across the fit-ba pitch
to the thin mirage
of the swings and chute;
scattered with glass.

Breathe that steamy musk
on the Curriehill Road, not mutton-shanks
boiled for broth, nor the chlorine stink
of the swimming pool where skinny girls
accuse each other of verrucas.
In her bathhouses women bear
warm pot-bellied terracotta pitchers
on their laughing hips.
All that she desires, whatever she asks
She will make the bottled dreams
of your wee lasses
look like *sweeties.*

Spangles scarcely cover
her gorgeous breasts, hanging gardens
jewels, frankincense; more voluptuous
even than Vi-next-door, whose
high-heeled slippers
keeked from dressing gowns
like little hooves, wee tails
of pink fur stuffed in the cleavage of her toes;
more audacious even than Currie Liz
who led the gala floats
through the Wimpey scheme
in a ruby-red Lotus Elan
before the Boys' Brigade band
and the Brownies' borrowed coal-truck;
hair piled like candy-floss;
who lifted her hands fom the neat wheel
to tinkle her fingers
at her tricks
            among the Masons and the elders and the police.

The cool black skin
of the Bible couldn't hold her,
nor the atlas green
on the kitchen table,

you stuck with thumbs
and split to fruity hemispheres –
yellow Yemen, Red Sea, *Ethiopia*. Stick in
with the homework and you'll be
cliver like yer faither.
but no too cliver,
no *above versel*.

See her lead those great soft camels
widdershins round the kirk-yaird,
smiling
as she eats
avocados with apostle spoons
she'll teach us how. But first

she wants to strip the willow
she desires the keys
                to the National Library
she is beckoning
        the lasses
        in the awestruck crowd . . .

Yes, we'd like to
        clap the camels,
to smell the spice,
admire her hairy legs and
bonny wicked smile, we want to take
PhDs in Persian, be vice
to her president: we want
to help her
        ask some Difficult Questions

she's shouting for our wisest man
to test her mettle:

        Scour Scotland for a Solomon!

Sure enough: from the back of the crowd
someone growls:
                whae do you think y'ur?

and a thousand laughing girls and she
draw our hot breath
and shout:

THE QUEEN OF SHEBA!

History in a new scheme. I stretch
through hip, ribs, oxter, bursting
the cuff of my school shirt, because
this, Mr Hanning, is me.
'*Sir! Sir! Sir!*
– he turns, and I claim
just one of these stories,
razed places, important as castles,
as my own. *Mum!*

We done the slums today!
I bawled from the glass
front door she'd long desired.
What for? bangs the oven shut,
Some history's better forgot.
                              So how come
we remember the years
before we were born? Gutters
still pocked with fifties rain,
trams cruised dim
street-lit afternoons; war
at our backs. The black door
of the close wheezed
till you turned the third stair
then resounded like cannon.
A tower of bannisters. Nana
and me toiled past windows
smeared in blackout, condemned
empty stone. The neighbours had flitted
to council-schemes, or disappeared . . .

Who were the disappeared? Whose
the cut-throat
razor on the mantelpiece, what man's
coat hung thick with town gas, coal
in the lobby press?
                    And I mind
being stood, washed like a dog
with kettle and one cold tap
in a sink plumbed sheer
from the window
to the back midden
as multistoreys rose

across the goods yard,
and shunters clanked
through nights shared
in the kitchen recess bed.

I dreamed about my sister in America
I doot she's dead. What rural
feyness this? Another sibling
lost in Atlantic cloud,
a hint of sea in the rain _
the married in England,
the drunken and the mad,
a couple of notes postmarked Canada,
then mist: but this is a past
not yet done, else how come
our parents slam shut, deny
like criminals: *I can't remember, cannae*
mind, then turn at bay: *Why?*

Who wants to know? Stories
spoken through the mouths
of closes: who cares
who trudged those worn stairs,
or played in now rubbled back greens?
What happened about my granddad? Why
did Agnes go? How come
you don't know

that stories are balm,
ease their own pain, contain
a beginning, a middle –
and ours is a long driech
now-demolished street. *Forget it!*
Forget them that vanished,
voted with their feet,
away for good
or ill through the black door
even before the great clearance came,
turning tenements outside-in,
exposing gas pipes, hearths
in damaged gables, wallpaper
hanging limp and stained
in the shaming rain.

History, Mr Hanning.
The garden shrank for winter,
and mum stirred our spaghetti hoops
not long before she started back
part-time at Debenhams
to save for Christmas,
the odd wee
luxury, our first
foreign
holiday.

A MIRACLE

When the lassie who started it
insisted on TV that she
and her wee brother

had seen the statue of John Knox
shoogle on its pedestal, and milk
tears start in his stony eyes,

from behind the bings, the buses arrived.
Tribes of auld wimmin
and their simpleton sons

filed through the yetts
settled under rugs
and rustled their sweeties.

Gobs of tallow stuck to the plinth.
Babies' booties dangled
from that upflung arm.

So began the custom
whereby, on a certain Sunday,
Knox, adorned in tinsel

gets carted on a bier
round the Edinburgh wynds;
pipers lead the way,

playing 'Comin' Through the Rye'.
By then the lass had disappeared.
– Until, that is, years later,

when, a famously glamorous
Hollywood actress, she announced
her intention to retire

home to Scotland,
buy Holyrood Palace,
and stand for president.

RAYMOND FRIEL

I was born in Greenock in 1963 and twenty-four years later left it, and Scotland, behind. The move wasn't particularly planned or motivated by any desperate desire to get out. It just so happened that in those days the Scottish Office was even more generous than the parliament is now and was willing to part-subsidise a cushy post-graduate stay in Oxford. Two years later (having seen my supervisor maybe three times for a civilised chat over a glass of red) I extricated myself from an academic dwam and trained as a teacher under the English and Welsh dispensation. My future career in the classroom was therefore mapped out down south.

The next six years were spent in London. It was here I met and married my (Welsh) wife, and here that the first and second of our three (English) sons were born. I remember at the time being seized by a kind of atavistic panic that my own son was English. A miserably racist response, which thankfully quickly faded. It was also around this time that I met Richard Price and we started Southfields, in which we teased out the whole vexed question of exile and émigré (as well as publishing a lot of good poetry from all over the place). Much of my own poetry at this time was also taken up with the dutiful working out of cultural identity.

The move outside the property-obsessed enclosure of the M25 came with a teaching job in the south-west of England. We moved to Somerset, where we've lived for the past four years. Here there is a very different sort of Englishness compared to the south-east. It's softer-edged, slower-paced. We're also close enough to Glastonbury to feel the gentling effect of the New Age folk: pipes in the High Street. Arcadia it's not (who wants to live in Arcadia anyway?). But it's home; it's where I work; it's where my children are growing up, in spite of my attempts at parenting; and it's where, in the occasional gaps, I write poems.

Publications:

Bel-Air (Southfields Press, 1993)
Seeing the River (Polygon, 1995)
Renfrewshire in Old Photographs, with Richard Price (Mariscat, 2000)

Schooldays

A soaked-to-the-skin wait
In the motley tail-end
That made up the numbers,
Then told to go and defend.

My big news at tea-time
Was that I *got a kick* –
A short-lived toe-ender
In the goalmouth panic.

But some of them had style:
Chesting it down, past
One and angled in off the bin,
Raising a nonchalant fist.

A po-faced Miss Pinelli,
Clean page and today's date;
Hands aching to record
Some boozed-up empire's fate.

The projects, more fun,
Like The Industrial Age –
The Use of Child Labour
A stick boy on the page.

McCreary, the hard man,
Blurting out 'I hate this!'
Collared out to the front,
Still defiant, 'What *Miss*?'

One time he called her a cow:
God, the scattering of chairs
As she raced after him out
The door to riotous cheers . . .

But dead comfy up the back,
I could usually retreat
Into pure vacancy and stare
Down at Cartsburn Street –

Where the heavy-booted men
Came drawn by the siren,
A shuffling procession
Into forests of iron.

HOGMANAY

At the bells
We stood up stiffly
And tinged the cut crystal
To the new year.

Dad slipped off
To sprinkle the rooms
(And anyone in them)
With holy water.

Left in peace,
I breathed in
At the open window
Where the night used to be so full

Of ships' horns
Blasting the sky
With gargantuan flatulence;
Blurred close encounters.

Tonight, though,
Merely a sad pamp
Lingers a moment
Over the town.

Lights go out;
Somewhere the river
Wrinkles in the dark,
Prowling west.

The dead shift
Under its cold pelt,
Dulse-entangled.
They will not come back

Transfigured
In half-lit, creepy tales.
We don't go in
So much for myths,

Believing more
Often than not,
That life's exactly
What it looks like.

WORKING-CLASS POET

Someone else had set the thing up.
She never had the time these days.
All the features editor told her
Was the Holiday Inn at 12
To meet some poet. The next big thing,
Apparently. Whitbread. Television.
Set text. She'd never liked poetry . . .

Afternoons drowsing over Wordsworth, Keats.
Something about pathetic fallacy.
(Funny how some phrases stick.)
She'd read nothing by what's-his-name.
Sod it. She'd have enough in no time:
Difficult background; the drinking;
Wild eyes. No problem.

She sat in the piano music
Of the lobby; a large gin, dead,
On the low table by her knee.
'Same again?' She smiled weakly back
At the porter and leant forward
To fold her cigarette into
Extinction. 12:47.

ONE LESS

All the time she talked about her mother,
Whose mission in life was to get her married
Into the right family; the latest
Was vetted for background and salary,
Which bombed me right out: Catholic student
With a one syllable Irish surname.
She talked about her father and her brothers,
Her grandmother, who listened to her,
Her friends, of course, and her friends' boyfriends;
And *her* boyfriends, which was the worst of it.
I never did get used to that, hearing
Her discuss so-and-so and look at me
As if I was to give an opinion.
That never seemed to bother her at all.

It bothered me all right. I used to think,
If she's telling me all this about them,
What do the rest of them know about me?
It was a different world. Anyway,
The whole thing lasted about three months;
And when it was pretty much all over,
I turned up at the flat for dinner
And told her, before she set the table,
That I really thought we should finish it.
She was perfect: she called me a lowlife
And wished me a slow death from stomach cancer,
Stormed about the room and slammed the door
Said I could bloody well starve then
And cried and went and stood by the window.
Five minutes later she gave me a hug
And made me promise we'd always be friends.
Sure. I left the flat and took a right towards
The routine pleasures of Dumbarton Road;
Leaving her to it, leaving her one less
To worry about, one less to worry.
Though there were, I remember, moments
When I fell for the whole scenario:
Taking a half-pissed walk in the twilight
Through Kelvingrove park, picking off leaves,
Reading aloud from our book of erotic verse;
And she would give me a sideways look and smile,
As if she knew exactly what that did to me.

THE CENTRAL PICTURE HOUSE

In 'the ranch'
the pallid gaze of the audience
is lifted under hell-for-leather hooves
of last-ditch, bugling cavalry
(the eyes of the heroine
moistening with gratitude
to be spared
a fate worse than death).

Outside, in the hungry years,
real cowboys use blades
and know what school you went to;

the cavalry's token bell
no comfort
to the inert wreckage up the alley.

DON PATERSON

'For me, bad poems try to offer solutions, while good poems leave a little more chaos, mystery, fear or wonder in the world than there was before.'

Don Paterson was born in Dundee in 1963. After a long stretch in south-east England, he now lives in Kirriemuir with his partner and their many offspring. He works as a writer, editor, musician and games reviewer. He has been the recipient of several literary awards, including a Forward Prize and the T. S. Eliot and Geoffrey Faber Memorial Prizes; he also writes drama for the radio and stage, and is Poetry Editor at Picador Books. For the last eleven years he has co-led, with the saxophonist Tim Garland, the jazz ensemble Lammas, for whom he also composes much of the music; they have recorded five albums together, the most recent being *Sea Changes*. He currently reviews PC games for *The Times*.

Publications:

Nil Nil (Faber, 1993)
God's Gift to Women (Faber, 1997)
The Eyes (Faber, 1999)

As editor:
Last Words: New Poetry for the New Century, with Jo Shapcott (Picador, 1999)
101 Sonnets: From Shakespeare to Heaney (Faber, 1999)
Robert Burns: Poems Selected by Don Paterson (Faber, 2001)

AMNESIA

I was, as they later confirmed, a very sick boy.
The star performer at the meeting house,
my eyes rolled back to show the whites, my arms
outstretched in catatonic supplication
while I gibbered impeccably in the gorgeous tongues
of the aerial orders. On Tuesday nights, before
I hit the Mission, I'd nurse my little secret:
Blind Annie Spall, the dead evangelist
I'd found still dying in creditable squalor
above the fishmonger's in Rankine Street.
The room was ripe with gurry and old sweat;
from her socket in the greasy mattress, Annie
belted through hoarse chorus after chorus
while I prayed loudly, absently enlarging
the crater that I'd gouged in the soft plaster.
Her eyes had been put out before the war,
just in time to never see the daughter
with the hare-lip and the kilt of dirty dishtowels
who ran the brothel from the upstairs flat
and who'd chap to let me know my time was up,
then lead me down the dark hall, its zoo-smell,
her slippers peeling off the sticky lino.
At the door, I'd shush her quiet, pressing
my bus-fare earnestly into her hand.

Four years later. Picture me: drenched in patchouli,
strafed with hash-burns, casually arranged
on Susie's bed. Smouldering frangipani;
Dali's *The Persistence of Memory*;
pink silk loosely knotted round the lamp
to soften the light; a sheaf of Penguin Classics,
their spines all carefully broken in the middle;
a John Martyn album mumbling through the speakers.
One hand was jacked up her skirt, the other trailing
over the cool wall behind the headboard
where I found the hole in the plaster again.
The room stopped like a lift; Sue went on talking.
It was a nightmare, Don. We had to gut the place.

An Elliptical Stylus

My uncle was beaming: 'Aye, yer elliptical stylus –
fairly brings out a' the wee details.'
Balanced at a fraction of an ounce
the fat cartridge sank down like a feather;
music billowed into three dimensions
as if we could have walked between the players.

My Dad, who could appreciate the difference,
went to Largs to buy an elliptical stylus
for our ancient, beat-up Phillips turntable.
We had the guy in stitches: 'You can't . . .
er . . . you'll have to *upgrade your equipment.*'
Still smirking, he sent us from the shop
with a box of needles, thick as carpet-tacks,
the only sort they made to fit our model.

(Supposing I'd been *his* son: let's eavesdrop
on 'Fidelities', the poem I'm writing now:
The day my father died, he showed me how
he'd prime the deck for optimum performance:
it's that lesson I recall – how he'd refine
the arm's weight, to leave the stylus balanced
somewhere between ellipsis and precision,
as I gently lower the sharp nip to the line
and wait for it to pick up the vibration
till it moves across the page, like a cardiograph . . .)

We drove back slowly, as if we had a puncture;
my Dad trying not to blink, and that man's laugh
stuck in my head, which is where the story sticks,
and any attempt to cauterise this fable
with something axiomatic on the nature
of articulacy and inheritance,
since he can well afford to make his *own*
excuses, you your own interpretation.
But if you still insist on resonance –
I'd swing for him, and every other cunt
happy to let my father know his station,
which probably includes yourself. To be blunt.

Nil Nil

Just as any truly accurate representation of a particular geog-
raphy can only exist on a scale of 1:1 (imagine the vast,
rustling map of Burgundy, say, settling over it like a freshly-
starched sheet!) so it is with all our abandoned histories, those
ignoble lines of succession that end in neither triumph nor
disaster, but merely plunge on into deeper and deeper obscurity;
only in the infinite ghost-libraries of the imagination – their
only possible analogue – can their ends be pursued, the dull
and terrible facts finally authenticated.

François Aussemain, *Pensées*

From the top, then, the zenith, the silent footage:
McGrandle, majestic in ankle-length shorts,
his golden hair shorn to an open book, sprinting
the length of the park for the long hoick forward,
his balletic toe-poke nearly bursting the roof
of the net; a shaky pan to the Erskine St End
where a plague of grey bonnets falls out of the clouds.
But ours is a game of two halves, and this game
the semi they went on to lose; from here
it's all down, from the First to the foot of the Second,
McGrandle, Visocchi and Spankie detaching
like bubbles to speed the descent into pitch-sharing,
pay-cuts, pawned silver, the Highland Division,
the absolute sitters ballooned over open goals,
the dismal nutmegs, the scores so obscene
no respectable journal will print them; though one day
Farquhar's spectacular bicycle-kick
will earn him a name-check in Monday's obituaries.
Besides the one setback – the spell of giant-killing
in the Cup (Lochee Violet, then Aberdeen Bon Accord,
the deadlock with Lochee Harp finally broken
by Farquhar's own-goal in the replay)
nothing inhibits the fifty-year slide
into Sunday League, big tartan flasks,
open hatchbacks parked squint behind goal-nets,
the half-time satsuma, the dog on the pitch,
then the Boy's Club, sponsored by Skelly Assurance,
then Skelly Dry Cleaners, then nobody;
stud-harrowed pitches with one-in-five inclines,
grim fathers and perverts with Old English Sheepdogs
lining the touch, moaning softly.
Now the unrefereed thirty-a-sides,

terrified fat boys with callipers minding
four jackets on infinite, notional fields;
ten years of dwindling, half-hearted kickabouts
leaves two little boys – Alastair Watt,
who answers to 'Forty', and wee Horace Madden,
so smelly the air seems to quiver above him –
playing desperate two-touch with a bald tennis ball
in the hour before lighting-up time.
Alastair cheats, and goes off with the ball
leaving wee Horace to hack up a stone
and dribble it home in the rain;
past the stopped swings, the dead shanty-town
of allotments, the black shell of Skelly Dry Cleaners
and into his cul-de-sac, where, accidentally,
he neatly back-heels it straight into the gutter
then tries to swank off like he meant it.

Unknown to him, it is all that remains
of a lone fighter-pilot, who, returning at dawn
to find Leuchars was not where he'd left it,
took time out to watch the Sidlaws unsheathed
from their great black tarpaulin, the haar burn off Tayport
and Venus melt into Carnoustie, igniting
the shoreline; no wind, not a cloud in the sky
and no one around to admire the discretion
of his unscheduled exit: the engine plopped out
and would not re-engage, sending him silently
twirling away like an ash-key,
his attempt to bail out only partly successful,
yesterday having been April the 1st –
the ripcord unleashing a flurry of socks
like a sackful of doves rendered up to the heavens
in private irenicon. He caught up with the plane
on the ground, just at the instant the tank blew
and made nothing of him, save for his fillings,
his tackets, his lucky half-crown and his gallstone,
now anchored between the steel bars of a stank
that looks to be biting the bullet on this one.

In short, this is where you get off, reader;
I'll continue alone, on foot, in the failing light,
following the trail as it steadily fades
into road-repairs, birdsong, the weather, nirvana,
the plot thinning down to a point so refined
not even the angels could dance on it. Goodbye.

PROLOGUE

A poem is a little church, remember,
you, its congregation, I, its cantor;

so please, no flash, no necking in the pew,
or snorting just to let your neighbour know

you get the clever stuff, or eyeing the watch,
or rustling the wee poke of butterscotch

you'd brought to charm the sour edge off the sermon.
Be upstanding. Now: let us raise the fucking *tone*.

Today, from this holy place of heightencd speech,
we will join the berry-bus in its approach

to that sunless pit of rancour and alarm
where language finds its least prestigious form.

Fear not: this is spiritual transport,
albeit the less elevated sort;

while the coach will limp towards its final stage
beyond the snowy graveyard of the page,

no one will leave the premises. In hell,
the tingle-test is inapplicable,

though the sensitives among you may discern
the secondary symptoms: light sweats, heartburn,

that sad thrill in the soft part of the instep
as you crane your neck to size up the long drop.

In the meantime, we will pass round the Big Plate
and should it come back slightly underweight

you will learn the meaning of the Silent Collcction,
for our roof leaks, and the organ lacks conviction.

My little church is neither high nor broad,
so get your heads down. Let us pray. Oh God.

A PRIVATE BOTTLING

So I will go, then. I would rather grieve over your absence than over you.

Antonio Porchia

Back in the same room that an hour ago
we had led, lamp by lamp, into the darkness
I sit down and turn the radio on low
as the last girl on the planet still awake
reads a dedication to the ships
and puts on a recording of the ocean.

I carefully arrange a chain of nips
in a big fairy-ring; in each square glass
the tincture of a failed geography,
its dwindled burns and woodlands, whin-fires, heather,
the sklent of its wind and its salty rain,
the love-worn habits of its working-folk,
the waveform of their speech, and by extension
how they sing, make love, or take a joke.

So I have a good nose for this sort of thing.

Then I will suffer kiss after fierce kiss
letting their gold tongues slide along my tongue
as each gives up, in turn, its little song
of the patient years in glass and sherry-oak,
the shy negotiations with the sea,
air and earth, the trick of how the peat-smoke
was shut inside it, like a black thought.

Tonight I toast her with the extinct malts
of Ardlussa, Ladyburn and Dalintober
and an ancient pledge of passionate indifference:
Ochon o do dhóigh mé mo chlairsach ar a shon,
wishing her health, as I might wish her weather.

When the circle is closed and I have drunk myself sober
I will tilt the blinds a few degrees, and watch
the dawn grow in a glass of liver-salts,
wait for the birds, the milk-float's sweet nothings,
then slip back to the bed where she lies curled,
replace the live egg of her burning ass
gently, in the cold nest of my lap,
as dead to her as she is to the world.

Here we are again; it is precisely
twelve, fifteen, thirty years down the road
and one turn higher up the spiral chamber
that separates the burnt ale and dark grains
of what I know, from what I can remember.
Now each glass holds its micro-episode
in permanent suspension, like a movie-frame
on acetate, until it plays again,
revivified by a suave connoisseurship
that deepens in the silence and the dark
to something like an infinite sensitivity.
This is no romantic fantasy: my father
used to know a man who'd taste the sea,
then leave his nets strung out along the bay
because there were no fish in it that day.
Everything is in everything else. It is a matter
of attunement, as once, through the hiss and backwash,

I steered the dial into the voice of God
slightly to the left of Hilversum,
half-drowned by some big, blurry waltz
the way some stars obscure their dwarf companions
for centuries, till someone thinks to look.

In the same way, I can isolate the feints
of feminine effluvia, carrion, shite,
those rogues and toxins only introduced
to give the composition a little weight
as rough harmonics do the violin-note
or Pluto, Cheiron and the lesser saints
might do to our lives, for all you know.
(By Christ, you would recognise their absence
as anyone would testify, having sunk
a glass of *North British*, run off a patent still
in some sleet-hammered satellite of Edinburgh:
a bleak spirit, no amount of caramel
could sweeten or disguise its after-effect
somewhere between a blanket-bath and a sad wank.
There is, no doubt, a bar in Lothian
where it is sworn upon and swallowed neat
by furloughed riggers and the Special Police,
men who hate the company of women.)

O whiskies of Long Island and Provence!
This little number catches at the throat
but is all sweetness in the finish: my tongue trips
first through burning brake-fluid, then nicotine,
pastis, *Diorissimo* and wet grass;
another is silk sleeves and lip-service
with a kick like a smacked puss in a train-station;
another, the light charge and the trace of zinc
tap-water picks up at the moon's eclipse.
You will know the time I mean by this.

Because your singular absence, in your absence,
has bred hard, tonight I take the waters
with the whole clan: our faceless ushers, bridesmaids,
our four Shelties, three now ghosts of ghosts;
our douce sons and our lovely loudmouthed daughters
who will, by this late hour, be fully grown,
perhaps with unborn children of their own.
So finally, let me propose a toast:
not to love, or life, or real feeling,
but to their sentimental residue;
to your sweet memory, but not to you.

The sun will close its circle in the sky
before I close my own, and drain the purely
offertory glass that tastes of nothing
but silence, burnt dust on the valves, and whisky.

THREE LYRICS

Love invents the year, the day
the hour and its melody;
love invents the lover, even
the beloved. Nothing is proven
against love that the mouth you kissed
so hungrily did not exist.

Lines for two sides of a fan:
– I desire you to forget –
– I forget you to desire –

I'd paint you, alone
on the latter-day urn
of an old photograph,
or the mirror's false depths –
alive to your heart,
dead to your poet

ANGELA McSEVENEY

I was born in 1964, the youngest of five sisters. I was brought up and educated entirely in Scotland (Ross-shire, Livingston and the Borders), settling back in Galashiels when I was about ten. I was at Edinburgh University (1982–6), where I completed a General Arts degree on the second attempt. I had been writing poetry since I was fourteen or so, managing to have a few accepted by small magazines; however, my academic struggles, health problems and extreme shyness shook my confidence badly and for a while I wrote very little. I was too much of a bag of nerves to have dared set foot in a writers' group, but in third year I began to take work to Ron Butlin, who was the University's writer-in-residence and then to Liz Lochhead, who held the post the following year. With their encouragement, I began to submit poems to magazines again and after that it was a fairly straightforward path via inclusion in small mags, anthologies and so on to my own book *Coming Out With It* in 1992.

Since graduating, I have worked mostly as a Library Assistant, Cleaner and Seasonal Assistant at a museum in Edinburgh's Royal Mile, combined with many happy hours as a volunteer in a charity shop. For the past couple of years I have been employed as a personal care assistant.

The fact that I almost always have some sort of job on the go, sometimes very tiring, absorbing work, may be one of the reasons that I can go for long periods without writing anything, sometimes several years. It used to bother me, but not any more; when I do start writing, the poems come in a rush, a very disturbing and exciting experience. I don't search out subjects, I just let ideas happen – a metaphor, a phrase, a reflection, often something said in a conversation – and everything grows from there. I don't have any ambitions beyond whatever poem I'm working on, but, so saying, I am at the moment thinking in terms of putting together another book.

Publications:

Poems in Other Tongues (Verse, 1990)
Coming Out With It (Polygon, 1992)

The Lump

Rolling over in a hot June night
I cradled my breasts in my arms
and felt a hard knot of tissue.

I was fifteen.
My life rose up in my throat
and threatened to stifle me.

It took three attempts to tell my mother.
She promised that my appointment would be
with a woman doctor.

A nurse called my name.
I didn't have cancer.

The stitches in my skin reminded me
of a chicken trussed for the oven.

I felt ashamed
that the first man to see
me had only been doing his job.

For the Best

I don't doubt you did it for the best.

After all I was twenty –
about time somebody did.

One of us was old enough to be my father,
the other to have known better.

I never said the word frigidity
– only went cold with the fear of it.

You rubbed me up the wrong way
and knowing that I must make the best of it.

The Fat Nymphomaniac's Poem

Tall men turn me on.
An immense man makes me petite and feminine.

For him I'm so much less the cow in a china shop.
My rugby tackle won't send him flying.

If there's more of him pound for pound
I can lay me down not smothering anyone.

Night Shift

I would wake up when I heard Dad
coming in at the front door.

The others slept through his early morning noises:
a toilet flush, one cup of tea boiling.

There seemed no place for him
at home all day Saturday
and most of Sunday.

His skin paled
apart from one weather-beaten patch
at his throat.

'It's no life for a man,' he sometimes grumbled
'this living like a mole.'

During school holidays I made
no noise at home.

Mum went to parents' night alone.
She was sick of darning where industrial acid
ate away his clothes.

At five o'clock I'd be sent
to waken Dad for tea.

The curtains in my parents' room
were almost always closed.

Who's Who

When it arrives for processing
on my library office desk I flip through *Who's Who*

as self-consciously as if
I were scanning the Personal Columns.

Your list of achievements
are too familiar to impress
but it's an unlooked for thrill
to read your unexpected middle name.

One morning
I datestamp with more vigour than usual
a magazine with your face on the cover.

I almost drop a cup
when you ease yourself over the airwaves
into my kitchen;

spinning round to stare
blushing at the radio

I smooth my apron,
tuck back a loose strand
of greasy hair.

Dunblane

I see the words first
at an *Evening News* stand
'Scottish' 'School' 'Massacre'.

They defy syntax
They don't make sense.

Readers walk by me
heads bowed, scanning print.

At work an hour later
I haven't shed a tear
but blunder about dazed, wrung out.

I scrounge that day's newspaper
from the wastepaper basket and keep it
for the crossword at teabreak.

It was printed this morning
in a different world
which I see receding from me
behind those unknowing headlines.

Tomorrow it will be
latest details, seven-page features,
a killer's profile.

But for now they babble on
about Blair, Europe, Railtrack
and a report on the cost of child-rearing
which sums up

'Having a child
could be the most expensive decision
of your life.'

IMPRINT

This new room I'm living in
should hold no memories,
at least not mine . . .

they must have come with me,
shaken out like moths
from my unpacked linen.

There's a fresh outlook
from the window,
unfamiliar voices leak through the ceiling
from new neighbours overhead,

but the same agonised daydreams
of slow seduction
roll in beside me
in my strange bed.
Hope blossoms in this place
like the blowsy patterns
on old-fashioned wallpaper

that perhaps it will be here
that he'll mount, settle into me,
his body big and bristling like a bear,

me cradling him,
mouthing at his shoulder,
thighs ajar.

ROB MacKENZIE

I was born in Glasgow in 1964, but grew up on the island of Lewis. For university I went to Edinburgh, to study environmental chemistry. I now lecture in atmospheric science at Lancaster University, having spent the twelve years after Edinburgh in the south-east of England, doing research into photochemical smog and stratospheric ozone depletion. Alongside my academic career, I have also been a writer for all my adult life. I come from a Gaelic-speaking community, but don't speak the language. I come from a community remote from the cultural hegemony, but have spent ten years at Cambridge University. I do science.

Publications:

Books and pamphlets:
Kirk Interiors, pamphlet (Ankle Press, 1993)
The Tune Kilmarnock, pamphlet (Form Books, 1996)
Off Ardglas (Invisible Books, 1997)

Anthologies and multi-author:
The Invisible Reader, edited by P. Holman and B. Penney (Invisible Books, 1996)
Other. British Poetry since 1970, edited by R. Caddel and P. Quartermain (Wesleyan University Press, 1999)
Foil: Defining Poetry 1985–2000, edited by Nicholas Johnson (Etruscan, 2000)
Atoms of delight, edited by A. Finlay (pocketbooks, 2000)
Wish I was Here, edited by A. Finlay and K. MacNeil (pocketbooks, 2000)

ANALYSIS

What would you 'wake up or slip
your agenda'd suit were I to split
your strange head like a pistachio?
'd you see the mother tongue? Ridged
nervy stuff the hand of your father? Or
would I be doing the vision, in my own
head your correspondent fancies, forms
cut like books, smoking like photographs?
Seems for twice the looking here's half
the sense. My every anti-Presbyterian
bone is in these tensed fingers, though maybe
it's just the case that we forgot to say grace.

COMFORT FOR THE REVD. ANGUS SMITH, NESS

'f there was rain, flat black Cambridge'd
bubble and flake like varnish, leave nothing
but an expert nomenclature, pink suspensions,
and some algorithmical solace.

I doubt you see it a collapsed Edinburgh,
minister, lacking the sheer colleges, sharp
etiquette for grace and nothing
beyond High Table falsification, nothing revealed.

Stony ground for revival when the Sunday ferry
sails even toward Stornoway now?
A camel's hope for Cambridge if even on Lewis
the coves slop out'f The Narrows Friday night?

I'd've agreed, among the yellowing accents, until I fell
in with a midsummer woman, labial ring,
dreadlocks and cotton, scarf-collared dog and
everything about her careful and dirty and painted.

'far from the South as a childhood
on the island: subject to draughts, strong beer,
peculiar convictions. She's reconstructed
a village from her own faint sense of it,

for most of the world like Ness
in the 1960s
(if short of the kirk and guga and fine football team.
For all that an island, convex like Lewis).

You were a high tower then, minister, in 'sixty-five
when you stopped traffic, turned the tide of Skye ferries.
The precipitate rhythms in your voice
beat back the supercilious timetable:

I desire to go to the ferry on the Sabbath day –
to stand or sit or lie down – to be a barrier,
and theology fell like a log in front of the lorries,
toppled by a culture with the post-modern

in its pouch like tar, ready for the stump.
It's rigid, and pointless defeat, then, but
only on that one shore, minister, only
if we allow their theory that all we have

is an empty Sabbath. And only if we'll not
look up and see the blythe-bidden opportunity,
the new travellers and the disassembling South,
the new congregations of love and morality.

COMFORT FOR DAVIE

Seems Old College's the bottle stashed
behind the Royal Mile, Crags and Castle
squeezing right enough, and tight,
the tenements to check some casual scan
of our inheritance: Simson's *Euclid* and
the limits of MacLaurin; Dugald Stewart,
Ferrier and the Clerk Maxwell mouldering
outwith remote architectural algebra . . .

Four from the Highlands, two blones, stepping up
North Bridge, breathing tea and proud cake,
fuddled in gowns and Edinburgh's suddron face.

Four years taken, pressed for the trickling vintage
's you know yourself, Davie, syne taught us
too of th'elitist intent of 'twenty-six and 'eighty-nine.

Four tries in all to stifle conversation's
art and cathode-blast our Frankish tongue,
philosophy, to th'expert discipline and Babel. Yet

four, kilting smalltalk still, first-foot up the Bridge – architect
at law, philologer priest're two; humming tomographer
and archaeologist, besotted with Bataille, the rest – while

Old Toun's false-self sticks to the dirt on the street.
The Castle, St Giles', the Gutted Haddy; even our grandest
gestures are no longer ours, for fear of theft, gifted.
To leave at last, vacuity, peace of the fake space,
costume drama, th'ineluctable jargon and death by inadventure.
This could be all of The University and its City –
the expert fear, sterility and thrall – but for the harvest,
but for Hogmanay! I mean, those wild bells for Sartre,
swilling Lovelock, Laing's hand black with Kierkegaard
and hot tea clouding in the breath once more, like Rothko . . .
there's spirit yet our City can't encapsulate and snuff.

Four points of the star, Davie, How many more
're keeping that trickle hot in the throat
of hogmanay and hairst? *Slàinte mhath dhaibh!*

Off Ardglas

The sea's some kind of grey off Ardglas, the air
and the sky're giving up height on plates. Left,
Stac Geal has the widow's swell on
and a lapful of china from the light. The rocks've
gone some strange loose flesh colour with the gulls.

You know it well enough, Ardglas, the spur
single-tracked and the ribs fenced. See
the bearded cars white-settling, sheep in closed
session, children trading cigarettes and saliva
in the lee of the Free Church manse?

Here's lazybeds collapsed and a mattress
of potato. Here the awkward oilskin's caught
only itself on the byre hook, dripping pullets,
and nothing has the time of Murdo's loom.
Something of my forehead's in the scene.

A Home for the Words Lost by 'Contemporary' Poets

The the and the a and the and and
because by and of the way if that
to be in or on or at or besides
in which is and are and can and
do perhaps of course it seems am

I meaning us as in we meaning me as
in all of a the or an a that is by
and about through even you to a he as in she
who were where what with yes and with
who is it I no but aye since I no no
buts but who are we what we are and
will be more many more more than one.

KATE CLANCHY

Kate Clanchy was born in Glasgow in 1965 and was educated in Edinburgh and Oxford. She won an Eric Gregory Award in 1994. Her first book, *Slattern*, was published in 1996 and won the Forward Prize for Best First Collection, the Saltire Prize for the Scottish First Book of the Year, a Scottish Autumn and a New London Writers Award. In 1997 she was awarded a Somerset Maugham Award and was shortlisted for the John Llewllyn Rhys Prize. After several years in the East End of London, she moved to Oxford in 1998 and works there as a teacher and freelance writer.

Publications:

Slattern (Chatto and Windus, 1996)
Samarkand (Picador, 1999)

MEN

I like the simple sort, the soft white-collared ones
smelling of wash that someone else has done,
of apples, hard new wood. I like the thin-skinned,
outdoor, crinkled kind, the athletes, big-limbed,
who stoop to hear, the moneyed men, the unironic
leisured sort who balk at jokes and have to blink,
the men with houses, kids in cars, who own
the earth and love it, know themselves at home
here, and so don't know they're born, or why
born is hard, but snatch life smack from the sky,
a cricket ball caught clean that fills the hand.

I put them all at sea. They peer at my dark land
as if through sun on dazzling waves, and laugh.

THE WEDDING GUEST'S STORY

Shortly after ditching me, a matter of weeks,
in point of fact, she bought a remarkable
backless dress and got hitched to an ex-army chap
who climbs up rocks on Sundays: not the sort,

that chap, if I might explain, to stop for stragglers
or to soak up sun. He'd strike for the top
in skin tight kit, lycra shorts and pick, straining
straps around the crotch. In spite of which,

I took the half-meant invite straight, sat tight
throughout, let that dress flash a foot of flesh
to the hushed cathedral, and in my mind
I slowly climbed the low, secret steps of her spine,

swung for a while on my rope in the tuck
of her waist, scrambled sweating, swearing,
over the slopes of her shoulder blades,
to slump on the summit, weak, sobbing with loss.

SLATTERN

I leave myself about, slatternly,
bits of me, and times I liked:
I let them go on lying where
they fall, crumple, if they will.
I know fine how to make them walk
and breathe again. Sometimes at night,
or on the train, I dream I'm dancing,
or lying in someone's arms who says
he loves my eyes in French, and again
and again I am walking up your road,
that first time, bidden and wanted,
the blossom on the trees, light,
light and buoyant. *Pull yourself
together*, they say, quite rightly,
but she is stubborn, that girl,
that hopeful one, still walking.

THE PERSONALS

The one with herpes sounded best –
who didn't mention Solvency,
nor *s.o.h.*, nor Arts Degree,
didn't say he'd *l.t.m.*
a younger lady, petite, slilm,
n.s., South-East, for Arts Pursuits –
but talked of this secret sore of his,
his soiling, suppurative lust.

RASPBERRIES

The way we can't remember heat, forget
the sweat and how we wore a weightless
shirt on chafing skin, the way we lose
the taste of raspberries, each winter; but

know at once, come sharp July, the vein
burning in the curtain, and from that light
– the block of sun on hot crushed sheets –
the blazing world we'll walk in,

was how it was, your touch. Not the rest,
not how we left, the drunkenness, just
your half-stifled, clumsy, frightened reach,
my uncurled hand, our fingers, meshed,

– like the first dazzled flinch from heat
or between the teeth, pips, a metal taste.

GILLIAN FERGUSON

'What do you want to be when you leave school?' my twelve-year-old self was asked. 'A poet,' I replied in a nano-flash. The Careers teacher looked stunned – before giggling nervously – she clearly wasn't sure what subjects to advise for aspiring poets. No doubt one of the reasons I ended up doing an Honours degree in Philosophy at Edinburgh University, and just as there are no job adverts saying 'POET WANTED – *short hours, high pay, long holidays*', neither were there any saying 'PHILOSOPHER WANTED', with similar conditions, and so I worked first – after the requisite stint starving on the dole, growing moley in a dark, damp basement – as an honest artisan making jewellery and painting silk scarves, as well as selling drawings and doing the odd illustration. I was then happily surprised to get a fantastic job as Tutor in Arts at the Open University, before moving into journalism. I have variously worked at *Scotland on Sunday* and *The Scotsman* at interviewing celebrities and authors, travel writing, features and book reviewing, before realising that being a TV critic is a lovely job, and doing it at *Scotland on Sunday*, and later at *The Scotsman*. I went on to become a columnist at *The Scotsman*, before moving recently to write a column for *The Herald*. I also write a humorous column for the *Financial Times* weekend magazine, and have just begun to broadcast my columns on John Peel's BBC Radio 4 programme, *Home Truths*. But, despite trying since that first Careers meeting, I still haven't really figured out how to get more time to write!

Publications:

Gillian has now received three Writers' Bursaries in the Scottish Arts Council's Writers' Bursary Scheme, including the top award for *Baby: Poems on Pregnancy, Birth and Babies* (Canongate, 2001). Her first book of poems, *Air for Sleeping Fish* (Bloodaxe, 1997), was shortlisted for the Scottish First Book of the Year, and she was a prizewinner in the *Daily Telegraph* Arvon International Poetry Competition. Selections of her work appear in Maura Dooley's anthology of new women poets of the 1990s, *Making for Planet Alice* (Bloodaxe, 1997), in *New Blood* edited by Neil Astley (Bloodaxe, 1999), and the *Faber Book of 20th Century Scottish Poems* (Faber, 1993). She is just completing a book of short stories and a first novel, and has also

written an ecological fable. Gillian is the winner of the £25,000 Creative
Scotland Award for Literature.

Winter Walk

Under a white skin of ice,
the river's clear veins push
air for sleeping fish.

Sun shatters on the hills'
blue spines, showers snow
with flashing dust.

In a dribbling cave we find
stone's slow tears
have made organ pipes of icicles,

a graveyard of unicorns.
You unroof two fluted horns
for your leaf-eyed head,

dance under armed trees.
I gather petticoats of starched web,
a blood-crown of cut haws.

Through many wind-shaped drifts
I hold your glove-furred paw
until air and fields blush.

Blue-breathed creatures let us stay
under these dragoned clouds
as birds' hearts flutter into silence,

the bloomed dusk falls,
under the knife of night;
the cold fires of space spark –

frozen in our own myth
with the moon veining our wooded path,
printing our feet with wildcat and deer.

Dear Norman
(for the late Norman MacCaig)

I blew in from my own young night
and demented Edinburgh November,
magnetised leaves tangled in Ophelia hair.

Whisky soon lay like a cat
on my stomach – its water, like you,
ran briskly forty years ago;

each year we celebrated with a Silk Cut –
mist peered at our lung-blown rival,
a dovetail of poems fanned in your hand.

How your chameleon mind, frail giant,
whose words skewer fragments of the world –
butterflies in boxes of books –

alchemised the blades of wit
to feathers. Your wife dead;
our pain surpassing all soberness.

Your hieroglyphs translated my pages,
laughter poulticed dry tears;
words summed like scars on stone.

Your tongue still speaks like light
in black holes of belief –
I remember my homeward, hovercraft feet.

The Swimming Pool Ghost

In splintering shallows at the local pool,
a ghost shifts – a shoal of pink minnows
that never comes up for air again.

A terminal dive into three feet of thin water.
Corrugated spine. Skull grenade.

Climbing from the slow skin
of emptied indoor water,

a goggled woman scoured
her shocked body raw.

You can mistake him for the breathless lengths
of underwater swimmers, but pass clean through –
a touch of cold current as he disperses.

No mermaids here.
No scenic carcasses of sunken ships.
Nothing of how my friend saw his death
as he drowned in a beautiful place:
a Mexican bay in the evening
like a basin of blood.

Water slapped kisses on his lips,
a mute choir of fancy-coloured fish
mouthing in the waves –
lungs could breathe water
like the living sponge.

The swimming pool ghost
ripples around children –
churning cherubs with plastic wings –
because there was no time
to make tableaux of his death,
for mouths cushioning bedside air
with comfortable words.

Because he died in the wrong metaphor
like a baby dropped in a font.

Because sudden death is crime
against the spirit, he waits
at the scene for a just court.

When the pool is drained,
will he swim in air
like a wingless salmon,

or rush to the sluice –
to dive, be swallowed
by bottomless sea.

PRAM RAGE

Onward in our chariot, baby, Ben Hur, in the evening-ghosted streets. Fast white wheels luminous, hardly seeming to touch ground, except on cobbles which make you giggle, like pigeon explosions in the park.

But in the day town we are slowed, a wing-clipped bird, by legs and feet frequent as weeds and more irritating – excuse me, *excuse me*, EXCUSE ME! But a pram has made my words loud as mouthing fish and what's more, the secret of invisibility has been discovered by my pram, despite its brightly coloured hide – model 'chameleon' obviously. Trip, bump, then tuck at *me! Bash my scarcely sleeping baby's head with that fat bag and I'll rip you limb from limb, sir.*

And at doors, why do people assume that I shall wait and wait and wait while a babbling stream of shoppers pass on through – it's never *my* turn. And while I'm on the subject, why does the whole of humankind, except other mothers, even young feminists, presume me stupid, slow, second class, just because I push a pram? Do degrees, high professions, just plain brains, competence, experience and talent, strangers' manners, vanish just because you've given birth? And does it make you deaf? – *A leopard-skin changing bag and mat, how very strange. Is that a BOY in a pink hat?* (Gasp!) *People shouldn't bring these pushchairs into shops* . . . What would you suggest, bovine madam? My baby sails, flies? My family go naked, starve now we are three, and stay indoors as punishment for having the next generation which will pay your pension . . . *Maybe*, my baby says – if he could.

And OK, maybe I have got milky, splashy stains on my top like a Florence statue, an odd sock, my hair is far from advert fresh. Maybe I have too many bags bulging from my pregnant pram and my hungry baby is girning until the next breast-feeding place distant as Everest, but must you look at me in that 1950s way as if I was a failure as a mother, and a person. Piss off! It's hard but I'm happy.

I imagine a protest, all of us on wheels, prams and wheelchairs en masse in the main street; we clog the doors of shops, let doors slam (revengefully) in startled faces, swarm slowly over stairs demanding lifts and where there are some, push in front and fill, create escalator hell – that'll teach'em to appreciate the choice, lazy gits. I see us weaving back and forth like fences round the wheel-less, aware only of ourselves, clipping heels and glaring if they complain. But we kiss all those who respect and help us in our struggle, especially with steps.

In the meantime – just until I've time, I mean, my husband buys a pushbike bell and mounts it on the handlebar. A cardiac effect – see them scatter in the street, like rabbits foxed, hee, hee. I half expect to see us on the news – *In the first confirmed case of pram rage* . . . so many altercations have there been, but I feel like a pioneer of wheels in a square world, a humble but important offshoot of the Suffragettes. To all parents, I say, join the cause – *Push Your Pram With Attitude!*

ORBIT OF THREE

Planets and stars understand
the luxury of love creating
me from my own materials
like God breathing flowers
from the seeded dust. As
abundant blue earth depends
on the sun, I am to you. You
water me. Eye-light leapt the
red boundaries of blood, stain –
glassed my heart; turned the
deaf *thud thud* counting life's
hurrying hours into drums,
duets, urging me on, on.

And we have made a moon,
out of nothing, like magicians
learning God's best trick.

SCAN

In me a moonscape of organs,
bloodless, maybe a monster;

my blood thuds. Until a black
bubble. Silent, slow as a flower,

opening from limb buds,
an anemone pulse of fingers.

Under my thick skin veil,
not me, plugged; blind,

bulb-headed, spinning invisible
tissue on bones fine as fish.

Mouse-big, sparrow-hearted,
it becoming *you*, new from

nothing; the miraculous alien,
eel-supple in blank dreams.

And like men loving the blue
planet, the world is changed.

STUART A. PATERSON

Born Truro, 1966, family returned to Scotland in 1970, to Ayrshire, where I was raised and educated in Kilmarnock. Attended the University of Stirling after working in varied and sometimes baffling lines of employment. Worked as a writer in the community in Ayrshire with various agencies and a wide range of community groups. I was Dumfries and Galloway/SAC Writing Fellow from 1996 to 1998. Have lived in Manchester since 1998, working in the areas of residential childcare and care of young adults with learning difficulties.

I no longer live in Scotland and write very little now. Both of these will change. I don't think of myself, certainly, as a 'New Scottish Poet', whatever that's supposed to mean, and never really did. 'New'; when does the poet cease to be 'new', after a requisite 'well-received first volume', or peer-acceptance within the defined critical arena? 'Scottish'; do we really still feel a need for our writing to be identified according to map references, and a sense of 'national selfhood'? I hope not but suspect differently. 'Poetry'; this definition's best left to others to whom such definitions seem to matter an awful lot.

Poetry still matters to me, the ongoing process that, I feel, shouldn't be subjected to group-inclusiveness or definitive statement. Other things matter to me: love, family, mates, place, work, Kilmarnock Football Club, good pubs, music, the future (its huge uncertainties), travel, movies and certain unplanned stages of drunkenness. And myself. Sometimes they have to be captured, explored, debated, slated, celebrated. Poetry can be good for that. Which does me. 'Nuff said.

Publications:

Mulaney of Larne and Other Poems (University of Leiden, 1991)
Saving Graces (diehard, 1997)

A Rush of Memory by Polmaise

At eleven I kissed the neighbourhood sweetheart,
Twelve she was, a stoneless peach then, furless
And ripe from the bough. It was a slap
Of wet concentration and closed eyes, tongueless
In the innocence of elevenishness and in
The spidery lair of a bin cupboard during
A preparatory dare for the coming school day.

At fifteen I kissed my first girlfriend,
Seventeen she was, a hairy rootmonger of men
All tousled from unmade beds. It was a suck
With a pull like a vacuum-cleaner. Tongueless
No more she forced the safety of my lips,
Seemed like she wanted my tonsils for a souvenir,
Welding our mouths with glue. I gargled later.

At sixteen I kissed my first love
For a whole three months, she was blond and frail
The way that kewpies are. It was summer,
And once I lay on top of her, in a field, young,
Hard as a hill, the dog's head cocked, no longer
Hoovering flies. If we'd gone one day
Without seeing each other we'd have died.

At seventeen I kissed a date ON THE TIT!
Twenty-one she was, immensely-nippled, almost
(But not quite) able to feed me, suckling, snorting away.
Mouths were irrelevant as we freed them to grab at
The mysterious sculpting and folds of flesh.
I tried to kiss her goodnight one time, she laughed
And groped me. Kissing was never the same.

At twenty-two I kissed a girl, cold dry
Funeral of love at a Galston bus-stop, our first kiss,
One of farewell from two kindred souls
Who never dared broach the borders of cloth
Yet held hands for comfort in a friendless world.
As I watched her go, my lips hung open to reveal
A tongue for talking. Kissing was learning to speak.

Not long ago, skinned of promises,
I kissed a girl near a ruined castle, shaded
By majesty of sequoia, drawn to cool stone,
Lapped by water, wing, the essential solitude of kisses.

FIFE

Dappled moorings by the grey
return to canvases in
Edinburgh antique shops showing
Crail or Kingsbarns in 1800.

The net-boys by the catch
smile, unaware, a legacy.
Low-slung harbour cottages
reek years away. Old crewmen,

worn by salt-spray, on
the breaking wall sniff for
lobster cooked wailing
on a high flame, watching

young ones lowered to boats.
City-dwellers on an open sea
of calm harbour shriek
camcorder laughs for Castlemilk.

Beyond walk more tourists
over dry cobbles, snapping
at the small auctions of lives
like a shoal of fat halibut.

Each day the spray is colder,
just a little grimier. Each
morning sees another wrinkle
frame a sun-caught smile.

DREAM STATE

a country so awake that
dreaming is for the sleepless,
but I think a back-here-then

when you'd maybe catch a fox
ear-deep in rubbish most
mornings, raking through full bins

for bones, *fragranta vesca*
honeying a hard soil in
new June, small tender fruits

for mouths yet too soft to take
ribes sylvestre's sharp blood
and tell-tale stain, football cards

in nationally-arranged piles
on the mantelpiece, Dalglish
and Keegan good company

one-dimensionally, food
like stovies, kedgeree, plain
but Scottish delights: to our young

lapping tongues, a nationalism
of proteins, a huge country
of undiscovered tastes

to fill the thoughts of small heads
put to bed before their world grew,
flag rose, fox came raking through

our back yard, when you'd maybe
catch the dream state long before
it woke to morning's red sky

laid along the contours of
a massive upset dustbin
something ransacked while we slept.

ALASDAIR FRASER[1]

This kind of man cuts down trees,
saws to kill and not to make them sing
as if in resurrection, and looks the type
you'd meet who serves an audience
with the drinks and not himself.
That kind of motion carrying him,
and himself carrying it, seems improbable
as the huge oak bent by high winds
or eternally collapsing before the chain

then springing full-blown
from the root time and again.
It's the music makes the movement
and, just as surely, movement the music.
Like the oak strained into and against
that irresistible wind, the best
is unseen and, probably, unheard.

[1]Alasdair Fraser is one of Scotland's finest fiddle players of recent years.

No-Way José

José you must have been
The original fat and spotty boy
In a Latino sort of way,
The last in line at playtime
When they picked the teams
For contact Lambada,
The poor wee burst
And soggy enchilada
Pushed to the side of the plate,
The date that senoritas
Would stay in to wash
Each other's hair
Or make burritos to avoid.

José, yours would be the face
That stopped the barroom gringos
In their Mescaled hoary jingo
When you walked into the place,
Yours would be the feet
That stumbled every second beat
Of every village-square bolero,
Yours would be the head
That wore the only raised sombrero
In the shade.
And you'd be first to go
In every dubbed Spaghetti Western
Ever made,
The one who had the nervous
High-pitched laugh and rotting teeth
Who pissed off Charles Bronson
Or Lee Van Cleef.

José, you'd be the spanner
In the opening scene fiesta,
The only one who'd stay awake
In the siesta.

José, can you see
That you are me
With a Mac before your surname,
Me, the same burst enchilada
Or overcooked *potatas bravas*
Who became the vegetarian haggis,
The red line who was never thin,
The crumbs at the bottom
Of the shortbread tin,
The Gordon who was never gay,
The Scotsman who never flew.
I was that tartan José.

I was you,
Who all that time in Mexico
Was not to know
You had a doppelganger ego,
Spotty twattish fat
And Scottish last-in-line amigo
In every playground,
Every backstreet where
The likes of us are found.

A sort of
By-the-way no-way José.

RODDY LUMSDEN

Much has changed for me since the first edition of this book. Back then, I had won an Eric Gregory Award and was waiting in vain for Faber to turn their interest into a first collection, but I had only written a handful of poems in over two years. I was spending so much time in the late, lamented St James Oyster Bar that I began to get mail there. I was working part time as an office manager and as a quizmaster in pubs – writing quizzes every week sapped my creativity. Early in 1994, an SAC bursary bought a computer, which changed everything. I wrote over seventy poems that year, some of which were not so bad.

These days I'm in (too?) deep – this week, I have just seen off the manuscript for my third collection and the proofs of my second book as editor. I am lucky enough to be making a living (of sorts) from writing and the things around: freelance editing (mostly for Anvil), residencies, commissions, teaching in schools, taking my regular advanced class, reviewing, judging competitions, giving readings all over the UK – on the 'page' and 'performance' circuits – and beyond. I sit on the Council of the Poetry Society and write regularly for their publications. Puzzle fans may have seen the nasty Brain Games I compile for *The Scotsman*.

Increasingly, I consider the book a necessary evil. I compose in my head; the text is an attempt to approximate the churnings of that process. There are still some poets (the bashful, the whiny, the schoolma'ms, the show-offs) whom I prefer on the page, but poetry's heart lies in the oral tradition. Few things are more stirring than seeing a skilled poet read well. Also, increasingly, I enjoy reading and writing work which has a certain rawness and spontaneity. Many of the poets I like most wore their flaws like medals and I grow weary of work which is mannered and honed, like a fat man in a tight, expensive suit. If that sounds like an apology for style over substance, ach, well I suppose it is. Some peers think I'm wasting my talents by using humour, by being 'quirky', by writing about men and women instead of the 'big themes'. The philosophising might come later – each to their own – but I still want to touch skin, not innards.

Publications:

Yeah Yeah Yeah (Bloodaxe, 1997)
The Book of Love (Bloodaxe, 2000)
Roddy Lumsden is Dead (Wrecking Ball, 2001)

As co-editor:
The Message (Poetry Society, 1999)
Anvil New Poets 3 (Anvil, 2001)

FATTENING

I tell her that the glistening is goodness,
that the glistening is stars. Reachable.
All that we ever wished for and more besides.

We both know what the glistening is: that it's
the ounce knob of butter I've stirred into
her soup. That I'm treating her like a child.

It's true to say that I want her body back
for my own reasons too. I gave up
philanthropy per se when I stepped off the Ark.

I stand in the open bathroom doorway, fix her
with a stern look as she squats to pee.
Her days of going in alone are over for the time being.

A glass bottle full of mouthwash catches me
on the temple. 'Now we're both martyrs,'
she'll say, admiring the yellow of the bruise.

But I'm doing the right thing, aren't I? Didn't we
make promises once, lying out in long grass
at . . . where was it? We take turns on the scales,

while through in the next room, on the stereo,
some long ago crowd raises a cheer as,
one by one, they recognise what song this is.

COMING

Outside the cinema, all evening long,
there is a young man waiting on
the girl who isn't coming.

I watch him stand and smoke and weep,
or crouch down, head in hands,
till one last audience files home to sleep.

And only now do I get to thinking
how the tenpenny hole in his trouser-seat, to me,
is the winking light of a buoy at sea

that marks what is hidden
and the way death comes in to land,
perfect and sudden.

YEAH YEAH YEAH

No matter what you did to her, she said,
There's times, she said, she misses you, your face
Will pucker in her dream, and times the bed's
Too big. Stray hairs will surface in a place
You used to leave your shoes. A certain phrase,
Some old song on the radio, a joke
You had to be there for, she said, some days
It really gets to her; the way you smoked
Or held a cup, or her, and how you woke
Up crying in the night sometimes, the way
She'd stroke and hush you back, and how you broke
Her still. All this she told me yesterday,
Then she rolled over, laughed, began to do
To me what she so rarely did with you.

An Older Woman

Mid-1990s, Scotland, dead of winter
And more than old enough to be my mother.
She hailed a taxi in the city centre,
Dropped me off a hundred yards before her
And we were naked fifteen minutes later;
A Brookes & Simmons dress, her bra and knickers
Were delicate and in contrasting colours.
I didn't stop to think if there were others,
Responded prompt and proudly to her orders.
And now I wish to speak to celebrate her
Although I don't know anything about her
Except the spray of freckles on her shoulders
And that she said the world revolved around her.
I know exactly what to do without her.

Piquant

Just as, surely, sweat is consommé
or scallions scowled in a jelly-pan
or golden acid, wrathful in a stoppered jar

and other body fluids I shan't mention
are sulphur, globster, stinkhorn, horse or Brie,
then there are these late-on summer days

when, just where nostril meets the upper lip,
a film appears, part sweat, part oil
with a perfect, clean white chocolate smell,

two parts ginger to ninety-eight parts milk
and which, when I lean in to take this kiss,
says *fool for sugar*, says *mammals one and all*,

says *never again a love like this*.

ACID

'She was right. I had to find something new.
There was only one thing for it.'

My mother told it straight, *London will finish you off,*
and I'd heard what Doctor Johnson said, *When a man is tired*
of London, he is tired of life, but I'd been tired of life

for fourteen years; Scotland, never thoroughly enlightened,
was gathering back its clutch of medieval wonts
and lately there had been what my doctors called a pica

(like a pregnant woman's craving to eat Twix with piccalilli
or chunks of crunchy sea-coal): I'd been guzzling vinegar,
tipping it on everything, falling for women who were

beautifully unsuitable, and hiding up wynds off the Cowgate
with a pokeful of hot chips drenched in the sacred stuff
and wrapped in the latest, not last, edition of *The Sunday Post*

where I read that in London they had found a Chardonnay
with a bouquet of vine leaves and bloomed skins, a taste
of grapes and no finish whatsoever, which clinched the deal.

MY LAST SUPPER

A truck rams through the window of the café.
It's only there a second, but I see it
clear as a mirror, coming straight towards me,
my glass of milk, my plate of chicken curry,
my *Private Eye*. How painful that would be,
to be sucked into the innards of a lorry
and how easy it seemed earlier to tell you
I love you, at last, to toss it in, among
our talk of crises we are living through
as if it was a line from some old song
you've never heard, but I have known forever.
The Turks chat as the radio chimes merrily:
the terror in the blue eyes of the driver,
the pocket-money sleaze of R&B.

The Consolation

Though I hate to cheapen a poem
with slang, it needs to be said
that our brief time together
went *straight to video*,
though when it was shown at the Odeon
one hot night in Weston-Super-Mare,
by mistake, there was a standing ovation
while up in Redcar two misfit teenage girls
had seen it so often
you could see their mouths move in unison,
overdubbing our half-hearted sweet-talk
as they watched it for the sixty-third time.

Roddy Lumsden

RICHARD PRICE

I was born in 1966 and grew up in the half-urban, half-rural county of Renfrewshire, to the south-west of Glasgow. I now live in the rurban territory that's to the west of London, just inside a crook of the Thames and an arc of the M25.

I was state-educated in Scotland, trained as a journalist, and then took a degree in English and Librarianship at the University of Strathclyde. I received a double first, and went on to complete a Ph.D. on the novels and plays of Neil M. Gunn. I couldn't find a job in Scotland, but found work with The British Library in London, where I am now a Curator of Modern British Collections.

I have been interested in little magazines since secondary school and have co-edited several Scottish reviews – *Verse, Gairfish* (with W. N. Herbert), and *Southfields* (with Raymond Friel and David Kinloch). *Painted, spoken* is the poetry magazine I edit at the moment. The intention has always been to allow a genuine range of Scottish poetry to reach, at the very least, the intellectual and creative communities in Scotland. Each magazine has always included avant-garde work seldom published anywhere else in the country, if at all. Similarly, Vennel Press, the press I set up with Leona Medlin in 1990, publishes what I believe are outstanding collections which would not be published otherwise.

In the early 1990s I was part of a loose grouping of poets I called 'The Informationists': Robert Crawford, W. N. Herbert, David Kinloch, Peter McCarey, myself, and Alan Riach. One of the ideas of Informationism was to rewire the new of the everyday to itself: to cross wires, to hot wire, to short-circuit. By this I mean to engage with the new worlds and jargon of 'the information society'; to find poetic analogies in form as well as content to technological invention and global discourse. Though a crucial part of Informationism was an enthusiasm for aspects of what is in some respects a new world, an ironic and satirical response to world-villagism was also – for some – part of the improvised project.

I try to make poems as *poemy* as the great works of cinema are filmy. Since Informationism, my work continues to problematise poetic narrative and oral/textual differences in vocabulary, syntax and rhythm. This sounds like a dry strategy for poetry, but the heart of my work is elegy and the lyric: this is *because* of a self-conscious negotiation with language, not despite it. But I'm not good at explaining my own work: poems to me are the most articulate forms of expression full stop and I'd prefer to let them speak for themselves.

Publications:

Poetry:
Sense and a minor fever (Vennel Press, 1993)
Tube shelter perspective (Southfields Press, 1993)
Marks & Sparks (Akros, 1995)
Hand held (Akros, 1997)
Perfume & petrol fumes (diehard, 1999)
Gift horse, with Ron King (Circle Press, 1999)
Renfrewshire in Old Photographs, with Raymond Friel (Mariscat, 2000)
Frosted, melted (diehard, 2002)

Translations and anthologies:
Contraflow on the Superhighway [an Informationist Primer], co-edited with W. N. Herbert (Gairfish/Southfields Press, 1994)
Eftirs/Afters [French modernists], with Donny O'Rourke (Au Quai, 1996)
César Vallejo: Translations, Transformations, Tributes, co-edited with Stephen Watts (Au Quai/Southfields Press, 1998)

Research:
The Fabulous Matter of Fact: The Poetics of Neil M. Gunn (Edinburgh University Press, 1991)
La Nouvelle Alliance: influences francophones sur la littérature écossaise moderne, co-edited with David Kinloch (ELLUG, 2000)
The Star You Steer By: Basil Bunting and 'British' Modernism, co-edited with James McGonigal (Rodopi, 2000)

TREE-BIRD

I'm lending you this poem –
it's yours.

Do you remember the owl-hawk, white as a guiser –
the dusk's sucky blanket tucked round our caravan
and the bird rid of us

like, at break-ripe, the fruit of the tree-bird tree,

the applefist which splits
into a beak and feathers,
a yellow tern
before Newton can say
Golden Delicious.

(It's a legend, you know, among fishers
who ken damn few trees
and they all shrubbery –
in this world, geese crack out of barnacles,
crabs lisp, and jellyfish are wedding veils
for mermaids who've vetoed
shivering grooms
in the wide aisle of a low ebb.)

I want to be the bird that's my hand in your hand,
to be the osprey that can dismember itself
like the lines of a poem,
climb the sky, dive, fish
and come back to itself
like a trick,
like the end of work.

WITH IS

To ravel with you in ripening light.
To worry and adore
the stacking cups of your spine.

What I come with
is a dubious country,
a prejudice against people like us:
nationals who've dropped to couples,
two martens agog
under a tired Scots pine.

Our table is empty,
a summer curling pond.
Come on out on the town!
I've the nightbus map you lent me
when I was only a Scot.

AT EASE

Scotland hits eighty in May.

An electric mower blows its nose
The explaining murmur is my father by the ladders;
the MacMillan visitor, months into this
conversation,
is at ease.

With my shirt off, everything is ridiculous:
dad in shorts and people in the wrong places.
Inside, like church, when mum says garden
she means an English one.

MY FATHER'S RECORD COLLECTION

The hard black Corryvreckan
is static.
All the blues are quiet
in the white-washed attic.

There's a dead shining black,
a brittle hour.
Between Beethoven and Broadway,
a pressed black flower.

JOHN GALLAGHER

Speak to me, John Gallagher,
at work if no the house.
I've took up ma hem for you,
skooshed scent in ma blouse.

Ma says you're a boy fae the Port,
a druggie and no all there.
She minds your sensitive hands
were fists at the Kilma Fair.

Come to the shop, John Gallagher,
meet me on ma break.
If you're no a Prudential man
that's a risk I'll have to take.

THE WORLD IS BUSY, KATIE

The world is busy, Katie, and tonight
the planes are playing, fine, alright, but soon
the folk behind those blinks will nap, sleep tight
as you will too, beneath a nitelite moon.
The world is busy, Katie, but it's late –
the trains are packing up, the drunks are calm.
The fast, the slow, has gone, it's only freight
that storms the garage lane. It means no harm.
The world is busy, Katie, but it's dark –
the lorries nod, they snort, they spoil their chrome.
They hate to be alone. They look to park
just off the road. For them, a lay-by's home.
The world is busy, Katie, like I said,
but *you're* the world – and tired. It's time for bed.

HAND HELD

No smile, smiler, blink and camera-shake.
A top's neck of milksoak and talc smell, Katie,
and babyskin's and spit's: bits of this-that's-you
(push-crashed into then then, but now
and holding), hands as loved as hands, hands!,

and

whatever your clear eyes are meaning
you mean it brightly.

HERON

A greying Senior Lecturer in Fish Studies (Thames Valley), he stands in frozen hop concentration, regarding a lectem only he can see. Still, he gets results. He's hoping for a chair.

PIGEONS

Pedestrianise the High Street? Crumbs!

KINGFISHER

Blue. I mean green. Blue, green.   Gone.

ANNE FRATER

I was born in Stornoway in 1967 and brought up in Upper Bayble on the Isle of Lewis. Educated at Bayble School and the Nicolson Institute (Stornoway) and Glasgow University, graduating in 1990 with M.A. (hons) Celtic and French, then in 1994 with a Ph.D. in Celtic (Scottish Gaelic Women's Poetry up to 1750).

Since then, I have had various jobs in the media, ranging from sub-titler to scriptwriter to television and radio researcher until I moved back to Lewis in 1999. I am currently based at Lews Castle College as a lecturer on the University of the Highlands and Islands Gaelic degree course.

Language, love and politics are still my main preoccupations when it comes to writing poetry, although the degree of optimism or despair has changed. The future for my first language, Gaelic, seems less gloomy than it did when I first started writing, although it is still nowhere near 'safe'. It seems that for every positive action regarding the language, there is an equal and opposite negative backlash. On the political front, being a Nationalist, things are looking brighter now we've got our own parliament, if not our independence (yet!). As for the other topic, knights on white chargers are still a bit thin on the ground . . . !

I don't think my experiences of life have been very much out of the ordinary, so I hope that even what I regard as my most personal poems are easy to relate to.

Publications:

Fo ' n t-Slige/Under the Shell (Gairm, 1995)

Anthologies:
An Aghaidh na Sìorraidheachd/In the Face of Eternity (Polygon, 1990)
An Anthology of Scottish Women Poets (Edinburgh University Press, 1991)
Siud an t-Eilean/There Goes the Island (Acair, 1993)

LIT' GUN SHALAINN

Sgian dubh na stocainn
agus Beurla na bheul;
moladh lit' sa mhadainn
's e cur muesli na bhòbhl;
'Chan fhaighear nas fheàrr na 'n t-uisge-beatha.'
Ach 's e Martini bhios e 'g òl . . .
Nach ann truagh a tha 'n cluaran
le boladh an ròis!

Unsalted Porridge

A *sgian dubh* in his stocking
and English on his tongue;
praising porridge in the morning
as he puts muesli in his bowl;
'You can't get better than whisky.
But it's Martini that he drinks . . .
Isn't the thistle pitiful
when it smells of the rose!

Danns' air a' bhalla . . .
Casan saor a' cluich puirt
air clachan cruaidh,
's a' uèir-ghathach air a lomadh
le bualadh nam bas . . .
No man's land
loma-làn le daoine
's iad a' dol seachad air Teàrlach –
chan ann gun fhiost
ach gun sgrùdadh –
agus na càirdean a' feitheamh
le gàire nan gàirdean . . .
agus gàir' aig na gàrdan
's gun fheum ac' air gunna
airson bacadh a thogail agus blocan a leagail . . .
Cailleach a' tighinn
gu geata Bhrandenburg,
nach eil fhathast air fhosgladh
cho farsaing ri càch,
saighdear òg a' dol thuice
's i a' seasamh, gu daingeann
's a' coimhead a slighe
mar cheumannan ceadachaidh
na chlàr fo a casan,
ga slaodadh,
ga tarraing,
's i gluasad a-rithist,
's a' coimhead an òigeir,
's a' toirt dùbhlan dha
a tilleadh air ais.
Làmh air a gualainn,
greim air a h-uilinn,
's i gun chothrom
a dhol an aghaidh a' churaidh
bha ga stiùireadh dìreach
gu Brandenburg,
gu teampall a saorsa . . .
A-raoir
gun imcheist
bhiodh e air peilear a chur innt'.

9TH NOVEMBER 1989

Dancing on the wall . . .
Feet freely playing tunes
on hard stones,
the barbed wire made smooth
by the beating of hands . . .
No man's land
brimming over with people
as they pass Charlie –
not furtively
but without scrutiny –
and their friends wait
with a smile in their arms . . .
and the guards laugh,
as they need no guns
to lift barriers
and knock down bricks . . .
An old woman comes
to the Brandenburg Gate,
which is not yet open
as wide as the rest,
a young soldier goes to her
and she stands firm
looking at her path
laid out at her feet
like steps of permission,
pulling her,
drawing her,
and she moves again,
and she watches the youth
daring him
to turn her back.
A hand on her shoulder,
a grip on her elbow,
and she is powerless
to resist the brave
who leads her straight
to Brandenburg,
to her temple of freedom . . .
Last night
without hesitation
he would have shot her.

SMUAIN

'Alba saor no na fàsach.'
Saorsa no gainmheach
canaidh iad ruinn an aon rud:
'Gheibh sibh sin . . .
ach cumaidh sinne an ola.'

DÀ RATHAD

Carson a bu chòir dhomh gabhail
na slighe ceart, lom, fada?
Ged a tha an rathad air a bheil mi cam
agus tha na clachan a' gearradh mo chasan,
agus tha dìreadh an leòthaid
gam fhàgail gun anail,
chan e an aon rud
a tha mise coimhead romham
latha an dèidh latha.
Agus shuas air an leathad
chì mi timcheall orm,
chì mi gu bheil barrachd ann dhòmhs'
na slighe cheart, fhada, lom.
Tha thusa cumail do shùilean air an aon rud
ceart, dìreach air do bheulaibh –
agus chan fhaic thu gu bheil an saoghal
ag atharrachadh timcheall ort.

A Thought

'Scotland free or a desert'.
Freedom or sand
they'll say the same thing to us:
'You can have that . . .
but we'll keep the oil.'

Two Roads

Why should I follow
the long, smooth, straight road?
Although the road I take is crooked
and the stones cut my feet
and climbing the hill
leaves me breathless
I am not confronted
by the same prospect
day after day.
And up on the hill
I can see around me,
I can see that there is more in store for me
than a straight, long, smooth road.
You keep your eyes fixed on one point
right in front of you –
and you cannot see
that the world is changing around you.

SEMAPHORE

An e na brataich cheàrr a tha mi 'cur a-mach
's nach tuig thu an teachdaireachd
a tha 'gluasad anns a' ghaoth?
An e am pàtaran a tha ceàrr
neo na dathan
's gu bheil thusa 'leughadh rud nach eil mi 'g ràdh?
Neo a bheil thu ri cleas Nelson:
a' toirt a' chreids nach fhaic thu
gus nach bi agad
ri freagairt a thoirt dhomh?

GEAMHRADH

Tha sneachda nis
far an deach mi 'nam theine
agus reothadh
air an àit' anns an do leagh mi.
Tha sealladh mo leannin
a' tuiteam air clach.
Cha thuit mise tuilleadh.
Tha cànan mo ghaoil
a chaoidh 'na tosd.
Tha 'n geamhradh air tilleadh.

Semaphore

Is it because I'm hanging out the wrong flags
that you can't read the message
that's moving in the wind?
Are the patterns wrong
or the colours
makingyou read it all wrong?
Or are you, like Nelson,
pretending you can't see
so you don't have to give me
an answer?

Winter

There is snow now
where I was aflame
and frost
in the place where I melted.
The look of my love
falls on stone:
I will not fall again.
The language of my love
is silenced forever.
Winter has returned.

TRACEY HERD

I was born in East Kilbride in 1968. I graduated from Dundee University with an M.A. in English and American Studies in 1991, returning there seven years later to take up the post of Creative Writing Fellow (1998–2001). My first appearance in print was in the Bloodaxe anthology *New Women Poets*, ed. Carol Rumens in 1990. I won an Eric Gregory Award in 1993 and a Scottish Arts Council Bursary in 1995. My first book, *No Hiding Place*, was published by Bloodaxe in 1996 and shortlisted for the Forward Prize for Best First Collection.

In 1998 I travelled to Russia (Moscow and Ekaterinburg) for a British Council/Bloodaxe Books Poetry Festival; Russian history has always been one of my passions, and I visited the site where the Tsar and his family and servants were executed in 1918.

My second book *Dead Redhead* was published in June 2001, and in it I've tried to weave together the threads of my obsessions: Nancy Drew, Hollywood, racehorses, Russian and American history, and fabulous, doomed women. Since I began writing, these have been, more or less, my themes.

Growing up on the east coast of Scotland, I entertained no thoughts of becoming a writer until I discovered American poetry of the 1950s and 1960s when I was eighteen. I began writing then with no aim other than my own enjoyment. I wanted to capture the essence of people (and horses) the way the camera does in a film: fleetingly, but definitively. I'm working on my third book of poems just now, along with a play about the Green River Killer.

Publications:

No Hiding Place (Bloodaxe, 1996)
Dead Redhead (Bloodaxe, 2001)

GIRL DETECTIVE

My father is a famous lawyer.
He adores me. There is no mother
to get in the way. She died when I was three,
leaving the plump, friendly housekeeper
who is concerned for me.
I have been titian-haired and delicately pretty
for three-quarters of a century.
I have an eye for a mystery.

I am often praised for my cool head,
despite having been drugged,
gagged, bound by all manner of villains.
I have tripped over tree roots, fallen
down stairs. I have seen stars,
choked on cloths soaked in chloroform.
It's enough to make a girl scream
but I prefer the cold stare and the stinging retort.

No villain has ever gotten the better of me.
Not one. They are, without exception,
swarthy and unattractive, probably foreign.
The women are crueller than the men
but they break down more easily in the end.
They talk in stage whispers, in a special code.
They have raised indiscretion to an art,
turning up in rest-rooms and at gas-stations,
passing notes and dropping handy clues.
The Chief says be at H.Q. by three.

Wherever I'm headed, they'll be.
It's uncanny: Montreal, New York, the Adirondacks
or overseas. I have travelled
a pale, whimsical version of the world
on a limitless stream of dollars.
I catch my villain and hand him over.
He is scrubbed from the face of the earth forever.
There will be plenty of others.
I shut my front door on the world.

Once, between cases, frozen in time,
I dreamed I died and was buried
in a simple ceremony
on the outskirts of River Heights.

They laid me down next to my mother's body.
After the mourners had gone
I simply climbed, Houdini that I am,
out of the hole in the ground
back into the arms of my beloved father.
I kissed his face, then turned mine
into the cold October sun. It was evening.
We linked arms and walked quietly home.

STALLION GRAVEYARD, KENTUCKY

The grass is lush but well tended.
The graves are ornaments
backlit to perfection by the sun.

Nashua, striking in bronze,
turns his handsome head
to his Negro stable-boy
in a savage gesture of love.

This is Bluegrass Country
and here lie the noble dead of Kentucky.
Some fell in their lovely prime
wrestled by lightning to the ground.
Others grew fat and almost tame.

On the first Saturday in May, at dawn,
the horsemen come to Churchill Downs.
The field is bloodlit viridian: guns
and cannon tear the silks of summer.
A fallen army stirs.
Their names are battle cries:
Cavalcade, Whirlalway, Gallahadion,
Count Fleet, Assault, Dark Star,
Dust Commander.

GIA

In drugstores across America
on laminated cards at points-of-sale
her lips are the glistening focus,
freshly painted with Melon-Shine,
the season's new shade from Maybelline.
In magazines, she struggles against a fake storm
with an umbrella by Christian Dior.

New York: a seventies summer.
A small apartment, spartanly furnished.
The morning is already warm,
the windows flung wide open
to catch the sun's first sweet rush
before the sidewalks bake and crack.
On the cover of August's *Vogue*
the model's complexion is as flawless
as a fresh snowfall
and her eyes are open very wide
in a halo of mink and klieg lights.

Southampton, Long Island: a week-long shoot.
Her chestnut hair is piled high on her head.
She rests her bare feet on a rock
and her hands paddle in the sparkling blue water.
The tide slaps against the track-marks
that run from wrist to elbow.

She is prowling in a thin black dress
on the roof of a building two hundred feet up
in the heart of the garment district:
black stockings, heels, slant eyes, a scowl.
A freezing wind sways the building.

In the darkroom the pictures float
in their tray of developing-fluid.
The emerging face is defiant and sad.
The eyes are dead, the fabulous body
is stripped of its flesh.
He lifts out the bones of the drowned girl.

OPHELIA'S CONFESSION

Every day God pats my head and calls me
angel, his little broken woman
and gives me flowers as if I hadn't had enough of these
and I choke back my rage and he mistakes this
for distress as I stand there shaking
in my little sackcloth dress.

Had I ever had the choice
I'd have worn a very different dress,
slit from breast to navel and far too tight
and I'd have smoked and sworn and been
out of my head on drugs, not grief, and the flowers
would have been a tattoo around my ankle,
not an anchor to drag me down, and as for
being a virgin, I'd have slept with both men and women.

I would never recommend a shallow stream
and what was no more than a daisy chain
as being the ideal way to die.
It was far too pretty but I had to improvise
and I was a poet, far more so than him,
who threw out every word he ever thought
as if that might have kept his sorry life afloat.

I didn't drown by accident. I was a suicide.
At least let me call my mind my own
even when my heart was gone beyond recall.

Today, a car crash might have been my final scene,
a black Mercedes in a tunnel by the Seine,
with no last words, no poetry,
with flashbulbs tearing at my broken body
because broken was the way I felt inside,
the cameras lighting up the wreckage of a life.
That would, at least, have been an honest way to die.

The Water Babies

Each night, Joan Crawford would tie her red hair back
from her smooth forehead with a bandeau,
scooping out the cold-cream
from a white porcelain jar, to cleanse
her skin of the foundation and thick powder
then she'd scowl at her freckles
and rub her face with ice-cubes till it stung.

Marilyn would buy a new pair of jeans,
wriggling her hips into the stiff blue denim
then lie in a cold bath for hours
till they'd shrunk to fit her
like a second skin. But still her skin
was too thin. Her hair was mousy then,
streaming down her back in unruly curls.
She lifted weights, she ran the back alleys of Hollywood.
She loved the sea, would swim with powerful strokes
out far from shore: she'd parade in a pink swimsuit
twirling a parasol, leaning down to sketch
names in the sand and smile her smile
till they taught her to pull her lips down over her gums.
When George Barris took the final shots,
she wrapped herself in a Mexican-knit cardigan
against the mist, her hair clumped, her face
pasty and dry, her eyes cast down
looking for the lost names in the sand.

Natalie Wood's brown eyes and chestnut hair,
her journals of life's small joys, her mediocre
acting skills that didn't matter when you looked
at *that* face, drowned in a boating accident
off Catalina, no witnesses, no saviour,
her lungs filled with the stars reflected in the dark
Pacific. There was no poor dialogue to spoil the scene,
just the doe-eyed beauty, mute and pale, her body
lit from within by tiny stars.

KEVIN MacNEIL

I was born and raised on the Isle of Lewis, desperate, from a young age, to be either a writer or a spaceman. (This was before I realised there's little difference between the two.) Being raised on an island has necessarily had a profound effect on my work. For one thing, writing is a fine antidote to the claustrophobia an insular upbringing will impart on the mind that is even remotely sensitive. Writing, this most liberating of disciplines, has given me access to places (countries, seas, worlds) I had previously only dreamed about.

Growing up on an island means, of course, being surrounded by the sea. And I am obsessed by the sea. Like the mind, the sea is deep, vast, mysterious, partly fathomable (but partly unexplored), and has many moods. The sea can sometimes surprise, ideas can spring up naturally, elegantly, like dolphins leaping; thoughts surface, drift, arrive, near-random, as flotsam and jetsam to the shore. There is also the hazard of going too deeply into your own mind; this is an inherent danger, just as diving entails the physical risk of the bends. The sea is a fluid treasure-store of images. The seahorse, for example, is a tiny emblem of perfection. When I write, I am beachcombing, I am diving, I am voyaging.

Literature, of course, feeds off fighting tensions and I have always found it more natural (and, admittedly, more discomforting) to explore negative aspects of formative experience. I write frequently about love because it is (surely?) the driving force that powers the universe (Dante's 'The love that moves the sun and the other stars'). And because it is inexhaustible (Joyce, ever so clever, 'Love loves to love love'). And because . . . well, you know circumstance.

I have been both rewardingly heightened and brokenly diminished by love and I've always felt that in writing about it I might come to terms with it. Love, like poetry, can be beautiful, transfixing, life-changing, overwhelming, destructive, unfaithful, dynamic and unforgettable. It so happens that love, like poetry, feels natural and compulsory.

Enough words about words. I am an insignificant person, the bewildered product of a sorely diminished culture, and I have nothing to offer but a few poems wrought from inscrutable experience by a pen that sometimes trembles and sometimes dances.

Publications:
Love and Zen in the Outer Hebrides (Canongate, 1998)
Wish I Was Here, edited by Kevin MacNeil and Alec Finlay (pocketbooks, 2000)
Baile Beag Gun Chrìochan/A Little Borderless Village, edited by Kevin MacNeil (Highland Council, 2000)
Dalle Ebridi A Malta, main contributor (Sensibili Alle Foglie, 2000)
Be Wise Be Otherwise (Canongate, 2001)

As editor:
The Red Door: The Complete English Stories, 1949–76, by Iain Crichton Smith (Birlinn, 2001)
The Black Halo: The Complete English Stories, 1977–98, by Iain Crichton Smith (Birlinn, 2001)

Forthcoming:
Singing for the Blue Men (a novel)

UILLEAM SONA'S SONG OF LEWIS

*(To Murchadh Beag – and Lewis in general –
on the occasion of his departure)*

Eyeland of brinebitten stone, eyeland stedee an grey, eyeland of kristsheein nureeshment, to mee yoo are chust like some hyootsh froe-sin saa-mon, quietlee wise in the Celteek way. Great preepacitsht fish gifteed from God, yoo are as if sleepeeng, yea, eevin undur skies as hevee as a neekname's eye-rinee: an I tshooteefoolee pletsh yoo my undyeeng love, what with mee beeing premeeur bard of the villitsh. *Seadh*, it is of yoo-ur bald an tighteyed men I must seeng, an of yoo-ur heveewait *cailleachs*, speweeng fresh gossip into the constint salt air. Loois, yoo solid grey windswept fish, this salt is God's way of preserveeng yoo. Yoo are an Eden to us, yoo-ur tshoodishil gardinursh, an I shall also seeng of yoo-ur sweengs an roundabouts, like murdurursh, so rightlee strangild eetsh Saturday night: for it woss not hilaritee whitsh got mee where I am today. That credit, of coursh, goes to my Granee. But oh! sharpur than vineegur woss the time I left yoo, *a ghràidh*, undur some preetenshis powursh: an oll yon collitsh tot mee woss that thou hast thine own calidoneein anti-sysitheeng, with thine urlee doe-ursh an yet purminint dreenkeeng. O, eyeland of kworees an fish, Loois *a ghaoil*, my veree sustinins – *hapurr* kareektursh yoo protshoos! They are a bettur medisin than laftur or booze. It woss onlee today Murchadh Beag woss compelt by the Lord to leev the place – Murchadh who, aftur won parteekyoolur sevin day bendur, woss transforimt by Grace. O, and cam untshaynt-sheeng tshurtshyard, gardin of stone, Eden of sensibil practeesis, though I have *not yet found the coorim*, I take my tablits safe in the nolitsh that yoo-ur fragrint an bounteefool presins, like ingraind vurshis of kristsheein text, like the print flavurd rapur that cradils the fish, will be within me and about me for all my dry days.

sona – fortunate, blessed; *seadh* – well, anyway; *cailleachs* – old women; *a ghràidh* – term of affection; *a ghaoil* – term of affection; *hapurr* – such (emphatic); *not yet found the coorim* – not yet been converted, i.e. to the Free Church.

SNOW AND SALT

Trudging Princes Street in an unexpected winter
heavy with Ishouldhaves and a Gaelic carrier bag,

I can no more shake you off than
convert the Wall of China into a rollercoaster.

(How noble it is to be a man and thus have influence
over love or weather just as a flea adds

to the gravity of earth and hence the stability of Jupiter.)
Can we bring about a change in love? I believed once

that snow was a chill test, silent, bearable,
like the air in a ship which exiles share.

Yet, in this snowstorm, unending and timeless
as white jazz, as thoughts of a girl filled my eyes

with tears, snowcrystals settled on each of my irises.
Improbable, snow, I should love you! Like a comet, you
     bring us relevance.

I picture you drifting through aeons of starry flakes
passing on (unnoticed, say, as one-sided love is),

later to surface, purer, water that is more
than water, a snow-white comet launched in the night

of our grandfathers' grandfathers, whose purpose drops it
with a blinding fizzle into the brine

of a shining green sea-loch, as though to absorb
the first taste of salt could set in motion

a sea change, an ice age, a thirsting for dilution.

ALL THE CLOUDS

And it would be simpler to contain all the clouds
in a single jar unlidded
than expect this love to be returned.
Just as the wind – breathless – carries a song
and never quietens its bustle to listen,
just as a bird's shadow streams over a lake,
just as our country exists and it doesn't,
and just as our world's original dawn
will never again equal itself, but rises blushing
that it be admired as a constant failing,
so you are here and are not here,
your face a bright mist in my dreams gently fading.

FOR THE CURTAIN TWITCHERS

chust reemembur the dumb old man
one brethless, gossipeeng day
who leend against a window
an steemd it up so mutsh
he beleevd the window emtee,
the whole eyeland grey

LOST LOCH FLOATING

Lost loch floating
behind the mist
summer
is over.

AN ACARSAID

na rionnagan a' deàrrsadh 'san uisge
na rionnagan a' deàrrsadh na mo chridhe
an Cuan Sgìth mar sgàthan dorch
's do phòg mu dheireadh
air mo ghruaidh fhathast
balbh, fuar, fad air falbh
mar seann ghealach
a' cuimhneachadh air acarsaid eile

FACLAN, EICH-MHARA

nam bhruadar bha mi nam ghrunnd na mara
agus thu fhèin nad chuan trom
a' leigeil do chudruim orm
agus d' fhaclan gaoil socair nam chluasan
an dràsda 's a-rithist
òrach grinn ainneamh
man eich-mhara, man notaichean-maise
sacsafonaichean beaga fleòdradh

The harbour

the stars shining in the water the stars shining in my heart the Minch like a dark mirror and your farewell kiss still on my cheek – dumb, cold, distant – like an old moon remembering another harbour

Words, seahorses

i dreamt i was the seafloor and you were the weight of ocean pressing down on me, your quiet words of love in my ears now and again, golden, elegant and strange, like seahorses, like grace-notes, tiny floating saxophones

Introduction

from the First Edition of *Dream State*

Donny O'Rourke

Dream State presents the work of a new generation of Scottish poets. Since Scottish culture (like this anthology) has the advantage of Scots and Gaelic, two distinct and thriving poetic tongues, Scotland's newest poetry is especially rich.

In addition, these writings serve as bulletins from, and memorials to, a transforming stretch of a small country's history. A substantial number of the poems are about the state of Scotland, both actual and envisioned; yet there is nothing narrowly chauvinistic about them.

If Pound was right and poetry really is 'news that stays news', much of the verse gathered in the book has nothing to fear from the long run. As usual, Edwin Morgan puts it very well:

Normally it ought to be enough to be called a poet, *tout court*, but I feel the present moment of Scottish history very strongly and want to acknowledge it, despite the fact that my interests extend to languages, genres, and disciplines outwith Scotland or its traditions. Much modern Scottish poetry differs from poetry in the rest of the British isles by being written in Gaelic or in some form of Scots, but my point would be even if it were written in English it may be part of a hardly definable intent on in the author to help build up the image of poetry which his country presents to the world. If Scotland became independent tomorrow, there is no guarantee that it would enter a golden age of literary expression. Yet I am sure I am not mistaken in sensing, even among those who are less than sympathetic to devolutionary or wider political change, an awareness of such change which in subtle ways affects creative endeavour, suggests a gathering of forces, a desire to 'show' what can be done. The 'Scottishness' may be no more than a writer deciding to remain and work in Scotland, though wooed elsewhere; and despite my phrase 'no more than' I regard this as being important. More and more writers now take this decision. The result will be, I hope, that dedication to the art of writing will not be unaccompanied by the other dedication – to a society, to a place, to a nation – which can and will run the whole gamut from the rabid to the near-invisible.

That is the gamut this book hopes to run and I make no apology for quoting Morgan at length, because his influence on Scotland's younger poets has been enormous. In the verve and variety of his verse, the insight and generosity of his teaching and in the copious modernity of his imagination, Morgan is very much this anthology's presiding spirit. Writing in 1979 in the magazine *Aquarius*, he was responding to the coming to power of the Thatcher government and Scotland's power-lessness after a rancorously-contested, listlessly-enacted referendum had failed to secure even limited self-government.

Most of the writers in this book felt a similar need to 'acknowledge the moment.' For some, the Thatcher election was the first in which they had been eligible to vote. Our inability as a nation to opt in suffi-cient numbers for the constitutional expression of what had long been culturally obvious did not for the most part propel young writers into political activity. Disillusionment with party politics tended to find expression in cultural commitment. Of course, some explicitly political poetry was written then, and since. And yet a kind of queasy quietism does seem to have prevailed as far as day-to-day dialectics were con-cerned. The 1980s saw poem after poem present and represent this new Scotland. Or (more exactly) *Scotlands*. For the poetry was characterised by a vigorous pluralism as ideas and ideals of nation and nationhood were explored, and Scots and Gaelic took on a new impetus. Not just, or even first, in poetry. In pop and in painting. In classical music. In design. In prose. In the media. An unprecedented cultural confidence – and a *popular* cultural confidence at that – offset the torpor and timidity of the politics of the decade. Often it seemed that the poets, more confidently than the politicians, were dreaming a new state.

At a time when the map of Europe, after various velvet revolutions, is once again being bloodily redrawn, one would want to be careful about the title *Dream State*. Used here (and borrowed from a Stuart Paterson poem) the phrase should imply no narrow nationalism. As Alasdair Gray points out in his polemic *Why Scots Should Rule Scotland* 'the first people in Scotland to call themselves Scots were immigrants', and 'Wee Scotlanders' have played no part in this cultural renaissance: a Scot leaving Scotland remains one, anyone coming to live here *becomes* one. But at the same time as some writers have moved away, poets such as Robert Crawford, David Kinloch and Iain Bamforth have returned to Scotland, fulfilling Morgan's hopes for 'a society, a place, a nation', and using history to help revive and revivify the spirit and matter of Scotland.

> . . . I came back here to choose my union
> On the side of the ayes, remaining a part
>
> Of this diverse assembly – Benbecula, Glasgow, Bow of
>   Fife
> Voting with my feet, and this hand.
>   'A Scottish Assembly'

A forthright, fervent but questioning and complexly modern Scottishness informs much of the new Scottish poetry. By craftily and confidently entitling his poem (and indeed the collection it comes from) 'A Scottish Assembly', Robert Crawford thrusts poetry into the vacuum created by the lack of a legislative forum. Of course poetry *isn't* a substitute Shelleyian parliament and Crawford is kidding no one, himself least of all. But poetry can help focus and foment feeling that has no parliamentary outlet. The Scotland that Crawford speaks from and to (and therefore occasionally for) is a more self-assured and cheerful place, for all its recent social and economic travails than the country on whose behalf MacDiarmid picked up his moral mega- phone in the 1920s.

> A Scottish poet maun assume
> The burden o' his people's doom
> And dee to brak' their livin' tomb.
> (*A Drunk Man Looks At The Thistle*)

Just as Edwin Morgan (born in 1920) followed MacDiarmid's lead in dreaming up Scotlands – some of them even science fictional – so poets born in the 1950s and 1960s have joined Morgan in envisioning their own, other, better, Scotlands.

Of course, not all writers are equipped, or minded to accept such responsibilities, and lyric poetry in particular has always had a predisposition towards the personal and private. Of the writers assembled here, John Burnside, Meg Bateman, Angela McSeveney and Elizabeth Burns write an inward poetry, though a poetry that is never complacently solipsistic. More outgoing poets have their meditative moments too, *their* dream states. It isn't only in poetry that the last fifteen years or so have seen many people retreating from the crassness and craziness of much contemporary life. Their reveries are here too. As the folk singer Phil Ochs pointed out, 'in such an ugly time beauty is the true protest.'

In hoping for a poetic 'gathering of forces' Edwin Morgan expected no specific political allegiance and imposed no residency clause. Economic or emotional imperatives have kept a good number of young Scots poets furth of Scotland. That is the case with the sharply contrasting poets Carol Ann Duffy and John Burnside, each of whom left Scotland as a child and so can be said to have had little choice in the matter. Both were born in 1955 and are included in Douglas Dunn's *Faber Book of Twentieth Century Scottish Poetry* as well as in Bloodaxe's *The New Poetry*. They are this anthology's senior representatives and its starting point. Although neither has lived here for more than twenty years, the leaving of Scotland is a recurring theme in their work. As highly successful, complexly Scottish poets, writing at two kinds of remove from Scotland, Duffy and Burnside, both still comfortably under forty, establish a useful perspective. They represent a break between the established Scottish-domiciled poets who were born around 1950 – Ron Butlin, Andrew Greig, Frank Kuppner, Brian McCabe, and Tom Pow – and the poets born at the end of the decade, such as Peter McCarey, Alan Riach, Elizabeth Burns, David Kinloch, Graham Fulton and Robert Crawford.

Together, Duffy and Burnside have enjoyed considerable success issuing outstanding books from Anvil and Secker respectively. They may have left Scotland as children but Scotland, clinging tenaciously as ever, has not left them. Although they have made it clear in separate interviews that neither is comfortable being regarded as an exile, ('I just don't live there anymore', as Burnside put it) both have written poems of displacement centred on their country of birth.

Carol Ann Duffy's family moved from Glasgow to Stafford when she was just four. Her poem 'Originally', takes André Breton's conviction that 'childhood is the only reality' and twists and deepens it. In Duffy's poem 'All childhood is an emigration'. The wee girl's cry, 'I want our own country', is one that echoes far beyond one uprooted childhood in the Potteries. In another poem, the Scottish phrase, 'what like is it' (for 'what's it like') triggers nostalgia for mother and motherland both:

I am homesick, free, in love
with the way my mother speaks.
'The Way My Mother Speaks'

The way Carol Ann Duffy speaks, whether in her monologues, in her love lyrics, or in her observational pieces, reveals one of the most supple and compelling voices in the poetry of the Dis-United Kingdom; one that sounds something like a more astringent and sardonic version of her friend Liz Lochhead's. 'Translating the English', something Carol Ann Duffy has been forced to do since primary school, introduces us to a wink-wink wideboy, doing a spot of back-of-a-lorry freelancing in the Heritage Industry. He'll sell the tourists anything. Or almost anything.

You will be knowing of Charles Dickens and Terry Wogan
and Scotland. All this can be arranged for cash no questions.
Ireland not on.

In our Banana Monarchy, Scotland too, is seldom 'on'. Duffy's verse is a surveillance camera trained on the greedy and the seedy. She misses nothing except the distant decencies of the recent past.

No one has better caught the vicious vacuousness of England in the 1980s. In another virtuoso (and Morganesque) monologue, a *Sun* headline writer boasts oafishly of his masterpiece; the poem is called 'Poet for our Times'. And that's precisely and eloquently what its creator is too. Duffy, for all her sometimes erotic and intimate lyricism, also writes outspoken poems about the condition of the state.

John Burnside, by contrast, is a poet of eternity, of dream. Although his break with Catholicism is less vituperative and final than Duffy's, it is a sufficiently marked severance to prevent him being considered as a conventional Catholic poet. His even-tempered, exquisitely-worked poems burn with a steady votive glow. Their externally focused, yet profoundly inward intensity gives Burnside's poems a vigil-like watchfulness; a meditational calm. Yet Scotland nags away at him too. 'Dundee' begins:

> The streets are waiting for a snow
> that never falls:
> too close to the water,
> too muffled in the afterwarmth of jute

This is the weather forecast by T. S. Eliot. But even without the snow-fall of grace, redemption is possible for: 'the one who stands here proven after all'. It is not, I think, coincidental that this 'proving' occurs in Scotland, or for that matter Dundee, the city of *Discovery*, and self-discovery, features prominently in this anthology.

Given John Burnside's underplaying of the notion of exile, a poem entitled 'Exile's Return' might be suspected of irony. It seems guilty only of ambivalence about an 'identity/to be assumed like tartan'. To ask 'Do we know/where we are in these tourist hills?' is to seek bearings that are at least partly spiritual. Burnside, whose father left Cowdenbeath for Corby in the early 1960s has a poem called 'Flitting', whose very title exposes differences between Burnside's two cultures and their languages. His flitting one suspects was very much a removal, a dislocation that draws him back in search of solace. Yet the past and its comforts cannot always be relied upon:

> Memory, you should have known,
> is a double agent:
>
> one of those gaberdine
> people in films, a smiling
>
> Harry Lime.
>
> 'Anamnesis'

Burnside has spoken of his fascination with Orson Welles. (Author of *F for Fake*, and, in *The Third Man*, the embodiment of the deceitful double agent.) But if his poems go to a film occasionally, they never lose themselves in it. The cinema is just another means of investigating the gap and overlap between being and seeming. Duffy has a fondness for the movies too. But she uses her film clips to zoom in on specific states of mind, particular people. John Burnside's is the poetry of the tacit, the implicit. Of the poets selected here, his disciplined brushwork is the deftest, his verbal surfaces the most delicate. John Burnside is the book's most 'domestic' poet and Home, whether in 'home rule' or the search for roots or emotional stability, is certainly prominent in this anthology. Burnside's homing instinct is pronounced, fervent and quietly expressed. This is characteristic:

> Silence is possible, and after dark
> it almost happens: silence, like a glove,
> the perfect fit you always hoped to find.
>
> 'Silence is possible'

The serenely ontological poetry of John Burnside not only demonstrates that silence is possible; it observes it.

Duffy and Burnside allow the reader to share revealing vantage points from which a real but lost Scotland can be glimpsed. Almost polar in their formal and tonal distance from each other, these poets represent at times this anthology's two governing tendencies. On the one hand, a public poetry, a poetry of the state and its affairs that is often engaged and frequently enraged; on the other a more private, ruminative and detached verse, a poetry of dream. It's an over-simplification but I think an allowable one to see these extremes in the poetry produced in Scotland in the 1980s and early 1990s, and to see poem after poem combining 'state' and 'dream' in differing proportions. Naturally, this being Scotland 'whaur extremes meet' and where the theme of 'doubleness' haunts our literature, these polarities regularly collide in the work of the *same* poets. Whitman's grandiloquent *carte blanche* 'very well I contradict myself. I am vast. I contain multitudes' has never seemed to me adequate to encompass the thrawn rivenness of the Scottish psyche. Carol Ann Duffy for instance is at once a *performing* and a *confiding* poet, one for whom Scotland is an emotional rather than intellectual entity.

Attempts to encompass, understand and explain Scotland are central to the practices and procedures of the group of poet-critics associated with the magazines *Verse* and *Gairfish*. Although these writers do not represent any kind of formal grouping, various factors link the work of Robert Crawford, W. N. Herbert, David Kinloch, Peter McCarey, Alan Riach, and Richard Price. All have published books of criticism. All except Riach and McCarey edit literary journals. Edwin Morgan has taught some and influenced all of them. Each writes a vividly-voiced and individual verse. Yet in its intellectual breadth, confident absorption and redeployment of poetic source material (MacDiarmid and Morgan especially), its capacity for cosmopolitan sophistication and a very Scottish directness, its rapport with both Europe and America, its deep interest in popular culture, Scottish history and the mass media, above all in its conscious (occasionally self-conscious) ambition to be newly Scottish and yet unbounded, the poetry of these six writers does have a good deal in common. Price has dubbed this group the 'Scottish Informationists', though it remains to be seen whether the label will stick.

Robert Crawford, the most prominent of them, has the clearest and most carrying voice and is beginning to establish a place for himself outwith the literary world where he has made considerable impact both as poet and critic. Douglas Dunn included him in his Faber anthology. He appears also in *The New Poetry*. Dunn's work was an influence on Crawford's long before they became colleagues at St Andrews University after the older poet's very public and conscious decision to return to Scotland. Possessed of an uncommonly cheerful poetic disposition, Crawford is inclined to hail rather than mourn the past. 'Opera', which demonstrates an almost Elizabethan relish for emblematic embellishment, brings together two of Crawford's preoccupations: industry and childhood. Remembering watching his mother working at her sewing-machine, the poet tells us:

> To me as a young boy
> That was her typewriter. I'd watch
> Her hands and feet in unison, or read
> Between her calves the wrought-iron letters:
> SINGER. Mass-produced polished wood and metal,
> It was a powerful instrument.

In 'Inner Glasgow', a sixties childhood of *Look and Learn* and 'pit bings' is contrasted with the de-industrialised present:

> Where docks are cultivated, hard nostalgia
> Steam-rivets us to ghosts we love,

In this Glasgow,

> . . . everybody looks the same and sings
> Of oppression, smokes, drinks lager, shouts out 'fuck'.

Typically however the poem *refuses* nostalgia, ending in affirmation: the adult will return to Glasgow to marry and to write.

Even stronger evidence of a new patriotism (by which I mean a clear-headed, historically sophisticated, sensitively *inter*nationalist and conditional affection for one's native place) is provided by Crawford's increasingly anthologised signature poem, 'Scotland'. Here, with a startling precision worthy of MacCaig, Scotland is seen from the air as a 'semiconductor country, land crammed with intimate expanses'. Instead of the lochs and brochs of conventional poetic diction, we find Scotland extolled in the jargon of the 'silicon glen' on which so much of our industrial future now depends. The poem's conclusion is one many young Scots are inclined to jump to,

> . . . among circuitboard crowsteps
>
> To be miniaturised is not small-minded.
> To love you need more details that the Book of Kells –
> Your harbours, your photography, your democratic intellect
> Still boundless, chip of a nation.

In his bold appropriation of the technical to express his Scottishness, Crawford exhibits a pedigree that owes something to late MacDiarmid and middle-period Morgan. Knowledge, its acquisition, categorisation and transmission – the poetry hums with it Much of it is of course owed to Scots who inspire Crawford to celebration as well as cerebration: Alexander Graham Bell; the founders of the *Encyclopaedia Britannica*, of the *OED*; J. G. Frazer, Logie Baird, Grierson, Reith, 'knowledge engineers' all, and many of them discussed in Crawford's prose book *Devolving English Literature* (1992).

Our immature and risible national obsession with the Scottish angle, our stolid determination to prove that even celebrities who are manifestly not Scottish can somehow be fielded in the Scottish team is hilariously sent up in Crawford's 'Alba Einstein'. Here the physicist is posthumously 'outed' as a closet Glaswegian inspiring the usual tacky panoply of identity-undermining cultural merchandising including 'the A.E. Fun Park', and 'Albert Suppers' complete with 'The Toast to the General Theory'. Aye, right enough! This is a woundingly witty poem about just how complex a collective inferiority complex can be. Crawford is comfortably, even ardently Scottish. Aware as a Scot of living 'between and across languages', he wastes no time debating which to use. Like all the poets in *Dream State* he uses the language that's to hand and most appropriate for what he wants to do. Of the comic potential which has always existed in the onomatopoeic expressiveness of Scots, he takes full advantage. By occasionally offering one of his

Scots poems and a bathetically undermining 'translation' of it on the facing page, in the way for example that Gaelic verse is often presented, he not only reminds us of the essential untranslatability of poetry (though he is an accomplished 'owersetter' from other tongues), but also questions wider relationships between the English and the Scots. This typographical split-screen, much used by Ashbery and Derrida, gives a double emphasis to Crawford's point about the complexity of modern communications.

There was nothing complex however about 'Ghetto-Blastir', Crawford's mid-1980s declaration of intent. It set out to cause a stooshie and did. The Scottish literary establishment at whom it was aimed got the message (very) loud and clear.

> Ghetto-makers, tae the knackirs
> Wi aw yir schemes, yir smug dour dreams
> O yir ain feet. Yi're beat
> By yon new Scoatlan loupin tae yir street

Crawford announced with a typically guileful play on dog's 'lead' and poet's 'leid',

> . . . we're grabbin

> Whit's left o the leid tae mak anither sang
> O semiconductors, . . .

And that change is precisely what he and his peers have engineered.

W. N. Herbert, who though slightly younger than Crawford, was his contemporary at Oxford, publishing with him *Sterts and Stobies* (1985), the shared pamphlet in which 'Ghetto-Blastir' first appeared, and handles Scots with even greater audacity. He argues (a bit disingenuously one suspects) that his Dundonian provides a S=C=O=T=S corollary to the L=A=N=G=U=A=G=E poetry emerging in the US. Too much of his output is organised around the personality of an identifiable seeing 'I', a poetic progenitor, for it to qualify as being language-led. The temptation of his gifts as a lyric poet of remarkable feeling and finesse are (thankfully) too alluring. But in their aural veracity and lexical brio, his experiments with the urban Scots of Dundee correspond to Tom Leonard's pioneering work in Glaswegian.

The sharp, cocky, yet tender 'Eh' (Dundonian for 'I') of Herbert's verse in Scots owes something to MacDiarmid on whose poetry he has published a critical study, *To Circumjack MacDiarmid* (1992), and to whom he offers homage in several poems. It also owes something to the

Americans Ginsberg and O'Hara and even something to McGonagall, whom he invokes in poem after poem. Master of a pungent postmodern pawkiness (a quality he shares interestingly enough with his fellow Dundonian, the singer-songwriter Michael Marra) Herbert finds in the city he left as a schoolboy a much more than local significance. Dundee, which regularly deputises on film as an Eastern European capital, is both more, and less, than Scotland, and as such well up to the sometimes cosmic demands Herbert makes of it. Dundee is, as he has delightedly noticed, an anagram of '*duende*', and Herbert's work can be construed as a kind of Tayside *canto jonde*. For him, as for John Burnside, Dundee is a place of 'provings'.

The 'Dundee Doldrums' written in his very early twenties after the example of Ginsberg, anatomise the city magnificently:

> Whaur ur yi Dundee? Whaur's yir Golem buriit?
> Whaur doon yir pendies lurks it?
> Broon brick, eldscoorit, timedustchoakit,
> blin windies – whaur's MacGonnagal's hert?
>
> '2nd Doldrum, Elephant's Graveyard'

Perhaps because his gifts are so many, so evident, and in inverse proportion to the notice they have attracted so far, Herbert takes a satirical interest in hierarchies and 'placings'. Though accomplished, Herbert's poems in English haven't quite the tang of his work in Scots. This places him at a disadvantage with critics outside Scotland. Many poems poke marvellously malicious fun at Scot Lit's High Heidyins and for all its mordant self-deprecation, 'Mappamundi', Herbert's 'poetic map o thi warld', exposes a real wound. Under the new dispensation, 'Ireland's bin shufted tae London' and 'Th'anerly ithir bits in Britain ur Oaxfurd an Hull.' A 'bittern storm aff Ulm' he may claim to be but his abilities and confidence move him closer to the centre of the literary map all the time.

Though anarchist in temper and a far from confirmed or conventional nationalist, Herbert (with his co-editor Richard Price) has used the magazine *Gairfish* to advance the cause of a 'McAvantgarde', one of whose most intellectually adventurous members is David Kinloch. An exact contemporary of Robert Crawford's, both at Glasgow and Oxford universities, and an editor with him of the international journal *Verse*, Kinloch writes a crammed, jammed, elusive poetry full of recondite Scots words and people, a poetry nonetheless capable of heart-tugging lyricism. Producing prose poems along more or less Rimbaudian lines *and* arias for the new Scotland, Kinloch (a university teacher of French) is a poet who has only recently found his own confident voice. Much of the explicitly and contentedly gay poetry Kinloch is now writing centres on 'Dustie-Fute', a juggler, an acrobat, a gay Orpheus, descended perhaps from Edwin Morgan's equally precariously poised circus performer, Cinquevalli. Certainly it is a relief (not just for him) that unlike Morgan he can write, as a *young* man, a poem like 'Warmer Bruder' at once a meditation of the fate of gay men in the concentration camps, a poem about Aids and a love lyric of understated power. Much more than 'simply' a gay poet, Kinloch is a *European* writer who has come home to Glasgow, and is determinedly saying for Scotland. 'The Tear in Pat Kane's Voice' ('tear' as in rip) reflects and adds to the *popular* culture of his city and his country.

> The tear in Pat Kane's voice
> Offers you a man's name,
> Whiter and harder than Alba:
>
> Adorno at his plain table,
> Rubbing out the barbaric lyrics
> Of post-Auschwitz poets

Like David Kinloch, Peter McCarey is steeped in French, making his living as a translator in Geneva. He also speaks Russian and developed his doctoral dissertation into a book, *Hugh MacDiarmid and the Russians* (1988). Sharing Edwin Morgan's love of Russian poetry and his keenness to translate from it, McCarey maintains a close link to Morgan that found practical expression in a series of collaborations in which the poets would a take it in turn to 'deconstruct' a well-known poem, publishing their versions together. These 'rehabs', as McCarey christened them, demonstrate his quasi-structural passion for adaptation and renovation; for what's underneath. Thus the May 1968 graffito 'Sous les pavés – la plage' finds a poem springing up around it, one in which 'money is buying itself up'. This is also what's happening in the Glasgow of the Garden Festival, symbol of Glasgow's continuing, civic regeneration where some very ambiguous rehabilitation is going on:

> It's good: I don't have far to go
> from my refurbished close
> to see the butcher's apron on a sign set
> boldly in the weeping sump . . .
>
> 'Garden City'

His whole (unpretentiously) semiotic search for meaning is 'a sign set boldly in the weeping sump'. McCarey keeps a sceptical eye on the same spoiled and despoiled state as Carol Ann Duffy, the Britain of 'Wimpey Super Singles' and mass-communicated hucksterism whose motto could be 'it's what the people who want you to want it want you to want'. Such poetry can be too cranially crammed for its own good; and a lot of it operates at dangerously low temperatures. But McCarey's voice is worth straining to hear.

His Scotland (viewed from Europe) is a lot less enchanting than Crawford's, Herbert's and Kinloch's. As the US Marine points out to the Holy Loch protester who wants America's missiles sited in the middle of nowhere, 'Lady/I'm from Brooklyn: believe me/this IS the middle of nowhere' . . . On McCarey's 'Mappamundi', Scotland is wee and peripheral, its identity determined negatively in relation to what it's not, its existential benchmarks provided more and more by America. In 'Not Being Bob De Niro', McCarey mounts a neo-Thomist inquiry into Scotland's contemporary condition, setting out his stall at the same time.

> I want to do things that will
> last because they have
> substance as well as quality.
> Didn't Duns Scotus say that?

He did. But it sums up McCarey's credo, his celluloid-like capacity to capture and fix. Or as a whole short poem has it, 'OED' (dictionaries again!):

> Every word in the language is laid out here
> with its meaning on a tag tied round its big toe.
> And here's me trying mouth to mouth.

These days Alan Riach's resuscitations are attempted from New Zealand, where he is a university teacher specialising in Scottish literature. He and Peter McCarey have a great deal in common. Both wrote doctoral theses on MacDiarmid. Both admire and correspond with Edwin Morgan. There's an ultra-contemporary, purposively fragmented cast to their minds. Neither has much time for notions of authorship pure and simple. Though stopping short (through a provident sufficiency of Scottish common sense) of naïvely accepting the structuralist slogans of 'the world as text' and 'the death of the author', Riach has worked witty and admiring variations on poems by Olson, Ashbery and Blackburn among others. These echo McCarey's rehabs and Herbert's 'doldrums'. Riach and McCarey have collaborated on a booklet length philosophical detective poem too integrally dense and narratively ravelled to permit inclusion here. They are the most comprehensively 'postmodern' poets in the anthology. Yet for all that, Riach has a plain-spoken, sonorous, lyric gift. Whereas MacDiarmid allowed information to overwhelm the lyric in his later poetry, all the 'Informationist' poets seek to sing as well as tell.

Selectively influenced by America, it is not only when he is deliberately reworking Black Mountain or New York School poems, that Alan Riach adopts an American accent. In the way that many of our pop and rock and jazz singers do he absorbs *while* remaining sincerely his own man. The Ashberian plangency of 'The Blues', 'You're out there somewhere, going to a concert in wide company . . .' is judicious and fine. Again like McCarey, Riach surveys Scotland from afar, in his case, Waikato. But for all the reminiscing, the evocations of childhood and loss, Riach has a classic Scottish immigrant's practicality and application. Allen Curnow can be heard in some of Riach's recent work. 'The Blues' is just one of the poems set in his adopted country that suggest that Riach has it in him to become an important *New Zealand* poet. But as a companionable and funny 'found' poem (not included here but well worth seeking out) reveals, he can still count on 'A Christmas Card from Edwin Morgan!'

The youngest of this loose grouping of 'Informationist' poets is Richard Price, who is an editor both of *Gairfish* and of *Verse*. A curator in the British Library in London, he has published a study of Neil Gunn's fiction. Born in Reading, raised in Renfrewshire, his Scottishness is elective, discriminating and passionately energetic. Price's Vennel Press has published a number of the poets in *Dream State*. His poems have a taut and tantalising obliquity about them, a lyric leanness that compounds their emotional force. Family, married love, cars, buses and trains again and again return him to the question of identity.

> I'd have called a 'flitting' but it was a year before I was born –
> to my father it was 'moving house.'
> He was Ma's envoy in Scotland:
> he'd just chosen a field
> that would grow into a bungalow
> and he'd pay for it
> whenever the bathroom,
> opening on the hall
> with a frosted glass door,
> trapped her, towelnaked
> before the postman
> and something to be signed for.
>
> 'Hinges'

'Flitting' is just as evocative a word and concept for Price as it is for John Burnside. Busily editing and agitating in London, Price has become one of our envoys in England. His poem 'With is' ends with a characteristic sense of removal:

> Our table is empty,
> a summer curling pond.
> Come on out on the town
> (I've the nightbus map you lent me
> when I was only a Scot)

Although he is a Doctor of Medicine rather than Philosophy, Iain Bamforth writes a well-read, uncompromisingly intellectual verse that's inclined to wear its learning brightly. While he shares philosophical, moral and aesthetic concerns with the poets considered above, he has published infrequent critical essays and edits no magazine. What really sets him apart from his contemporaries is his diagnostic gloom about Scotland, a dyspepsia he suffers more glumly than McCarey. Gramsci's 'pessimism of the intellect' has seldom been more balefully expressed. Crawford's 'optimism of the will' is mostly absent from these dour, dismal (and linguistically resourceful) poems. Bamforth's Scotland, a 'land of dissent and magnificent defeats', with its 'subtle theology of failure', a 'threadbare, ruinous country', where the 'servile myths, skite home' is a sermon his imagination broods on between sorties to Paris or New York, Polynesia or New Mexico. As widely read as he is widely travelled, Bamforth has a bulging steamer-trunk imagination. 'Alibis' features the 'ultimate collector', a figure whom this poet occasionally resembles. His Scotland has 'grown owlish with hindsight', a form of epistemological eyestrain these younger poets avoid, despite their close reading of Scottish history. Much exercised by his conception of Calvinist Geography, Bamforth puts theology to approximately the same use as Crawford puts technology. Like McCarey, he is an explicitly though not consistently postmodern poet interested in 'the semiotics of couscous' and 'the semiologists of bliss' and adrift in a world where recently it has 'all hardened into permanent lateness'. The arch, posed, Bohemianism of the poems he delivers 'in character' evoke not only the resilient Les Murray but also Ashbery or Ash at their most exquisitely salonesque and aphoristic – an almost gaudily gifted writer.

Kathleen Jamie's achievement depends less on the accretion of images and ideas than on their paring down. The honed flinty poems in *Black Spiders* got her noticed before she was out of her teens. She is one of the youngest poets in Douglas Dunn's Faber anthology and is part of the Scottish contingent in *The New Poetry*. There's a feisty candour to her work, a take it or leave it self-possession, a formal purity, that makes Jamie's the least paraphrasable, the most stripped down, the *sheerest* poetry in this anthology. Her collaboration with Andrew Greig, *A Flame In Your Heart* (not sampled here), in which she wrote in the persona of a nurse in love with, and pregnant by, a young Battle of Britain pilot (Greig), demonstrated a knack for monologue narrative and impersonation. Her own voice, whether in love, 'Things Which Never Shall Be', or in jest, 'Arraheids', in English, 'A Shoe', or in Scots, 'Xiahe', is attractive and assured. 'The way we live', Kathleen Jamie's best known poem, is looser and more headlong than a lot of her work; a joyous, jazzy inventory, it has affinities with the poetry of Morgan, and of Crawford and his ilk. Jamie's increasing fondness for Scots and her willingness to write explicitly about Scotland align her recent poems fairly closely with some of the writers considered above. She is however blazingly original. The staccato rhythms, the clear, curt, discourse, the juggling with the workaday and the wondrous – these mark Jamie out. It is in her work that the disparate poetics of John Burnside and Carol Ann Duffy are most satisfyingly balanced.

Thus a beachcombed shoe on the shore at Cramond occasions first a meditation, then a declaration:

> those shoes – stupid
> as a moon walkers'; ah
> the comfort of gravity.

The 'wedge of rubber gateau' becomes (literally) a 'platform' for affirmation:

> God, girls we'd laugh –
> it's alright once you're in
> it's alright
> once you're out the other side

Getting across is consistently a concern with Jamie. 'Permanent Cabaret', maroons its high wire artiste protagonist halfway, leaving her high and dry while:

> The audience wonder: is it part of the show
> this embarrassing wobbling,
> this vain desperation to clutch

Jamie, too, 'knowing nothing of fear', will take 'sparkling risks fifty feet high'

Another poem 'The Republic of Fife' finds her perched on her Fife rooftop, from which she can see 'Europe, Africa, the Forth and Tay Bridges'. Do *we* 'dare let go lift our hands and wave to the waving citizens of all those other countries'? Jamie's cosmopolitan and inclusive poetry is informed and often inspired by her journeys. Her travel prose is no less fine than her poetry. These fearless comings and goings sharpen her perspective on Scotland. Her tough-minded, though never flamboyantly intellectual, verse is as hospitably open and international as any currently being produced in Britain.

'Living in Berlin' and 'Poems of Departure' indicate that Elizabeth Burns, too, sees Scotland in context. Separation and suspension are recurring themes. In New York, 'in the place between daylight and darkness/in the place between your being here and leaving' the poet is 'wrenched between the old world and the new'. In Berlin she can see, 'wall's space like a tooth gap/explore soft new places with the tongue'. 'Valda's Poem', like several in this anthology, evokes MacDiarmid though it keeps him off stage. Here, it is his wife Valda who addresses us while Chris and Norman MacCaig make a recording indoors. What might have been a (justified) act of feminist revisionism turns out to have no axe to grind. It's a dreamy but meticulous reconstruction of a moment and a mood, something at which this poet excels.

Angela McSeveney is a more forthright poet. Her recent first book was entitled *Coming Out With It*. And she usually is. Hers is the most autobiographically revealing poetry in this collection. Many of her poems were written in and about a severe psychological crisis and amount to a very moving record of a bout of self-administered psychotherapy. Utterly devoid of self-pity, they succeed (as similarly motivated explorations often fail to do) as poems *and* therapy. Nor is McSeveney's exploration of her self only psychological. Her work is full of proddings, partings and inspections. After the removal of a non-malignant lump in her breast, the fifteen-year-old poet ponders her nakedness.

> I felt ashamed
> that the first man to see me
> had only been doing his job.
> 'The Lump'

This most tactile of poets is always picking at her wounds. 'For the Best' recalls an actual sexual encounter punning with the phrase 'You rubbed me up the wrong way' in describing a cackhanded initiation. Size and sex are constant preoccupations in McSeveney's poetry. Her customary tone in discussing these themes is one of a wryly protective self-deprecation as in the splendid 'The Fat Nymphomaniac's Poem'. Her Confessional candour allied to a sleekit sense of humour make Angela McSeveney a most engaging confider. That her poems are sparklingly clear makes being her confidant all the more pleasurable. She is not, however, her only subject. 'Night Shift' is a beautifully brought-off study in parental non-communication and 'The Pictures' tells a horrific tale with deadpan panache.

The openness and amiability of Jackie Kay's prize-winning *The Adoption Papers* was warmly praised when the story of her adoption as a black child by a white Scottish couple was published in 1991. Kay's expert handling of the poem's three voices – the two mothers' and the child's, her selection of telling detail, her narrative flair – these announced her as the intending dramatist she has since successfully become. Black. Lesbian. And a Scot: her status as an outsider is triply underscored. And yet hers is perhaps the friendliest and most 'upbeat' poetry in the book. A poetry that succeeds (as Liz Lochhead's does or as Tony Harrison's can) in being both consummate and popular. In its locus (The Campsies) and in its joyousness 'Pounding Rain' conjures up Morgan again:

> I stroked your silk skin
> until we were back in the Campsies, running
> down the hills in the pounding rain,
> screaming and laughing; soaked right through.

Fresh, chatty, funny, yet capable of great depth and seriousness, Jackie Kay's is one of the most hugely likeable new poetic voices. Her recent work not only consolidates her achievement but extends her range into a variety of genres and media: stage and TV drama, poetry for children, lyrics and social commentaries.

Also black, also lesbian, also living in England, Maud Sulter, a photographer and performance artist as well as a poet, has a less instantly recognisable voice, one influenced by a number of black American poets but a voice capable nonetheless of incantatory rage and tender fragility. 'As a Blackwoman' shows Sulter as angry, 'unpoetic' ('As a Blackwoman every act is a personal act'). Other poems are conventionally tender. 'Drich Day', a simple, sad, poem of leave-taking finds the poet and her loved one on the links at St Andrews with:

> nothing between us and Denmark
> except that tomorrow you leave me.

Much of Sulter's anger at sexual and class injustice is shared by Alison

Kermack, who, instead of finding or cultivating a voice of her own, has simply (and effectively) taken over Tom Leonard's. This sounds strange, and is. But *what* she has to say survives the ventriloquism, and Kermack's is merely the most extreme example of Leonard's influence on many young poets.

> it wiz hardur tay buleev in
> upwurdmubility
> when thay pit barbed wire
> oan toappy thi lectric fens
> thit ran roon thi skeem'
>
>   'Ikariss'

Meg Bateman's soulfully reflective poetry is at almost every conceivable remove from Alison Kermack's. Bateman's work, which I am able to appreciate only through its author's translations from the Gaelic, seems only circumstantially and incidentally contemporary: timeless verse written in, but not always of, modern Scotland. Hers is in a particular sense a 'dream state'. Bateman's academic interests are in the Gaelic religious poetry written by women in the fifteenth century. Her rhymed metrical verse is cast in traditional forms, whose force and felicity have been strenuously praised. Yet Bateman is a learner of the language, coming to it and indeed to poetry while at university in Edinburgh. That city forms the backdrop for much of her verse, a lot of it elegiac. Lost love and the adventures of an intricate heart are memorialised with almost Petrarchan dolefulness. But Bateman's passionate plaintiveness, the all too evident pain and searing sincerity move and convince. In recent years, happiness in Bateman's personal life has kept her muse away. 'A Letting Go Of Dreams' reads worryingly like a letting-go of poetry.

> No one man do I mourn
> but a life-time's longing,
> every unmade choice
> slipping from me
> because of you, fair man.

That loss would be *ours* to mourn. For Bateman is one of the most haunted and haunting of contemporary poets.

It is older Gaelic poets who appear to engage most energetically with the here and now, in particular, Fearghas MacFhionnlaigh, Crisdean Whyte and Aonghas MacNeacail. There are reasons of temper and tradition for Gaeldom's reluctance to modernise its poetic practices.

The urge to preserve not merely language but form is understandably strong. Anne Frater (the youngest poet in *Dream State*), a writer from the same Lewis village as both Iain Crichton Smith and Derick Thomson, is only slightly more 'modern' in outlook than Meg Bateman. At a time when Gaelic is *much* more discussed than spoken, she is, however, acutely aware of her cultural responsibilities. One might wish in fact for a little *less* responsibility and a little more youthful zest. With the recent government investment in Gaelic television (bringing soap opera and other contemporary genres into the language) and renewed interest in Celtic music, there is an audience beyond Gaeldom for a poetry as open and accessible as Bateman's and Frater's. What is lacking in Scotland, as opposed to Ireland, is much sense of young writers using an ancient language to grapple with the present. A vehement and vocal nationalist, Frater has many contemporary concerns; her '9th November 1989', a celebration of the Berlin Wall's destruction, shows that the there and then (and the here and now) can be grist for young writers.

> An old woman comes
> to the Brandenburg Gate,
> which is not yet open
> as wide as the rest,
> a young soldier goes to her
> and she stands firm
> looking at her path
> laid out at her feet
> like steps of permission,
> pulling her,
> drawing her,
> and she moves again,
> and she watches the youth
> daring him
> to turn her back.

Maybe there will be less turning back in Frater's work in due course.

This predisposition is not confined to Gaelic. Writing in a lovely, unaffected, gravid Scots, the Fife poet William Hershaw displays a similar predilection for the backward glance. Given the scale and suddenness of the industrial change visited upon the mining, fishing and other industries of Fife, a tendency towards the elegiac is hardly surprising. Hershaw does, however, use the past to inform the future. 'Comp' poignantly memorialises Hershaw's grandfathers, Comp and Wull, with their 'quiet and kenspeckle dignity'. What's being mourned here, with and through the passing of the two old miners, is the passing of a way of life. Of his place in the continuum of culture, community and family, Hershaw is acutely aware. 'They twa ware the making o me', he says attributing the 'sma worth' of his poems to his upbringing by his working-class parents. Given its restricted audience, all writing in Gaelic or Scots is an act of commitment. Well-versed in, and an adept translator from, the French poetry of the late nineteenth century, this poet is anything but unsophisticated. His commitment to birthplace, birthright and language is highly conscious. 'Januar Winds o Revolution', chides Fife and Scotland for their cowardice and complacency at a time when Eastern Europe was in ferment:

> The cauld wind o reality yowls sairly past the Labour Club
> Singan that in Prague, Berlin and Bucharest
> Are the fowk wi a speerit and smeddum.

Dreaming of a Scottish state, though in a more conventional Scots than Crawford or Herbert, Hershaw is a young Scottish poet readily prepared to assume with MacDiarmid 'the burden of a people's doom', while developing a sense of honest self-criticism.

This birthright for the Shetlandic writer Robert Alan Jamieson encompasses not only poetry in the fertile language of his native island but experimental verse, plays and novels in English. Finding inspiration in MacDiarmid's sojourn on Whalsay, Jamieson has written both poetry and criticism devoted to that poet. Jamieson's love of ideas, his tendency towards abstraction, his fearless and unembarrassed (and maybe even un-Scottish) willingness to 'think big' mostly find expression in English. Only Jamieson, of the young writers gathered here, bears any trace of Kenneth White's influence. In his native tongue and with native themes, Jamieson is more earthed and earthy, producing a gloriously rich and mysterious Scots whose Nordic shimmer requires recourse to the glossary, even for readers familiar with the language. Most of what he has to say about Shetland's (or Scotland's) oil, he has said adroitly in prose, but the verse sequence 'A Day at the Scottish Office' lays bare the national psyche and psychosis with a twitchy quirkiness reminiscent of the Davids, Byrne and Lynch. 'Resistin the National Psychosis (9 April 1992)' is this anthology's only poem occasioned by John Major's unexpected election victory, a reversal much hated in Scotland:

> I'm a diamond –
> I will never fuckin crack –
> Rough uncut and smaa
> I roll aroond yer jeweller's scale
> but I am unassayable –

Despite being less overtly political, the Paisley poet Graham Fulton comes on just as strong. He's read Bukowski; he attended workshops with Tom Leonard. You can hear them both in Fulton. But he has developed an original poetic personality that's aggressively his own. This is 'in your face' poetry, verse as stand-up comedy; even on the page every Fulton poem is a *performance*, while on the stage Fulton puts his work over with a pugnacity and aplomb uncommon among poets.

His is also a cinematic poetry, although this is a '*cinéma pauvre*' shot on 'super-eight', all grainy slo-mo and jumpcuts. Or then again, it can be grandiose and Cormanesque. But if Fulton is often Poe-Faced he is never po-faced. In Fulton's febrile imagination the television seems always to be on, spilling out Danny Kaye, or Neil Armstrong or John Boy Walton or The Monkees to take their chances with bit parts in a Fulton poetic snuff movie. Not so much post as hyper or mega-modern, Fulton's poems vibrate with a strobing, trippy sourness. Having been to the same America as Edwin Morgan, Fulton has brought back a scarier poetics. He is less a dream than a nightmare state. 'Charles Manson Auditions for the Monkees' represents a characteristic cultural conjunction (this one based on an actual event). It is also, like a lot of Fulton, tackily and blackly humorous:

> Charlie wants
> > to be an Axe-hero,
> Charlie has mastered
> > tricky chord changes,
> Charlie has memorised lines
> > that
> the Beatles haven't written
> > yet.

Emerging campily from the Golly Gosh Gothic of 'The Unmasking Scene' to wonder 'what I required to be an artist in the Eighties' the poet receives this answer:

> A vicious streak is
> > fine and dandy
> a fucked-up life can
> > come in handy

Quite. The grin-and-bare-it locale for these seamy shenanigans is a Los Angelised Paisley denied even the bilious bonhomie local boys John Byrne and Gordon Williams took refuge in. His Scotland often resembles Williams':

We knew our country was a small time dump
where nothing ever happened and
there was nothing to do.
And nobody had a name like Jelly Roll Morton.

Fulton's response to the various poverties around him is to hallucinate a poetry in which *anything* can happen, a verse which always has something to do – even if it's only striking attitudes all day.

Yet the anguish of real lives in hard times is not cheapened by Fulton's lurid posturing. His chippy lack of sentimentality, his excoriating ability not merely to describe but to *embody* frustration, the detached hipness of his technique, all these serve to amplify the scream. The width of contemporary Scottish poetry can be measured in the respective responses to de-industrialisation of a William Hershaw and a Graham Fulton. Where they concur is in their unwillingness to provide happy endings. In 'Goodnight John Boy', King Kong's demise is a reminder that, 'the bi-planes get us all in the end' a certainty that Fulton compounds by tailing off the poem in mid-sentence.

Raymond Friel is an Irish Catholic from Greenock who favours simplicity in his discourse. His is another sixties Scottish childhood cooried into and picked over for succour and significance. In his poems we watch as Greenock is transformed from a forest of iron into a 'dole town'. Teaching now in London, Friel can get a good unmuzzy look at Scotland and its past, the rituals, observances and nuances of which he reconstructs tenderly. The lower Clyde he comes home to, in order to celebrate 'Hogmanay', is a place transformed by the loss of livelihood and way of life. And the identity-shaping folklore that died with it. The old myths and dreams no longer serve. A state of grace has given way to stasis. Nowadays,

We don't go in
So much for myths,

Believing more
Often than not,
That life's exactly
What it looks like.

Don Paterson's is a world in which what you see is definitely what you get. The same age as Friel, he has already had his first volume made PBS Choice. His brusque, knowing tones are unmistakably contemporary. John Martyn's on the soundtrack. It's cool. Paterson is so cool he'll even interrupt his poems to make ludic, little postmodern guest appearances in them. Sometimes the poems seem to just scowl inscrutably, too mean to mean. None of which stops this being poetry of the first order. Paterson invites (and should fear nothing from) comparison with his English counterparts, Glyn Maxwell and Simon Armitage. The existential dreichness of Dundee and the wider world for which it acts as fall guy is caught precisely in the title poem of his first book *Nil Nil*. Paterson has configured Dundee as 'Undeed', a more torpid anagram than Herbert's *duende*. Life here is a goalless draw muddily slithered towards (Camus, never let it be forgotten, was a goalkeeper . . .). Paterson's Dundee, like W. N. Herbert's, is sometimes in America, sometimes farther afield. His verse dreams implausible connections:

> One day we will make our perfect journey –
> the great train smashing through Dundee, Brooklyn
> and off into the endless tundra,
> > 'The Trans-Siberian Express'

After a long residence in Brighton, Paterson, a rock musician as well as a poet, has recently returned to his native city as writer-in-residence at Dundee University. His 'Amnesia' has moments of Bamforthian excess, a *mise en scène* of Fultonesque Grand Guignol, but remains acridly quotidian, its tone reasonable, everything leading us to the matter of fact last line 'It was a nightmare Don. We had to gut the place.' There are chasms beneath the glacial flatness of Paterson's poetic surfaces. That obsolete memento mori of an epoch, the elliptical stylus provokes a beautiful poem about his father (one which took third prize in, the National Poetry Competition in 1991). The disruptive intrusion of another related poem into the one he has started, so far from seeming clever-clever, is sincere and moving, the circumstances of the elegy's making affecting and being included in what's made. The poem like the stylus, 'fairly brings out a' the wee details'. Paterson, stung by the memory of the shop assistant's condescension at his father's attempts to buy the old-fashioned stylus, ends the poem with the atypical avowal:

> I'd swing for him, and every other cunt
> happy to let my father know his station,
> which probably includes yourself. To be blunt.

To be blunt is something of a speciality with one of the youngest writers in *Dream State*, Stuart A. Paterson (no relation). His is a big-boned, firm-gripping, forthright poetry that's not above nuzzling the reader's ear. Paterson has no book of his own yet. But the range and assurance of his work bode well enough to hustle him into this one. So too with another Gregory Award winner, Roddy Lumsden, whom Graham Fulton could easily have accompanied, on 'The Misanthrope's Afternoon Walk'.

> They're all out today.
> The victims. The chipped on the shoulder.
> The chipped on the cheek, the scarred.
> The mental cripples. Baby mothers,
> Repros, pit bulls, tiny dummy-suckers,
> Bad moustached shouldn't-have been fathers.

Stylistically, 'Detox' seems to suffer its cold turkey under the influence of John Berryman and Carol Ann Duffy. Lumsden's Scotland is not particularly Scottish. The poems are worldly and unfazed, their ambience more redolent of Don Paterson than Stuart Paterson.

For all its swagger the younger Paterson's verse is genial, sentimental and oddly innocent. His skilfully expressed affection for Kilmarnock and its environs calls to mind Stewart Conn. He stravaigs with the wide eye of a Burns or a Whitman. His poetry loves and learns:

> At seventeen I kissed a date ON THE TIT!
> Twenty-one she was, immensely-nippled, almost
> (But not quite) able to feed me, suckling, snorting away.
> Mouths were irrelevant as we freed them to grab at
> The mysterious sculpting and folds of flesh.
> I tried to kiss her goodnight one time, she laughed
> And groped me. Kissing was never the same.

A love poet of unabashed candour, Paterson can also manage satire. 'The Leaving of Scotland' set on Ne'erday 1997 has Scotland asking for and being denied political asylum. Here is a dream state that sleep-walks. Explicitly nationalistic, it's appealing, though less crafty and crafted verse, than the comic cuts of Robert Crawford or W. N. Herbert. As I said before, *blunt*. But a poetry brave enough to dream of,

> a country so awake that dreaming is for the sleepless.

* * *

Scottishness, in poetry, as in everything else, is a hard quality to pin down. The novelist and screenwriter Alan Sharp has described coming from Scotland as being 'a very specific existential event'. Each poem in *Dream State* is that certainly. But in a country as small and complex as this one, being more specific is difficult. As Alastair Reid has pointed out, any statement about Scotland is likely to be true and just as unlikely to be the whole truth.

The whole truth is not to be found in this anthology. But the poets in it are true to their times and their talent. This means ignoring the tyranny of either or: not Burns, Dunbar; Muir versus MacDiarmid; Scots or English; free verse as opposed to rhyme – phoney dilemmas every one. Instead, following Morgan's example, these poets want it all. But if their poems are inclusive, they are also choosy. Their pluralism does not break down into a semiotic void in which everything signifies, nothing means, and anything goes. Every poet in *Dream State* writes to *communicate*.

In a world obsessed with information gathering and Communications, poetry's best hope is to provide more compelling information, to communicate more engagingly. These poets do that. They are also to an unprecedented degree, with the exceptions noted above, interested in the here and now which MacDiarmid's 'Gairmscoile' seemed to forsake.

> For we ha'e faith in Scotland's hidden poo'ers,
> The presents theirs, but a' the past and future's oors

Goethe's advice to the young poets of America, offered a century before MacDiarmid's *Penny Wheep*, seems more apposite. He bade them,

> concentrate on the present joyfully

Dream State reclaims the present. There is a renaissance going on in Scotland across all the arts. The word culture is on the unlikeliest of lips. But we shouldn't have a culture instead of an economy or a parliament. A fully authentic culture requires a fully authentic politics; and a fully authentic politics requires a state.

The Dream State offered here is vibrant and various, self-confident and self-critical. It knows its past and claims its future. Above all it is vigorously alive in Scotland's noisy and numinous now. It's like the modern Scotland Edwin Morgan was talking about: a Scotland no longer riddled with questions of identity, whose citizens just happen to be, and are happy to be, Scots. As 'King Billy', one of the Morgan poems many of these writers studied at school, has it.

> Deplore what is to be deplored
> and then find out the rest

The rest, or some of it, is *Dream State*.

Acknowledgements

We are grateful to the following copyright holders for granting us permission to reproduce the poems in this anthology. Every effort has been made to trace copyright holders, but if any have been inadvertently overlooked the publisher will be pleased to make the necessary arrangement at the first opportunity.

'Two Saints', 'Exile's Return' and 'Out of Exile' from *The Hoop* by John Burnside, Carcanet Press Limited, 1988. 'Urban Myths' from *Feast Days*, Secker and Warburg, 1992. 'The Light Institute' from *Swimming in the Flood* by John Burnside published by Jonathan Cape. Used by permission of The Random House Group Limited. 'Blue', 'Husbandry' and 'A Smoke' from *Asylum Dance* by John Burnside published by Jonathan Cape. Used by permission of The Random House Group Limited. 'A Normal Skin' from *A Normal Skin* by John Burnside published by Jonathan Cape. Used by permission of The Random House Group Limited.

'Four Views from the Camera Obscura', 'Pibroch' and 'Aberdeen' from *A Painted Field* by Robin Robertson, Picador, 1997. 'The Long Home', 'False Spring' and 'Wedding the Locksmith's Daughter' from *Slow Air* by Robin Robertson, Picador, 2002.

'Poet For Our Times', 'Translating the English, 1989', 'Originally' and 'The Way My Mother Speaks' from *The Other Country* by Carol Ann Duffy, Anvil, 1990. 'Ash Wednesday 1984' and 'Liverpool Echo' from *Standing Female Nude* by Carol Ann Duffy, Anvil, 1985. 'To the Unknown Lover' from *The Pamphlet* by Carol Ann Duffy, Anvil, 1998. 'Elvis's Twin Sister' and 'Mrs Darwin' from *The World's Wife* by Carol Ann Duffy, Picador, 2000.

'Mark Rothko's Lochs', 'The Pursuit of Happiness', 'D. Y. Cameron's Government of Light', 'Continuing' and 'Compliments from a Bitter Day' by Robin Lindsay Wilson © Robin Lindsay Wilson, reproduced by kind permission. 'Continuing' first appeared in *Private Cities*, Stride.

'Two Escapes', 'Going Down to the Crossroads with Robert Johnson', 'Behind the Blackboard', 'Yesnaby' and 'On the North Train' from *Whins* by George Gunn, Chapman, 1996.

'Not Being Bob De Niro', 'Garden City' and 'Sous les pavés – la plage' by Peter McCarey © Peter McCarey. 'Double-click on this', 'I have on at least two occasions', 'Today I scaled the ultimate', 'You've got fifteen seconds in which to', 'Unachievable hopes and unassuageable sorrows' and 'I've sung in otherwise empty buildings' from *Double Click* by Peter McCarey, Akros, 1997, © Peter McCarey, reproduced by kind permission.

'I Have a Dream' from *Birthmarks* by Mick Imlah published by Chatto and Windus. Used by permission of The Random House Group Limited. 'Past Caring', 'Flower of Scotland' and 'London Scottish' by Mick Imlah, © Mick Imlah, reproduced with kind permission.

'Tae Ma Mither and Faither', 'Johnny Thomson', 'On Hearing the Psalms Sung in Gaelic', 'Januar Winds o Revolution', 'Self-Portrait', 'The Visiting School Poet' and 'Turner Prize' by William Hershaw, © William Hershaw, reproduced by kind permission.

'At Loudoun Hill', 'A Short Introduction to my Uncle Glen', 'They Dream Only of Scotland' and 'The Blues' from *This Folding Map* by Alan Riach, Auckland University Press, 1990. 'Necessity of Listening' from *First and Last Songs* by Alan Riach, Chapman, 1995. 'Kilmartin Glen' and 'Clearances' by Alan Riach from *Clearances*, Scottish Cultural Press, 2001, © Alan Riach, reproduced by kind permission.

'Poems of Departure', 'Sisters' and 'Valda's Poem/Sleevenotes' from *Ophelia and Other Poems* by Elizabeth Burns, Polygon, 1991. 'For W. S. Graham' from *The Gift of Light* by Elizabeth Burns, diehard, 1999, © Elizabeth Burns, reproduced by kind permission.

'Sang oda Post War Exiles' from *Shoormal* by Robert Alan Jamieson, Polygon, 1986. 'Resistin the National Psychosis (April 9th 1992)', 'Lios Mhor', 'Saxby Five' and 'Speaking to the Ocean, Glasgow' by Robert Alan Jamieson, © Robert Alan Jamieson, reproduced by kind permission.

'Charles Manson Auditions for the Monkees', 'The Unmasking Scene', 'Goodnight John Boy' and 'Quiz Night' by Graham Fulton, © Graham Fulton, reproduced by kind permission. 'Cream of Scottish Youth' from *Knights of the Lower Floors* by Graham Fulton, Polygon, 1994.

'Praise of a Crofter' and 'The Stars of Autumn' from *The Shell House* by Gerry Cambridge, Scottish Cultural Press, 1995. 'Lines to Another Emily' and 'The Dark Gift' from *Mme Fi Fi's Farewell* by Gerry

Cambridge, Luath Press, 2001 © Gerry Cambridge, reproduced by kind permission.

'Opera', 'Scotland', 'A Scottish Assembly' and 'Alba Einstein' from *A Scottish Assembly* by Robert Crawford published by Chatto and Windus. Used by permission of The Random House Group Limited. 'Fur Thi Muse o Synthesis' and 'Ghetto-Blastir' from *Sharawaggi* by Robert Crawford and W. N. Herbert, Polygon, 1990. 'Masculinity' from *Masculinity* by Robert Crawford published by Jonathan Cape. Used by permission of The Random House Group Limited. 'The Result' from *Spirit Machines* by Robert Crawford published by Jonathan Cape. Used by permission of The Random House Group Limited.

'A chionn 's gu robh mi measail air/Because I was so fond of him', 'Aotromachd/Lightness' and 'Gille a' Sireadh Obair/Boy Looking for Work' from *Aotromachd agus dàin eile/Lightness and Other Poems* by Meg Bateman, Polygon, 1997. 'Ceòl san Eaglais/Music in Church' first published in *The Red Barrow*. 'Ugh Briste/Broken Egg' and 'Ealghol: Dà Shealladh/Elgol: Two Views' by Meg Bateman both published in *Etruscan Reader 9*, Etruscan © Meg Bateman, reproduced by kind permission.

'Men on Fire', 'Calvinist Geography', 'Alibis' and 'Rain Diary' from *Sons and Pioneers* by Iain Bamforth, Carcanet Press Limited, 1992. 'Up and Down the Ayr Road' from *Open Workings* by Iain Bamforth, Carcanet Press Limited, 1996.

'Algren', 'Great Western Road', 'Milk', 'Primary' and 'Wine and Wooing' from *The Waistband and Other Poems* by Donny O'Rourke, Polygon, 1997.

'The Rev. Robert Walker Skating on Duddingston Loch', 'Dustie-Fute', 'The Love That Dare Not', 'Envoi: Warmer Bruder', 'The Tear in Pat Kane's Voice' and 'Three Wee Frees: I Hinnie-Pigs' from *Paris-Forfar* by David Kinloch, Polygon, 1994, © David Kinloch, reproduced by kind permission. 'Bed' and 'Braveheart' by David Kinloch from *New Writing Scotland*, Carcanet Press Limited, 1997. 'Customs' by David Kinloch from *The Rialto*, Carcanet Press Limited, 1997.

'Fax/Fax' and 'Doras-Cuartachaidh/Revolving Door' from Fax and Other Poems by Rody Gorman, Polygon, 1996. 'A' Faireachdainn T' Fhàilidh/Catching Yer Waucht/Getting Your Whiff', 'Hosai' and 'Do Gheas/Spell, from *On the Underground* by Rody Gorman, Polygon, 2000, © Rody Gorman, reproduced by kind permission.

'A Flower for Federico García Lorca' and 'Spins and Turns' from *Souvenirs and Homelands*, Scottish Cultural Press, 1998. 'Blank' and 'Shandwick Stone' by Ken Cockburn, © Ken Cockburn, reproduced by kind permission. 'Blank' was first published in *The Red Wheelbarrow*, and ' Shandwick Stone' in *Present Poets*, National Museums of Scotland, 1998.

'As a Blackwoman', 'Drich Day' and 'If Leaving You' from *As a Blackwoman* by Maud Sulter. 'A Poem of Love' from *Zabat: Poetics of a Family Tree* by Maud Sulter, Urban Fox Press, 1989, © Maud Sulter, reproduced by kind permission.

'A Backlook', 'Mariposa Pibroch' and 'Dingle Dell' from *Forked Tongue* by W. N. Herbert, Bloodaxe Books, 1994. 'Ballad of the King's New Dialect', 'Cabaret McGonagall' and 'Ode to Scotty' from *Caberet McGonagall* by W. N. Herbert, Bloodaxe, 1996. 'Jacobite's Ladder' from *The Laurelude* by W. N. Herbert, Bloodaxe, 1998.

'Chapter 6: The Telling Part' from *The Adoption Papers* by Jackie Kay, Bloodaxe, 1992. 'Watching People Sing' and 'In my Country' from *Other Lovers* by Jackie Kay, Bloodaxe, 1993. 'The Birth and Death of Bette Davis', 'The Broons' Bairn's Black' and 'Pride' from *Off Colour* by Jackie Kay, Bloodaxe, 1998.

'The Republic of Fife' and 'The Queen of Sheba' from *The Queen of Sheba* by Kathleen Jamie, Bloodaxe, 1994. 'Things Which Never Shall Be' and 'Permanent Cabaret' from *The Way We Live* by Kathleen Jamie, Bloodaxe Books, 1987. 'Xiahe' from *The Autonomous Region: Poems and Photographs from Tibet* by Kathleen Jamie and Sean Mayr Smith, Bloodaxe Books, 1993. 'Forget It' and 'A Miracle' from *Jizzen* by Kathleen Jamie, Picador, 1999. 'Ships/Rooms' by Kathleen Jamie, © K. Jamie.

'Schooldays', 'Hogmanay', 'Working-Class Poet' and 'One Less' from *Seeing the River* by Raymond Friel, Polygon, 1995. 'The Central Picture House' by Raymond Friel from *Renfrewshire in Old Photographs*, Mariscat, © Raymond Friel, reproduced by kind permission.

'Amnesia', 'An Elliptical Stylus' and 'Nil Nil' from *Nil Nil* by Don Paterson, Faber and Faber Ltd, 1993. 'Prologue' and 'A Private Bottling' from *God's Gift to Women* by Don Paterson, Faber and Faber Ltd, 1997. 'Three Lyrics' from *The Eyes* by Don Paterson, Faber and Faber Ltd, 1999.

'The Lump', 'For the Best', 'The Fat Nymphomaniac's Poem' and 'Night Shift' from *Coming Out With It* by Angela McSeveney, Polygon, 1992. 'Who's Who', 'Dunblane' and 'Imprint' by Angela McSeveney, © Angela McSeveney, reproduced by kind permission.

Rob MacKenzie – all poems from *Off Ardglas* by Rob MacKenzie, Invisible Books, 1997. Also: 'Analysis' previously published by Verse and Sub-Voicive Programme; 'Comfort for the Revd. Angus Smith, Ness' previously published by Etruscan Books; 'Comfort for Davie' previously published by Gairfish; 'Off Ardglas' previously published by Verse and Kunapipi; 'A Home for the Words . . .' previously published by First Offense © Rob MacKenzie.

'Men', 'The Wedding Guest's Story' and 'Slattern' from *Slattern* by Kate Clanchy, Chatto and Windus, © Kate Clanchy. 'The Personals' and 'Raspberries' from *Samarkand* by Kate Clanchy, Picador, 1999.

'Winter Walk', 'Dear Norman' and 'The Swimming Pool Ghost' from *Air for Sleeping Fishes* by Gillian Ferguson, Bloodaxe, 1997, © Gillian Ferguson, reproduced with kind permission. 'Pram Rage', 'Orbit of Three' and 'Scan' from *Baby* by Gillian Ferguson, Canongate Books Ltd, 2001.

'A Rush of Memory by Polmaise', 'Fife', 'Dream State', 'No-Way José' and 'Alasdair Fraser' by Stuart A. Paterson, © Stuart A. Paterson, reproduced by kind permission.

'Coming', 'Fattening' and 'Yeah Yeah Yeah' from *Yeah Yeah Yeah* by Roddy Lumsden, Bloodaxe, 1997. 'An Older Woman', 'Piquant' and 'Acid' from *The Book of Love* by Roddy Lumsden, Bloodaxe Books, 2000. 'My Last Supper' and 'The Consolation' by Roddy Lumsden, © Roddy Lumsden, reproduced by kind permission.

'Tree-bird', 'With is', 'At Ease', 'My Father's Record Collection', 'John Gallagher', 'Heron', 'Pigeons' and 'Kingfisher' by Richard Price, © Richard Price. 'The World is Busy, Katie and 'Hand Held' from *Hand Held* by Richard Price, Akros, 1997, © Richard Price, reproduced by kind permission.

'Lit' gun Shalainn/Unsalted Porridge', '9mh den t-Samhainn 1989/9th November 1989', 'Smuain/A Thought', 'Dà rathad/Two Roads' and 'Geamhradh/Winter' from *Under the Shell* by Anne Frater, Gairm Publications. 'Semaphore/Semaphore' by Anne Frater, © Anne Frater, reproduced by kind permission.

'Girl Detective', 'Stallion Graveyard, Kentucky' and 'Gia' from *No Hiding Place* by Tracey Herd, Bloodaxe Books, 1996. 'Ophelia's Confession' and 'The Water Babies' from *Dead Redhead* by Tracey Herd, Bloodaxe Books, 2001.

'Uilleam Sona's Song of Lewis', 'Snow and Salt', 'All the clouds', 'For the Curtain Twitchers', 'Lost Loch Floating', 'an acarsaid/the harbour' and 'faclan, eich-mhara/words, seahorses' from *Love and Zen in the Outer Hebrides* by Kevin MacNeil, Canongate Books Ltd, 1998.

Photograph Credits

John Burnside by David Thompson, thanks to Jonathan Cape
Robin Robertson by Niall McDiarmid
Carol Ann Duffy by Sue Adler, thanks to Anvil Press Poetry
Robin Lindsay Wilson supplied by R. L. Wilson
George Gunn supplied by G. Gunn
Peter McCarey supplied by Polygon
Mick Imlah supplied by M. Imlah
William Hershaw by Bill Paton
Alan Riach by Campus Photography, the University of Waikato
Elizabeth Burns by Tim Curtis
Robert Alan Jamieson supplied by R. A. Jamieson
Graham Fulton by Steven Carlton
Gerry Cambridge by Anne Lennox
Robert Crawford supplied by R. Crawford
Meg Bateman by Elsie Mitchell
Iain Bamforth supplied by I. Bamforth
Donny O'Rourke supplied by D. O'Rourke
David Kinloch © Unglee, Paris
Rody Gorman by Steve McKenzie
Ken Cockburn by Roddy Simpson, 7 Oct 1999
Maud Sulter supplied by M. Sulter
W. N. Herbert by Stephanie R. Mickler
Jackie Kay by Ingrid Pollard, thanks to Bloodaxe Books
Kathleen Jamie by Phil Butler, thanks to Picador
Raymond Friel by Janet Friel
Don Paterson © Bob Barkany, thanks to Faber and Faber
Angela McSeveney by Ross Murray
Rob MacKenzie supplied by R. MacKenzie
Kate Clanchy supplied by Picador
Gillian Ferguson by Gillian Whisker, © 1999, thanks to Canongate Books
Stuart A. Paterson supplied by S. A. Paterson
Roddy Lumsden by Richard Nicholson
Richard Price by J. S. Canning
Anne Frater supplied by A. Frater
Tracey Herd © Moira Conway, thanks to Bloodaxe Books
Kevin MacNeil © David Tomorrowscape Whyte

Index of Poems

Index of Poets

hill

DATE DUE